THE LONG VIEW

ALAN PATON

The Long View

EDITED BY EDWARD CALLAN

FREDERICK A. PRAEGER, *Publishers*

New York • Washington • London

FREDERICK A. PRAEGER, PUBLISHERS
111 Fourth Avenue, New York, N.Y. 10003, U.S.A.
77-79 Charlotte Street, London W.1, England

Published in the United States of America in 1968
by Frederick A. Praeger, Inc., Publishers

"Beware of Melancholy" is reprinted from *Christianity and Crisis,*
XXV, No. 11 (November 1, 1965).
"In Memoriam: Albert Luthuli" is reprinted from
Christianity and Crisis, XXVII, No. 5 (September 18, 1967).
Both used by permission of Christianity and Crisis, Inc.
© 1965, 1967 by Christianity and Crisis, Inc.

Library of Congress Catalog Card Number: 67-24675

Printed in the United States of America

Editor's Acknowledgments

The essays in THE LONG VIEW form an important part of Alan Paton's literary work during the past ten years. They speak eloquently of the respect due to the dignity inherent in persons. They also outline a nonracial philosophy that may yet provide great hope, not only for the future of Africa, but for the world at large.

Compiling and editing these essays for American readers has been a rewarding experience. In the beginning, I had hoped for the benefit of Alan Paton's advice through every stage of preparing the volume for publication, but the pressure of events prevented this: The fortunes of his banned friends and colleagues in the Liberal Party and in the Defence and Aid organization gave him increasing cause for concern; and his wife's grave illness weighed heavily on him. Mrs. Doris Paton died on September 23, 1967, after a long illness, in the fortieth year of their marriage. Writing in the *Saturday Review* of September 9, 1967, Alan Paton paid this tribute to his wife: "I certainly had good fortune in marriage and children and friends. . . . Life has taught me—and this is my luck—that active loving saves one from a morbid preoccupation with the shortcomings of society."

Although I bear the sole responsibility for all opinions and attitudes expressed in the editorial matter, I should like to acknowledge a great debt of gratitude to Professor Joseph Jones of the University of Texas, who is editor of the South African volumes in Twayne's World Author Series, for permission to draw freely on biographical materials I had previously used in my critical study *Alan Paton;* to Mr. Harry Brague of Charles Scribner's Sons, for providing the text of Mr. Paton's Freedom House Address; to the editors of *Christianity and Crisis,* for permission to reprint copyright material; to Muriel Horrel, whose annual *Survey of Race Relations in South Africa* provided a most valuable source of information for the notes and introductions; and to the *Natal Daily News* for "Dr. Hendrik Verwoerd—A Liberal Assessment," which appeared in the issues of September 26–27, 1966.

I also wish to express my gratitude to Mr. Gilman Park and Mr. Louis Barron of Frederick A. Praeger, Inc., for advice and encouragement, and, in particular, to Mrs. Marian Wood, who edited the manuscript skillfully and expeditiously; to Mrs. Janice Lee, for secretarial assistance; to Professor Frederick J. Rogers, for reading the introductory essay and suggesting improvements; and to Mr. Donald R. Brown and Mr. Kenneth Harris of the Western Michigan University library, for their help in locating materials.

EDWARD CALLAN
Western Michigan University
February, 1968

Contents

PART THREE: WITH BELL, BOOK, AND CANDLE, 1963–67

Foreword

It must happen very seldom that the subject of a study such as this should be asked to write a foreword to it. It is in fact a study of my public life, and as I read it in its final form, I marvel at the labour that has gone into it, and at the amount of information that has been gathered by a person living in a country so far from my own.

It is almost always embarrassing to read an account of one's life and thought written by some other person. I do not find Edward Callan's account embarrassing at all and that is because he has been extraordinarily skilful in letting the writer and speaker write and speak for himself. If I am to be embarrassed, therefore, I can only be embarrassed by myself, and at the age of sixty-five, one is able to look at one's life more objectively, and to smile, even if sometimes ruefully, at what one was and thought and said in earlier days.

Most of the material presented here I wrote and spoke myself. I wrote, *inter alia,* of the time that must elapse and the work that must be done before the new nations of the world, and especially those of Africa, could achieve stability. I recognised that the ending of colonialism would be followed by a period of instability. It now seems to me that this period will be longer and more unstable than I thought.

This has another consequence. It means that white South Africa will be given a period longer than I thought to abate the hostility of the outside world. If the conservatives inside the ruling Nationalist Party do not succeed in their struggle to gain control, the Government will go ahead with its plans to permit racially mixed teams to go to the Olympics, and to accept Maori rugby players in the visiting New Zealand teams, and to relax *apartheid* restrictions for any black diplomats sent to South Africa. But simultaneously there will be made an intense effort to hasten the pace of separate development *within* the country, and to prove to the world that it actually can work, and can bring advantages to nonwhite South Africans.

In other words, the disarray of the African nations and the impotence of the United Nations have given the Government time, and the whole aim of Government policy will be to make that time as long as possible. That this time would be so far extended was something that I did not foresee. I am still of the opinion that neither separate development nor *apartheid* can endure, but they are going to endure longer than I thought.

In order to use this time without hindrance the Government has given itself totalitarian powers over those who might oppose or delay the implementation of their plans. Opposition, once so exciting, has become dangerous, and those who oppose have several choices. They can leave their country, or they can remain and offer what opposition is still permitted, or they can learn to live without power and in silence, or they can accept the grave consequences of vigorous opposition. I see no sign whatever that the Government will become more tolerant of opposition.

I cannot suppose that the publication of this material will do me much good at home, but I have no overwhelming desire to have good done to me at home. This is what I was and did and thought, this is how I lived or tried to live, and if I lived again, this is how I should try to live. I must add, however, that many of these pieces are much braver and stronger than their writer.

I thank Dr. Callan that he thought it worth his time and labour to make this book, and that, by his own interpolations, he has made it so intelligible to those who do not know my country.

ALAN PATON
Kloof, Natal
February, 1968

THE LONG VIEW

Alan Paton and the Liberal Party

by EDWARD CALLAN

Advocate of Freedom

SINCE 1948, WHEN HIS FIRST NOVEL, *Cry, the Beloved Country,* was published in the United States and Great Britain—and very soon afterward translated into more than twenty European, Asian, and African languages—Alan Paton's name has been widely identified with the cause of racial justice in South Africa. *Cry, the Beloved Country* was a work of art and not simply a record of South Africa's social ills; yet, Paton felt it mirrored the times authentically, and, in a Preface to the novel, he remarked, "Considered as a social record it is the plain and simple truth."

Paton well knew the facts and statistics of the South African social record. For more than ten years, as a practical social reformer and as Principal of Diepkloof Reformatory, he had marshaled the evidence before public and private bodies and presented it in the publications of the South African Institute of Race Relations and in the liberal biweekly *Forum.* His views on the social situation were not considered to be either personal or eccentric; nor, indeed, were they considered particularly original, for the reports of many other educators, welfare workers, and government commissions drew comparable conclusions. He was, therefore, justified in suggesting that *Cry, the Beloved Country,* considered as a social record, was the plain and simple truth.

3

Facing up to the plain and simple truth—his persistent questioning, for example, of why South Africa's blueprint for the perfect society of the future should require great suffering from so many individual men, women, and children living now—is still a characteristic of his writing. There may well be many who share Paton's compassionate understanding of the daily tribute of humiliation that racial arrogance exacts from those it deems inferior. But few share his gift for communicating this understanding through concrete instance, and still fewer share his resolution to go on communicating it in changed circumstances and in the face of censorship, intimidation, and scornful jeers that increasingly label him "sickly liberalist" or "cat's-paw of Communists."

Cry, the Beloved Country was written during 1946–47, at a time when some South Africans, under the leadership of Jan Hofmeyr, seemed ready to move forward toward a common society. Hofmeyr, who was General Smuts's brilliant Deputy Prime Minister and Paton's friend of many years, was determined to "go forward in faith, not fear." Furthermore, the prospect of his succession as Prime Minister coincided with a brief flowering of the liberal spirit among many South African servicemen recently returned from the war against Nazism. These circumstances, as well as Paton's own Christian ideals, justified the note of hope pervading the tragic atmosphere of *Cry, the Beloved Country,* and account for its subtitle: *A Story of Comfort in Desolation.*

But, in the same year that the novel was published, these hopes received an unexpected setback. Dr. Daniel F. Malan's Nationalist Party, whose declared policy was "Christian Nationalism," won an election victory after a campaign that introduced to the world the word *apartheid*—then understood to mean an intensification of South Africa's traditional color-bar policies. That same year, Jan Hofmeyr died, and, as Paton put it, "a great light went out in the land, making men more conscious of its darkness."

Among white liberals, these setbacks diminished the hope for some progress toward a common society in the immediate future, but they did not extinguish it. Rule by the Nationalist Party was, after all, neither new nor revolutionary; the Nationalists had been in power in South Africa before—under Hertzog, from 1924 to 1933, and, in coalition with Smuts, from 1933 to 1939. But, by 1952—when the new Minister for Native Affairs, Dr. Hendrik Verwoerd, introduced his Bantu Education Act—it had become clear that *apartheid* was no longer a mere election slogan but a new and systematic ideology of racial exclusiveness that regarded racial purity as the highest good. The years following 1952 saw a spate of new legislation and amendments to old legislation, all designed to perpetuate barriers between members of one race and those of another. This legislation sought to ensure that the permissibility of human activity would be determined by a single touchstone: absolute racial exclusiveness.

By 1953, both Smuts and Hofmeyr had died; under their successors, the United Party no longer offered any real opposition to the racial policies of the Nationalists. The two major parties differed in their attitudes toward Commonwealth links with Britain, but hardly at all in their attitudes toward the nonwhite peoples. After the Nationalists were returned to power with an increased majority in the 1953 elections, the interracial Liberal Association decided to reconstitute itself as a political party that would offer voters of South Africa, almost all of whom were white,* a clear choice of racial policies. To a racially organized society seeking to perpetuate itself through such legislation as the Population Registration Act (which classified everyone by race) and the Group Areas Act (which determined where one could live), the Liberal Party offered the direct contradiction of *apartheid*—a program for a nonracial society with equal civil status for all, irrespective of race. Alan Paton joined this new Liberal Party as one of its vice-presidents. In 1956, he was

---

* The right to vote was reserved for whites everywhere in South Africa except in the Cape Province, where Cape Coloured males could still qualify to vote. By 1955, Cape Coloured voters were removed from the common roll. They could not, thereafter, vote in general elections for candidates of the contending political parties, only in separate elections to select four white people to represent them in Parliament.

elected National Chairman; thereafter, as the party's Chairman or as its President, he steadily upheld its nonracial policies despite growing intolerance and intimidation and the repeated bannings of key party organizers and officials from political activity of any kind.

In the course of a very active and productive life, Alan Paton has consistently served an ideal of freedom that values human personality above any considerations of race, color, or doctrinaire politics. "The really evil thing about Hitlerism," he has said, "is that it committed unspeakable crimes against personality." As a teacher, writer, and penal reformer, and, more recently, as a reluctant politician speaking out on both national and international affairs, he has affirmed his belief in the dignity of personality and in its inner quality of creativity that enables men to realize their gifts fully only when they are freed from inhibiting fears and prejudices, as well as from external domination by others. He once described the postwar drive of Asian and African nations toward independence as a massive expression of the inner personal drive for creative freedom. "Just as we have freed our children," he said, "because we loved them and thereby conquered our fears, just so we can free the world, and release for the good of all humanity the gifts and energies of its people."*

Individual freedom, and the accompanying responsibility to cultivate one's gifts and creative potential, has been Paton's consistent touchstone. As a guardian of delinquent boys (while Principal of Diepkloof Reformatory, between 1935 and 1948), he put his faith in freedom as the supreme instrument of reform, and he took advantage of every occasion offered him, in speech or in writing, to propagate his belief in the primacy of freedom. Now, as President of the Liberal Party, he continues to believe in the primacy of freedom, but opportunities to propagate his belief are increasingly denied him. The South African Liberal Party has been rendered largely

---

* Alan Paton, "Religious Faith and Human Brotherhood," in A. W. Loos (ed.), *Religious Faith and World Culture* (Englewood Cliffs, N.J.: Prentice-Hall, 1951), pp. 189–99.

ineffectual through the "banning" of many of its leading members;* newspapers are increasingly reluctant to publish liberal opinion, including Paton's; the state-owned radio system (SABC) has repeatedly attacked him and refused him permission to reply on its transmitters. *Contact,* the publication where most of the essays in this volume first appeared, has had six editors and five staff members and correspondents banned; it has been forced to give up its registration as a newspaper, and it now appears only infrequently and in mimeographed form. *Contact* has tried to live up to the brave assertion it made when, forced to abandon regular printing, it produced its first mimeographed issue (August 28, 1964): "We will continue to publish as long as we have one person with one typewriter and one machine left to print or duplicate what we believe must be said from inside South Africa." And not once, even during the paper's worst trials, has Paton failed to produce his regular column, "The Long View."

The belief in the primacy of freedom that Paton has so consistently upheld rests ultimately, he says, on his Christian convictions. He has declared, "Because I am a Christian I am a passionate believer in human freedom, and therefore, in human rights."† In the context of life in South Africa, such a statement cannot escape interpretation as something other than a personal affirmation of faith, for, in the face of racial policies described by their proponents as "Christian Nationalism," it constitutes a challenge in the political

* A banning order is imposed directly by the Minister of Justice, at his discretion, on any person he deems to be wittingly or unwittingly "furthering the aims of Communism" as defined in the Suppression of Communism Act (1950). Individual banning orders may vary in their specific prohibitions, but all bans are for five-year terms and are renewable. They permit no appeal to the courts. All restrict the movements of the person named in them to a specified area. All prohibit attendance at public or even social gatherings. No statement by a banned person may be published in any form. In addition, banning orders list specific prohibitions on such matters as entering a school, law court, or publishing office; entering a harbor or railroad station; belonging to a specified organization; or communicating with any other banned or "listed" person. Recent legislation has increased the number of possible prohibitions.

† "Church, State and Race," *Christian Century,* LXXV, No. 9 (February 28, 1958), 278.

sphere. Furthermore, now that organized African parties like Chief Albert Luthuli's African National Congress and Robert Sobukwe's Pan-African Congress have been outlawed, and radical groups, including the Liberal Party, largely silenced, the role of actively opposing *apartheid* has devolved almost exclusively upon the churches, including the handful of Dutch Reformed Church intellectual leaders whose views run contrary to the mainstream of opinion in their church. One forum for these dissenting views is *Pro Veritate*, a monthly magazine published, since July, 1962, by the Dutch Reformed churches in Johannesburg and edited by C. F. Beyers Naudé, who resigned from the position of Moderator of the Southern Transvaal synod of his church to free himself to challenge certain aspects of *apartheid*. From the outset, *Pro Veritate* offended conservative members of the church by including a nonwhite clergyman on its editorial board and by its policy of giving a hearing to controversial views. It is a sign of the times that Balthazar Vorster, in one of his earliest public statements as Prime Minister, warned both Alan Paton and the editors of *Pro Veritate* that charges of treason might be preferred against them unless they modified their criticism of the status quo. On January 17, 1967, he said, "I warn these people and organizations who invite foreign intervention in our internal affairs, that we will not suffer such action much longer. It is nothing more than treason."*

Official disfavor is not the only hostile expression confronting Paton and the diminished Liberal Party. Much of white popular opinion holds them in contempt, and more and more white South Africans—English-speaking as well as Afrikaans-speaking—who formerly sympathized with liberal aspirations now, in fear of being branded "enemies of the people," remain silent or dissociate themselves from suspect persons and organizations.

To those who would ask what the future holds, one can only respond by pointing to "Beware of Melancholy," Paton's eloquent and moving essay, included in this volume, in which he concludes

* As quoted by D. L. Royle, in an Associated Press dispatch of January 17, 1967.

with the following exhortation to fellow South African liberals of all races:

Stand firm by what you believe; do not tax yourself beyond endurance, yet calculate clearly and coldly how much endurance you have; don't waste your breath and corrupt your character by cursing your rulers and the South African Broadcasting Corporation; don't become obsessed with them; keep your friendships alive and warm, especially those with people of other races; beware of melancholy and resist it actively if it assails you; and give thanks for the courage of others in this fear-ridden country.

In the light of "Beware of Melancholy" and of the humanity and reasonable spirit of other writings in this book, one is struck by the accuracy of Archibald MacLeish's characterization of Paton. In presenting Paton with the Freedom Award for 1960, at Freedom House, New York, MacLeish said:

To live at the center of the contemporary maelstrom; to see it for what it is and to challenge the passions of those who struggle in it beside him with the voice of reason—with, if he will forgive me, the enduring reasons of love; to offer the quiet sanity of the heart in a city yammering with the crazy slogans of fear; to do all this at the cost of tranquillity and the risk of harm, as a service to a government which does not know it needs it . . . is to deserve more of history than we can give our guest tonight.*

Toward a Nonracial Outlook: 1903–34

Alan Paton was born in the British colony of Natal on January 11, 1903, shortly after the Anglo-Boer War had ended. His father, James Paton, who had emigrated from Scotland to Natal before the war, was a civil servant in Pietermaritzburg, the colony's administrative capital. His mother, Eunice, was a third-generation South African of English descent who had been a teacher before her marriage. James and Eunice Paton were devout Christians in the non-

* The text can be found in Aaron Levenstein and William Agar, *Freedom's Advocate* (New York: Viking Press, 1965), pp. 153–54.

conformist tradition, and Paton says it was from them that he learned his first lessons in tolerance—"tolerance toward the Afrikaners, who were then a defeated people."

The great political event of Paton's childhood occurred in 1910, when the former Afrikaner republics of the Transvaal and the Orange Free State joined with the British colonies of Natal and the Cape of Good Hope to form the Union of South Africa. The Liberal Party in England, confident that liberalism was the wave of the future, encouraged this union of Anglo-Boer War antagonists, and, led by two former Boer generals, Louis Botha and Jan Smuts, the new Union embarked on a policy of reconciling white South Africans of British and Dutch extraction in a single shared patriotism.

Paton grew up in this atmosphere of reconciliation. His undergraduate writings in the *Natal University College Magazine* show that, like other liberals of the period, he gave this policy of reconciliation wholehearted support and that he was beginning, even then, to expand his conception of a common South African patriotism to include African, Coloured, and Indian inhabitants as well as the two white cultures. He was a member of the Students' Representative Council of Natal University College when the National Union of South African Students (NUSAS) was being formed— chiefly through the efforts of Leo Marquard, who was to become one of South Africa's outstanding liberals. In 1924, Paton's fellow students elected him as their representative to an Imperial Student Conference. The conference, set up to discuss student involvement in the cause of world peace, was held in Britain. Two letters Paton wrote while attending it are extant. The first is optimistic about the role of NUSAS in bringing about reconciliation between English-speaking and Afrikaans-speaking groups and thereby helping "to weld the whites of South Africa into one race of South Africans." The second reveals his sympathy with complaints voiced by conference delegates from India about the conditions among Indians in Natal. Paton pointed out, in this letter, that South African opinion against the Indians in Natal was "in many cases unjust," and he

urged the universities and student unions to take the lead in edu-
cating white opinion on this point.*

These letters, together with the full range of his cultural and
social activities during his university years (1920–24), substantiate
the brief self-description with which Paton introduced himself to
his readers in *The Land and People of South Africa:*

I am a white English-speaking South African, born in the largely
English-speaking Province of Natal. In childhood I never heard any
Afrikaans spoken, but learned at home to feel sympathy for the language and cultural struggle of the Afrikaner people; and later learned
to speak the language itself, studied its literature, and the history of
its people. All these attempts to appreciate and to understand were
strengthened by religious motives. Later at University (at college as
you would say) I learned to take an even wider view, and to understand
and to sympathize with the aspirations of the African and Coloured
peoples, and of our three hundred thousand Indians in Natal. This direction once taken, I did not deviate from it, and am now not likely
ever to do so.†

During his four years at Natal University College, Paton developed the wide range of humane interests—social, intellectual,
and religious—that have characterized his mature years. He ma-
jored in the sciences and went on to obtain a Bachelor of Science
degree with distinction in physics. But his frequent contributions to
the *Natal University College Magazine* attest to at least an equal
interest in literature and drama; his undergraduate writings included fifteen poems and two humorous plays (one of them in
Shakespearean verse). These poems—even the earliest of them—
show that he had achieved considerable fluency in the craft of verse,
but, except for two poems set on Anglo-Boer War battlefields, they
do not draw on South African social life for subject matter.

Besides being a member of the Students' Representative Council,
Paton took part in the affairs of several student organizations. His

---

* These letters can be found under the title "The Imperial Conference," in
Natal University College Magazine, IX (October, 1924), 9–12.

† *The Land and People of South Africa* (Philadelphia: J. B. Lippincott,
1955), pp. 80–81.

interest in one of these, in particular, was to have a profound effect
on the course of his later life. This was the Students' Christian Association (SCA), which was soon to provide the link leading to his
friendship with Jan Hendrik Hofmeyr. Paton shared with Hofmeyr
the conviction that South Africa should move forward toward a
common society "in faith, not fear." After Hofmeyr's death, in 1948,
it was continued loyalty to this conviction that impelled Paton to
forego his career as a literary man and to devote his talents to
carrying on Hofmeyr's work of keeping the liberal spirit alive in
South Africa.

In 1924, Paton had received his Bachelor of Science degree and
also had completed the course of studies required for certification
as a high school teacher. When he returned from the Imperial Student Conference in England, he took his first teaching post, at Ixopo
High School, a school for white children only. Ixopo is the small
rural town in the Natal hills introduced in the opening lyric ca-
dences of *Cry, the Beloved Country.* Spurred by this locale and
also, he thinks, by Hugh Walpole's Rogue Herries novels set in
the English Lake District, Paton attempted two or three novels of
white South African life. But he thought none of them worth preserving.

While teaching at Ixopo, he met Doris Olive Francis. They were
married at St. John's Anglican Church, Ixopo, on July 2, 1928. In
the same year, Paton accepted a post at his old high school, Maritzburg College, in his birthplace, Pietermaritzburg. The strong at-
tachment to the Anglican church that informs so much of Paton's
writing dates from this period in his life. In so far, for example, as
Cry, the Beloved Country is "a Christian interpretation of racial tensions and of the spirit by which they can be overcome," the spokesmen for the Christian spirit are all Anglican priests: Father Vincent
(a fictional portrayal of Paton's friend Father Trevor Huddleston),
the Reverend Theopholis Msimangu, and the Reverend Stephen
Kumalo.

During his years at Ixopo, Paton had joined with two other high
school teachers, Reg Pearce and Cyril Armitage, in establishing a

boys' camp in Natal. Begun in 1926, the camp had as its aim "to win boys . . . to Christian principles in life and society." It was an outgrowth of the vigorous branch of the SCA at Natal University College. Jan Hofmeyr, during his own university days in Cape Town and Oxford, had taken part in the work of the SCA, including the organization of clubs and camps for boys. Hofmeyr was an enthusiastic camper who, throughout his brilliant career—even as cabinet minister and Deputy Prime Minister—preferred camping to any other form of recreation. Through common links with the parent association in Cape Town, Hofmeyr came to Paton's second camp at Umgababa; then, as Paton relates in his biography of Hofmeyr, "year after year to the new camp site on the Idomba River, which site he helped the Association to buy and develop."*

Everyone in South Africa admired Hofmeyr's intellectual genius; his brilliant public career permitted no dissenting view. But not everyone admired the firm conviction he had arrived at by 1930, namely, that South Africa should aspire toward a common society recognizing the human significance of all men. Paton admired Hofmeyr's parliamentary championing of the liberal spirit. But, even more, he admired Hofmeyr's determination to act in public life in accordance with his Christian conviction of human brotherhood—a difficult and courageous posture to adopt in a society where so many were convinced that it was God who had set the races of man apart, and where it was easy to ridicule any such concept as "brotherhood."

To Paton, Hofmeyr's Christian conviction lay at the heart of the matter, including the heart of all political matters in South Africa. He characterized Hofmeyr's fiercest parliamentary opponents in the Nationalist Party as "outraged believers in that heretical Christianity which has made racial separation the highest of all goods, and racial difference a God-given gift which no ordinary man could set

---

* *South African Tragedy: The Life and Times of Jan Hofmeyr* (New York: Charles Scribner's Sons, 1965), p. 98. *Hofmeyr* (Cape Town: Oxford University Press, 1964), p. 136. The Scribner's edition is a slightly abbreviated version. Henceforth, the Oxford edition will be cited.

aside."* And Hofmeyr himself, as his public statements testify, became more and more convinced that South Africa's social and political problems had roots in ethical, and even doctrinal, considerations. As he put it in a memorable address as Chancellor of the University of the Witwatersrand, in March, 1946:

As long as we continue to apply a double standard in South Africa to determine our attitudes towards . . . European and non-European on different ethical bases, to assign to Christian doctrine a significance which varies with the colour of a man's skin we suffer as a nation from what Plato would have called the lie in the soul—and the curse of Iscariot may yet be our fate for our betrayal of the Christian doctrine which we profess.†

This address is remembered as the *Herrenvolk* speech, because in it Hofmeyr, a leading cabinet member, dared openly to compare the white South African mentality to the Nazi *Herrenvolk* (master race) mentality. But the remedy he advanced is perhaps not so well remembered. Hofmeyr proposed that a fifth freedom—freedom from prejudice—be added to the Four Freedoms of the Atlantic Charter:

I commend this fifth freedom as worthy that you should fight for it. I shall put it more strongly than that. May you be prepared to say with Thomas Jefferson, "I have sworn upon the altar of God eternal hostility against every form of tyranny over the mind of man"—and here in South Africa the greatest evil of all is the tyranny of prejudice.‡

In his biography of Hofmeyr, Paton notes that the university audience greeted this address with thunderous applause: "People crowded round him with shining eyes to thank him, and to thank God for him, and he, as always, replied to them formally, more constrained than they by the presence within him of this prophetic spirit."§

Was Hofmeyr's spirit truly prophetic? Or was Paton misled? When, in his *Herrenvolk* speech, Hofmeyr sought to illustrate for

* *Ibid.,* p. 264.
† Quoted in Tom MacDonald, *Jan Hofmeyr: Heir to Smuts* (London: Hurst & Blackett, 1948), pp. 12–13.
‡ *Hofmeyr,* pp. 422–23.
§ *Ibid.,* p. 423.

his audience the extent to which white South Africans "as a nation" were "slaves of prejudice," he chose one instance in particular:

By way of illustration of what prejudice means in South Africa I cannot do better than refer to the growing tendency to describe as a Communist—and therefore one who should be condemned by bell, book, and candle—anyone who asks for fair play for all races, or who suggests that Non-Europeans [nonwhites] really should be treated as equals of Europeans [whites] before the law.*

If readers of Paton's essays in the third part of this present volume, *The Long View,* keep in mind this illustration of what prejudice means, they will be able to decide whether Hofmeyr was truly prophetic or Paton was misled.

The Great Barred Gate Is Gone: 1934–44

There can be little wonder that a young man of Paton's qualities should find Hofmeyr's ideal worth serving. Paton had no aspirations toward the public life, but he had two desires that he admits have always been in conflict: the desire to write and the desire to do creative social work. Almost providentially, Hofmeyr's determination not to supply a double standard with European and non-European children opened up for Paton a unique opportunity to embark on creative social work.

In 1934, Hofmeyr held three cabinet portfolios: Education, Interior, and Public Health. He introduced legislation—since known as the Children's Act—that was to apply impartially to children of all races. This legislation transferred responsibility for reformatory institutions from the Department of Prisons to the Department of Education. As a result, new personnel were needed to supervise the transformation of the three existing reformatories (for white, for Coloured, and for African offenders) into educational institutions. Paton, who was then on sick leave from Maritzburg College, applied for one of the three new principalships. He was appointed to

* *Ibid.,* p. 422.

Diepkloof Reformatory, an institution housing some 700 African boys between the ages of ten and nineteen.

In 1935, Diepkloof Reformatory was a prison-like institution occupying about 1,000 acres of farmland on the outskirts of Johannesburg. It housed African youths convicted of crimes ranging from petty theft to murder. Apart from his own qualities of mind and spirit, there was little in Paton's background to prepare him for the task of transforming this virtual prison into a school. Yet, within three years, he was able to report, "We have removed all the more obvious aids to detention. The dormitories are open all night. The great barred gate is gone."*

In the perennial debate on the function of penal institutions, two viewpoints prevail. One view envisages them as places of restraint, designed to impress offenders with the truth of the dictum "Crime does not pay." The opposing view sees their primary function as that of restoring warped lives to social usefulness. This second view underlay the proposals of Hofmeyr's Children's Act, and Paton devoted his creative energies to proving its validity in his experimental work at Diepkloof Reformatory. To begin with, he put aside his literary endeavors—the novels and the poems; he also put aside work on his thesis for the Master of Education degree, even though he had completed the course work and passed the qualifying examinations with distinction. (Years later, he applied for the Bachelor of Education degree; on the basis of this completed work, he was awarded the degree with distinction.) He then set about organizing Diepkloof as a place of education and rehabilitation based on "increasing freedom, increasing responsibility, increasing privilege, and increasing temptation." Newly committed boys were housed in a closed dormitory. When they proved themselves trustworthy, they were transferred, in small groups, to the care of a housefather and housemother and given freedom to roam the surrounding farmland. Later, they were allowed to make weekend visits

---

* "Remarks by Mr. Alan Paton," *Minutes of a Conference on Urban Juvenile Delinquency Held at Johannesburg, October 1938.* Mimeographed. (From files of the South African Institute of Race Relations.)

to their families. The most trustworthy senior boys were permitted to work for employers outside the institution and to live in hostels, where they paid part of their earnings for their keep. There were, of course, failures and frustrations. (This side of Diepkloof Reformatory is personified in Absolom Kumalo, the young murderer in *Cry, the Beloved Country,* and also in characters in Paton's short stories and his play *Sponono.*) But Paton's experiments with increasing freedom and responsibility, which he deemed the "supreme instruments of reform," soon earned him a respected reputation in the field of penal reform.

Not all observers of the Diepkloof experiment were impressed by its measure of success, and some opposition was politically oriented, stemming from a basic disagreement with the principle that the Children's Act should extend equally to children of all races. In *Hofmeyr,* Paton noted that "one of the sourest observers" of the Diepkloof experiment was Dr. Hendrik Verwoerd, then editor of *Die Transvaler.* Verwoerd described Diepkloof as "a place for pampering rather than education, the place indeed where one said 'please' and 'thank you' to the black 'misters.' "* If Hofmeyr's action transferring reformatory institutions from the Department of Prisons to the Department of Education was a small but revealing sign of his social philosophy, the fate of Diepkloof after 1948 is an equally revealing sign of Nationalist social philosophy. For example, Paton had long recommended a separate institution for the younger boys in the reformatory. In 1948, the year he resigned from Diepkloof, the Department of Education accepted his recommendation and provided the money for a new school for the younger boys, to be called the Alan Paton School. Within a month of this decision, Dr. Malan became Prime Minister. His administration disapproved of the project for the Alan Paton School, and it was abandoned. Furthermore, his administration soon transferred the reformatory for African boys from the Department of Education to the Department of Native Affairs. Since only the institution for African

* *Hofmeyr,* p. 274.

boys was affected, this transfer undercut Hofmeyr's intention to apply the provisions of the Children's Act impartially to children of all races. For a time after Paton resigned, Diepkloof continued to be run as a school. In 1958, Dr. Verwoerd, then Minister for Native Affairs, closed Diepkloof and transferred its 800 inmates to rural youth labor camps, where they would be trained in farm labor under the supervision of warders. That same year, Dr. Verwoerd became Prime Minister of South Africa.

The present significance of the Diepkloof experiment lies not in its record of successful rehabilitation but in the subsequent decay of the thinking that had brought it into being as a remedial community. The Diepkloof endeavor was based on a creative approach to penal reform, advocated in many nations and officially approved in South Africa. Paton recorded that he had the privilege of working for thirteen years under a department "that had tried ably and honestly to give full effect to the provisions of the magnificent Children's Act of 1937," and, he went on, "I even had the extraordinary experience, almost unknown to Public Servants, of administering Diepkloof Reformatory for some years under no regulations at all, and this meant freedom to experiment that comes to few of us in our lifetime."* Paton had approached the problems of Diepkloof as part of the universal problem of penal reform, and he had applied principles of rehabilitation that were universally accepted as valid by contemporary reformers. Dr. Verwoerd and his colleagues in the Nationalist Party approached Diepkloof in the context of *apartheid,* not penal reform, and they disposed of it accordingly. Diepkloof had never been an integrated institution, but it had, under Paton, provided ordinary schooling, equipping African youths with skills intended to enable them to live in an urban environment. Dr. Verwoerd's ideal of "separate development," and its instrument, the Group Areas Act, presumed that there was no place for Africans in an urban environment, beyond the level of certain forms of labor.

---

* "Juvenile Delinquency and Its Treatment," *Community and Crime* ("Penal Reform Pamphlets," No. 3 [Pretoria: Van Schaik, 1949]), p. 53.

During his years as a reformatory principal, Paton sought every opportunity to promote his belief in freedom as the supreme instrument of reform. He lectured frequently on the subject and wrote on various aspects of crime and delinquency for the publications of the South African Institute of Race Relations and the Prison Reform League. During 1943–44, the South African liberal biweekly *Forum* commissioned him to write a series of six articles on crime and punishment, as part of *Forum*'s exploration of social reforms that should be undertaken in the postwar period. Paton's series was concerned, in large measure, with the details of constructing model prisons and other practical steps toward reform, but the underlying principle was the restoration of the individual—and the society. In general, Paton proposed that the best way to deter crime was to restore to each person a feeling of social significance: "To mean something in the world is the deepest hunger of the human soul, deeper than any bodily hunger or thirst, and when a man has lost it he is no longer a man."* Although, as Principal of Diepkloof, his specialty was the care and rehabilitation of African delinquents, Paton could not separate the causes of African crime from the general malaise of society, nor could he see any hope for eliminating crime among Africans unless the whole social structure based on prevailing racial attitudes underwent reform.

A Philosophy of Emancipation: 1944–53

Two psychological stumbling blocks stand in the way of any change in South Africa's racially organized society. One relates to the question "How can the white ruling group be induced to initiate a process of self-emancipation from inbred attitudes?" The other relates to the question "Since most whites have no experience of a nonracial society, how can they even grasp the concept?"

An interesting recurring theme in Paton's writing, which relates to the second question, is that of the experience of a white South

* "The Real Way To Cure Crime," *Forum*, IV, No. 44 (January 29, 1944), 24.

African who joins in some common purpose with fellow South Africans of other races. In his biography of Hofmeyr, for example, Paton dwells on Hofmeyr's address to a joint Bantu-European Student Christian Conference (SCC) at Fort Hare College in 1930. Paton refers to this interracial conference as a visible manifestation of the kind of racial harmony that might be possible in South Africa. Since 1930 was the year Hofmeyr finally came to believe that the future lay with a common society, Paton perhaps implies that his experience at this interracial conference was a turning point. Again, in *Cry, the Beloved Country,* the interracial funeral service for Arthur Jarvis provides the deep experience that prompts James Jarvis to seek to understand his son's liberal outlook. Since Paton is normally a reticent and self-effacing man, he clearly hopes that his own autobiographical vignette "A Deep Experience" (included in this volume) has some significance beyond its mere telling.

"A Deep Experience," written for the South African literary journal *Contrast* in 1961, recounts an event of 1944 that, Paton says, convinced him he would never again be able to think in terms of race and nationality. "I had never been militantly white but now I became militantly nonracial." The climax of "A Deep Experience" is an account of the funeral service for Edith Rheinallt Jones, who had devoted her life to the work of the Institute of Race Relations: "Black man, white man, coloured man, European and African and Asian, Jew and Christian and Hindu and Moslem—all had come there to honour her memory—their hates and their fears, their prides and their prejudices, all for this moment forgotten." This vision of a nonracial community became transmuted into the practical endeavor of the Liberal Party, which, to demonstrate the viability of a nonracial society in South Africa, based its own organization on nonracial principles.

Africans and other nonwhite South Africans can more readily adapt themselves to nonracial attitudes than can white South Africans who must emancipate themselves from the rigid cast of habitual assumptions about race. In one of its aspects, Paton's biography of Jan Hofmeyr is a perceptive account of a typical spiritual

quest—a self-emancipation from white South African racial attitudes. "Hofmeyr," Paton tells us, "was moving slowly towards a
shore but dimly seen of that country called by some Utopia . . . and
by modern liberals the Common Society. It was a voyage into the
unknown, and he had as compass nothing but his own convictions."* And again: "Hofmeyr was a white South African, with
white South African fears and prejudices and irrationalities, but he
knew them for what they were and was feeling his way out of the
bog into which he had been born."† Paton, throughout, stresses
Hofmeyr's slow and painful progress "characterized by advances and
retreats," and he keeps constantly before us the image of a man
"inching his way towards emancipation with fear and caution but
not without courage." Paton's careful plotting of the stages of
Hofmeyr's inner progress provides a chart for the mental and psychological voyage facing every white South African who would
launch out toward a common society. Since his own essay "A Deep
Experience" implies a somewhat comparable inner progress, and
since Edith Rheinallt Jones's funeral—the event that caused him
to become "militantly nonracial"—took place in 1944, we are led
to presume that Paton came to the full realization of his militant
commitment to a common society during the period of World War
II.‡

At the outbreak of World War II, white South Africans were
divided in their allegiance. (Paton's *Too Late the Phalarope* cap-
tures some of the atmosphere of the times.) Some looked forward to
a victory by Hitler; others volunteered to fight with Britain and the
Allies. Thoughtful South Africans were acutely conscious of the
racist frenzy that drove Hitler on. In the early 1930's, they had
felt the wind of the wing of madness when a sympathetic outburst
of anti-Semitism in South Africa accompanied the emergence of

---

* *Hofmeyr*, p. 175.
† *Ibid.*, p. 307.
‡ Paton's recent contribution to the *Saturday Review* series "What I Have
Learned" confirms this conjecture. In that essay, he says, "It was Adolf Hitler
who finally destroyed for me—and for many others—the romantic illusion."
Saturday Review, L, No. 36 (September 9, 1967), p. 20.

Nazism in Germany.* Hofmeyr recognized it for what it was and took a public stand against it; a few private men, with Paton among them, actively fostered the South African Society of Christians and Jews, and other interracial associations.

Paton volunteered for military service when the war began, but his occupation was deemed essential and he was not accepted. He assumed a number of volunteer duties including the chairmanship of the combined YMCA and Toc-H (Talbot House) War Services —a voluntary organization providing services for the armed forces similar to those provided by the post exchanges and Red Cross volunteer workers in the United States. The war also brought him personal tragedy, for his only brother, Athol, was killed on December 16, 1940, in the battle of El Wak, the first engagement between a South African unit and Axis forces.

Whether or not Paton's deep experience in 1944 constituted a turning point, his writings from this period express a deepening concern with problems of race relations. In spite of wartime pressures, he seized every occasion offered him to write about, and lecture on, crime and other problems of the community. And it is noteworthy that he did not hesitate on these occasions to blame white society for condoning conditions that engendered African crime and lawlessness. On one occasion, he declared:

The truth is that many of us are just as afraid of a stable, purposeful, knowledgeable, moral, temperate, and law-abiding non-European community, as we are of a corrupt and lawless community. If reason does not help us, then we cannot do other than import moral considerations. . . . Let us aim at doing what is just and right and good, and let go our fears.†

On another occasion, he dismissed South Africa's favorite, if futile, antidote for African crime, the laws requiring all Africans to carry identifying passes, as irrelevant: "The carrying of papers of identi-

* See *Hofmeyr,* pp. 255 ff.
† "The Prevention of Crime," *Race Relations: Special Crime Number,* XII, No. 3–4 (1945), 77.

fication is an irrelevancy. No piece of paper—unless it be the charter of social significance itself—can keep a man from crime."*

The recurring theme in Paton's writing during this wartime period was the need for restoration: restoration of a sense of purpose and responsibility to youthful delinquents; restoration of dignity and social significance to dwellers in the urban slums; and restoration of family life among Africans in cities, following the disintegration of tribal ties and old ethical standards.

One of Paton's *Forum* articles has a special interest in retrospect. In this article, "Who Is Really To Blame for the Crime Wave in South Africa?"† he discerns three key elements in South Africa's social condition. First, he identifies the disintegration of African tribal society under the impact of Western economy and culture as the underlying cause of increased urban crime. "For a long time," he says, "the full dangers were not seen, but fathers and sons and daughters went to work and sometimes never came back." Robbed of the powerful support of tribal custom, African families attempting to set up homes in cities "began to experience with bewilderment and shame the shocks of disobedient children, pregnant daughters, delinquent sons." Concurrently, home life decayed in tribal Reserves "where men did not come back and where women went away to look for them and often found someone else." This is, essentially, the picture of disintegration that appears in *Cry, the Beloved Country*.

Paton then turns to the question of how society is to be restored, and he argues that restoration requires education as well as opportunities for work and the growth of self-respect. He repeats the insistent theme of his earlier *Forum* articles: "Men obey the laws when they are pursuing some worthy goals, working for some good purposes . . . using their gifts."‡ But he goes on to make a third, less familiar, observation when he speaks openly of white fear of

* "The Real Way To Cure Crime," *Forum,* No. 44 (January 29, 1944), p. 26.
† *Forum,* VIII, No. 37 (December 15, 1945), 7.
‡ *Ibid.,* p. 8.

African advancement. He says that it is an unacknowledged fear that causes white society to deny Africans the right to develop their gifts in almost all trades and occupations above the level of menial tasks. "It is these gifts of which we are afraid," he declares. "And as long as we fear them we shall be at the mercy of other more terrible gifts developed in the school of poverty, ignorance, cunning."

There is nothing tentative or uncertain in the tone of Paton's writings on social conditions in the 1940's; he speaks from knowledge, with conviction and, above all, with urgency. If Paton arrived at his nonracial attitude after an intellectual and spiritual voyage in some sense resembling Hofmeyr's, it was one less characterized by advances and retreats. It more closely resembled the successive stages of Arthur Jarvis' "Private Essay on the Evolution of a South African," which, together with the funeral, awakens James Jarvis —in *Cry, the Beloved Country*—to an understanding of his son's liberal spirit.

In 1946, Paton undertook, at his own expense, an eight-month study tour of penal institutions in Britain, the Scandinavian countries, Canada, and the United States. As he later reported, in his *Freedom as a Reformatory Instrument,** he was prompted to undertake this tour by his interest in the unsolved problem of the relationship between freedom and constraint in penal practice. In general, he noted in his report, penal institutions for adults tended to emphasize either custodial detention or re-education, without achieving a satisfactory synthesis. He found some Swedish institutions to be exceptions, but most of the reforms he saw outside of Sweden were "reforms within the framework of custody, and leave out of account the importance of freedom and responsibility as the supreme reformatory instruments."

During this tour, while he was at Trondheim, Norway, the urge to write returned to him, and he composed *Cry, the Beloved Country* during lonely evenings in hotel rooms in Scandinavia, Canada,

---

* Pretoria: Penal Reform League of South Africa, 1948.

and the United States. It is unnecessary to dwell here on the novel and its subsequent public reception, except to point out that the compassion and insight that inform it could only be attained by someone who had undergone Paton's experience with poverty and frustration among urban Africans during his Diepkloof years. It has, perhaps, sometimes been overlooked that a principal theme of *Cry, the Beloved Country* is the acceptance of personal responsibility for the social advancement of others. The two main characters, Stephen Kumalo and James Jarvis, are ordinary "uninvolved" men who come to recognize that individual indifference infects society with moral paralysis and that they must personally assume the responsibility of taking whatever action is possible to change their world.

The success of *Cry, the Beloved Country* encouraged Paton to go on writing, and, in 1948, he resigned from public service as Principal of Diepkloof Reformatory to devote himself to the task of interpreting South Africa through the medium of literature. That same year, he gave his reasons in a talk broadcast over the SABC:

I have left the public service, but not with any intention of living in idleness or ease. I want to interpret South Africa honestly and without fear. I cannot think of any more important or exciting task. All my life, of course, I have lived actively in a world of problems and people, and I do not know if I shall be able to live the kind of life an author seems to find necessary. This is one of the things I must find out for myself.*

The year 1948 was that of the initial Nationalist election victory; before the year ended, Jan Hofmeyr had died at the age of fifty-four. This turn in the tide of South African affairs did not long permit Paton to live the "kind of life an author seems to find necessary." For a time, he succeeded; he wrote *Too Late the Phalarope,* a novel that looked deeper into the psychological and spiritual roots of racism than *Cry, the Beloved Country* did, for it was the idolatry of pure race that demanded the total immolation of its tragic vic-

---

* As quoted in Horton Davis, "Alan Paton: Literary Artist and Anglican," *The Hibbert Journal,* L, No. 3 (April, 1952), 263.

tim, Pieter van Vlaanderen, not a transgression on his part against a law of God. After 1953, the year that *Too Late the Phalarope* was published, Paton was drawn increasingly into public affairs, having, as he put it, "felt it a duty to follow Hofmeyr's course, and to collaborate with Margaret Ballinger, Leo Marquard, Jordan Ngubane, Peter Brown and others in the work of the Liberal Party founded in 1953."*

The Liberal Party—A Nonracial Society: 1953–56

Although there was no Liberal Party in the Union of South Africa before 1953, there was a liberal tradition drawing sustenance from humanitarian, religious, and constitutional sources. Humanitarian liberalism had its intellectual roots in eighteenth-century theories on the rights of man—theories that find twentieth-century expression in the pursuit of civil liberties. Liberal attitudes informed by religious motives were fostered first by missionaries, particularly Dr. David Livingstone and Dr. John Philip, and thereafter chiefly by those churches known in South Africa as "English-speaking churches." Constitutional liberalism had its roots in the nineteenth-century constitution, creating self-government, that was granted by Great Britain to the Cape of Good Hope. By the terms of this constitution, voters were registered on a common roll on the basis of property qualification, not race. At the time of the Act of Union, in 1910, the Cape Province still had its common voters' roll basically intact. The Cape liberals (English-speaking and Afrikaner alike) sought to extend the Cape's common-roll franchise to the whole Union. The other three provinces rejected this extension but agreed that the Cape should retain its common roll; hence, the Union constitution guaranteed that no change could be made affecting the common roll without a two-thirds majority of both houses of Parliament voting together.

In 1936, the Hertzog-Smuts coalition Government collected the necessary two-thirds majority and removed African voters from the

* "The Hofmeyr Biography," *Contrast,* III, No. 2 (October, 1964), 34.

Cape common roll, but permitted them to elect white "Natives' representatives" in separate elections. Cape Coloured (mixed-race) voters were not affected. After their 1948 election victory, the Nationalists, under Dr. Malan, sought to remove the Cape Coloured voters from the common roll to a separate roll, which would have permitted them to elect white "Coloured representatives" to Parliament. This move initiated a constitutional struggle that lasted until 1955; in that year, the Government achieved its aim by freely manipulating the constitution. As a consequence of this struggle, the Liberal Party came into being—though the immediate causes of its creation were disillusionment with the United Party and the return to power of the Nationalist Party, with an increased majority, in April, 1953.

The circumstances of the Liberal Party's coming into being provide a key to the meaning of the term "nonracial," which the party uses to describe its own attitude. Dr. Malan's first proposal for action on the Cape common roll aroused strong opposition on constitutional grounds. The United Party opposed the proposal in Parliament, and, outside Parliament, an active organization was formed dedicated to upholding the constitution on the specific issue of Cape Coloured voting rights. This was the Torch Commando, composed chiefly of veterans of World War II, led by the famous Battle of Britain fighter pilot Group Captain "Sailor" Malan. This movement, with its enthusiastic rallies, was, in a sense, the crest of the wave of South African traditional liberalism, but it broke on the traditional rock. The Torch Commando movement, although supporting the rights of nonwhites, split on the issue of collaboration with Coloured movements seeking the same goal. The liberalism of the Torch Commando was the traditional white liberalism that was prepared to support, and even to extend, existing nonwhite rights but was not prepared to make common cause with nonwhites in an interracial movement. By accepting a common cause and common membership, the Liberal Party, which emerged in 1953, broke with this tradition. This willingness to make common cause with others on a nonracial basis was so distinctive a mark of the spirit of the new Liberal Party that some, including Chief Luthuli in his autobiography, trace its origin to the Defiance Campaign of 1952, when Patrick Duncan (son of a former Governor General of South Africa) and Manilal Gandhi (son of Mahatma Gandhi) led groups of white and Indian volunteers to join Africans in defying *apartheid* laws. Nelson Mandela, of the African National Congress (ANC), has expressed similar views, and Jordan Ngubane, a former vice-president of the Liberal Party, dwells on African response to this willingness to make common cause in his *An African Explains Apartheid.**

The decision to found a Liberal Party was taken at a meeting of the South African Liberal Association in Cape Town on May 9, 1953. Margaret Ballinger, MP, was elected President, with Leo Marquard and Alan Paton as vice-presidents; Dr. Oscar Wolheim was elected National Chairman, with Leslie Rubin as National Vice-Chairman. To begin with, the party's membership was preponderantly white, but, by its tenth anniversary, it was preponderantly African.

At the time that the Liberal Party was formed, Alan Paton was passing through a period of uncertainty and frustration. Not only were political events on the national scene confused, but he had been forced to abandon the work he had in hand—his biography of Jan Hofmeyr. During 1952, he had decided to put aside work on the biography and proceed no further during Mrs. Hofmeyr's lifetime, because she began to dislike the idea of a biography that was not to be simply a record of her son's public life. To gain time to think, and to recoup spiritually, Paton went to work with his wife at the Toc-H tuberculosis settlement for Africans at Botha's Hill, Natal, to help the infant settlement build accommodations for 600 patients. Responding to a letter from the *Saturday Review* on the occasion of the publication of *Too Late the Phalarope,* in 1953, he stated simply:

* New York: Frederick A. Praeger, 1963.

At the moment my wife and I are at the Toc-H TB settlement at Botha's Hill. The task of the settlement is to help Africans who have had TB to return to normal life. We have given ourselves to this work for a year and are enjoying it. We are also working for the new Liberal Party whose aim is to accustom South Africa to the idea that our only hope is to open the doors of our society to all people who are ready for it no matter what their race or colour.*

While at Botha's Hill, Paton wrote *The Land and People of South Africa,* a book geared to the needs of high school students in the United States and Britain. He also wrote on the crisis in race relations in South Africa for various journals in Britain and the United States as well as in South Africa. At the end of his stay at Botha's Hill, in 1954, he accepted an invitation from *Collier's* to tour the United States and report on American race relations.† In the course of this visit, Yale University conferred on him the honorary degree of Doctor of Humanities, and he was also invited to address a World Council of Churches meeting in Evanston, Illinois.

Paton returned to the United States in 1956, when *Too Late the Phalarope,* dramatized by Robert Yale Libott, was staged on Broadway at the Belasco Theatre. He had, in the meantime, toured South Africa with photographer Dan Weiner to compile *South Africa in Transition;* Weiner's photographs, constituting the bulk of the volume, corroborate Paton's views on the inherent dignity of all human beings. It was during his 1956 visit to New York, when literary matters seemed once more about to occupy his interest, that Paton received the news of his election as National Chairman of the Liberal Party. Averse as he was to public political life, he accepted the election as a call to duty.

* "A Letter from Alan Paton," *Saturday Review,* XXXVI, No. 34, August 22, 1953), 10.

† His report on race relations in the United States appeared in two issues of the magazine: "The Negro in America Today," *Collier's,* CXXXIV, No. 8 (October 15, 1954), pp. 52–56; and "The Negro in the North," *Collier's,* CXXXIV, No. 9 (October 29, 1954), pp. 70–80.

No Ivory Tower: 1956–60

Paton was called on to lead the Liberal Party during three separate phases. He was its National Chairman during a two-year period of comparative calm between 1956 and 1958. In June, 1958, he sought release from some of the active responsibilities of the chairmanship to give greater attention to pressing obligations as a writer, including the task of completing his biography of Jan Hofmeyr. Peter Brown was then elected National Chairman with responsibility for active leadership, and Paton was named to the less onerous position of President. When Peter Brown was imprisoned during the national state of emergency that was in effect from March through August, 1960, Paton again assumed the duties of National Chairman. He undertook the active leadership once more in July, 1964, when Peter Brown was placed under ban, until former Senator Edgar Brookes became National Chairman, in October, 1964.

During Paton's first years as Chairman, the Liberal Party was represented in Parliament by four of its members who had been elected as Natives' representatives in the separate election for those seats in December, 1953.* In 1956, the party put forward a constitutional policy calling for three steps toward reform: first, the coming to power of a government determined to retain a single national unity and interracial cooperation; second, the summoning of a national convention, representative of all racial groups and having power to recast the constitution; and third, the enactment of a bill of rights guaranteeing fundamental human rights and liberties to members of all racial groups.

The Liberals had greater difficulty, however, in agreeing on a policy for voting rights that would be just and, at the same time, palatable to a white minority whose voters feared being swamped by the votes of a black majority. At first, the political realists fa-

* These were Margaret Ballinger (Cape Eastern) and Walter Stanford (Transkei) in the House of Assembly, and William Ballinger (Transvaal and Orange Free State) and Leslie Rubin (Cape Province) in the Senate.

vored a gradual extension of voting rights. Others favored adopting the motto popular among Africans "one man, one vote." By 1960, this second view prevailed, and the party revised its franchise policy to include extending "the right of franchise on the common roll to all adult persons." This total commitment, as well as the decision in the extraparliamentary sphere to give the party's official support to the economic boycott of South African goods planned in several countries, caused a number of leading Liberals including Walter Stanford, MP, to resign and to join the new Progressive Party, which seemed likelier to succeed in a parliamentary role.

The problem of common policy regarding voting rights demonstrates that certain unavoidable facts required the multiracial Liberal Party to view the South African political scene in double focus. No matter how single-minded its members might be about ultimate goals, only the white members had votes, and only voters could directly influence constitutional or parliamentary change. If the nonwhite members were to be anything more than mere spectators, their contributions to a nonracial society would have to be made outside the sphere of parliamentary action. The party recognized its dual role and attempted to make headway on two fronts: in the parliamentary sphere and through such extraparliamentary activities as investigating and publicizing cases of hardship caused by *apartheid* and providing legal aid and advice to those in need. Paton's writings of the period immediately after 1956 reveal his equal interest in both these aims. His *Hope for South Africa* and his *Contact* essays during the parliamentary election campaign of 1958 take cognizance of the restricted sphere of white politics. His pamphlets *The People Wept* and *The Charlestown Story*—parts of which are included in this volume—were based on field research undertaken by Liberal Party members; both emphasize the need to oppose the implementation of *apartheid* measures on the grounds of inherent injustice to nonwhites.

When Paton was released from his active duties as Chairman of the Liberal Party, in June, 1958, he had two tasks before him as a writer. One was the completion of the biography of Jan Hofmeyr, which he had put aside in 1952; the other was the writing of plays for a nonracial theater. On July 27, 1959, Mrs. Hofmeyr died, and Paton immediately resumed his work on the biography of her son. It took almost four more years to complete the book, because of such serious interruptions as the period of the state of emergency, in 1960, during which the manuscript was hidden as a precaution against seizure in a police raid.

Before taking up the biography again, he had written a play, *Last Journey,* based on the circumstances under which Dr. Livingstone's body was carried from the interior of Africa to Bagamayo, on the coast. The play was first performed in Lusaka, Northern Rhodesia (now Zambia), by the Waddington Players, an amateur group that provided the necessary interracial cast. Paton's next dramatic piece was the libretto for the musical *Mkhumbane,* with music by Todd Matshikiza. Paton wrote this drama as a contribution to the efforts of the Institute of Race Relations to provide dramatic media for the talents of African actors and actresses. *Mkhumbane,* directed by Malcolm Woolfson, had its world premiere at the Durban City Hall on March 28, 1960, under extraordinary circumstances. Those who set the date for the opening of *Mkhumbane* had no foreknowledge that March 28, 1960, would be a day of national mourning for those killed at Sharpeville and Langa, or that the play's scheduled week of performances would coincide with the most fearful and anxious week in recent South African history.

On March 21, 1960—the date selected by Robert Sobukwe's Pan-African Congress (PAC) for a nonviolent campaign against the pass laws—police fired on crowds of demonstrators at Sharpeville in the Transvaal and Langa in the Cape Province, killing and wounding many. On March 26, Chief Albert Luthuli, President of the African National Congress, ceremoniously burned his pass book and called on all Africans to stay away from work on March 28, in mourning for the victims. On March 28, Parliament introduced the Unlawful Organizations Bill, empowering it to ban both the PAC and the ANC. This bill was rushed through both houses of Parliament within a week. Meanwhile, on March 30, the Government declared a state of emergency. In the early morning hours of that day, the police arrested and imprisoned 234 men and women of all races, including the Liberal Party National Chairman, Peter Brown, and several other leading members of the party.

Against this background of fear and anxiety, with thousands of Africans marching through the streets of Cape Town and Durban, *Mkhumbane* was presented daily before racially mixed audiences. "During this momentous week," Paton recalls, "we played to full houses, people of all kinds and races, in Durban City Hall. It was indeed a moving experience to go into that hall and see there the absence of all fear and hate."*

The first weeks of the emergency were a time of great internal crisis in South Africa. There were huge, but disciplined, demonstrations by Africans in the streets of Cape Town and Durban, and there were also undisciplined riots and incidents involving arson (frequently directed against churches, schools, and clinics) in some African townships. This rioting and violence continued sporadically until April 7. On April 9, Prime Minister Verwoerd was seriously wounded in an assassination attempt by a white farmer who was later found to be mentally unsound. Just over the South African horizon, the Congo, torn by internal disorder and cruel racial killings, was increasingly becoming an international cockpit.

In this unparalleled atmosphere of crisis, Paton was called from his literary pursuits to act as National Chairman. "At real personal risk and cost," said *Contact*, "he ran the national office of the Party and led the Party in all ways."† His first task was to rally the Liberal Party while many of its most distinguished members were held as political prisoners.‡ The fact that the emergency regulations

---

* Letter to the editor of this volume, August, 1966.
† *Contact*, III, No. 17 (August 27, 1960), 6.
‡ These included, besides Peter Brown, several district leaders and executives —among them, Dr. Hans Meidner (Natal Chairman), Frank Bhengu (National Committee), Eric Attwell (Port Elizabeth Committee), John Lang (East Rand Chairman), Dr. Colin Lang (Liberal Party candidate, Transvaal provincial elections, 1959), and Elliott Mngadi (party organizer for Northern Natal).

contained stringent measures against adverse press comment (even publication of the names of detainees was prohibited) added to the confusion and uncertainty. In the midst of this uncertainty, Paton addressed Liberal Party meetings in several cities, putting forward the party's attitude to these events clearly and unequivocally. Addressing the Liberal Party national congress at Rondebosch, Cape Town, on May 27, 1960, he declared:

It is my duty, as acting National Chairman of the Liberal Party, to say what the party attitude is in this matter. We do not intend to operate an organisation agreeable to the Government; we intend to go on speaking and writing openly, we intend to communicate with any organisation if we think there is benefit in it, and we intend to go on putting forward our proposals in regard to the future of South Africa and its people, and we intend to go on maintaining a nonracial party, for it is only in nonracialism that we see any hope for the future. Although we are not living in a democracy, we intend to go on acting as though we were, as far as that is possible. And that is what every democratic South African ought to be doing. That is certainly what we are doing by meeting here this evening.*

Paton's writings in this present volume, particularly his May, 1960, presidential address and his essays on Africa in crisis, reflect the pressures of the times better than any summary account here could, but one additional source of strain within the Liberal Party at this time should be mentioned.

The year 1960 saw the virtual end of the Liberal Party as a parliamentary party, when the seats for Natives' representatives were abolished under the terms of the Promotion of Bantu Self-Government Act—the legislation that replaced parliamentary representation with local tribal autonomy in Bantu (African) areas. But, even before this form of representation came to an end, one of the Liberals in Parliament, Walter Stanford, had shifted to the new Progressive Party, which had been formed by twelve MP's who, previously, had constituted the liberal wing of the United Party.

* Extracts reproduced in "The Long View," *Contact*, III, No. 11 (June 4, 1960), p. 5.

Other prominent white Liberals outside Parliament also joined the Progressive Party organization. Among these were Dr. Oscar Wolheim, who had been the Liberal Party's first National Chairman, and Gerald Gordon, QC, who had represented the party in the 1958 parliamentary elections. Dr. Wolheim and Mr. Gordon issued a statement in September, 1960, taking issue with the party's new policy of "one man, one vote," and also with its increasing preoccupation with the extraparliamentary activity. Their statement, which crystallizes the Liberal dilemma, declared:

We have always been in favour of a qualified franchise and against the idea of "one man, one vote," our view being that the franchise should be exercised only by those whose education and civilized standards give them the necessary sense of responsibility. . . . Secondly we think that the function of a political party is to seek power to govern or to participate in government. This it can only do by appealing to those who have the vote. . . . The Liberal Party is today functioning mainly as a pressure group and we feel therefore that as a political party we can no longer support it.*

Coincidentally with this loss of some of its founding members, the Liberal Party gained wider support among Africans. One event that helped to nurture African confidence was Peter Brown's refusal to take advantage of the Government's readiness, in response to representations made in his behalf, to free him from prison. "He would leave jail only if his colleagues on both sides of the color line were released," said Jordan Ngubane. "This showed the Africans that the white liberal was determined to destroy white supremacy."†

During the difficult days of 1960, many Liberals were cheered by the news that Freedom House had selected Alan Paton as the recipient of the Freedom Award for 1960—an honor conferred in previous years on such distinguished men as Winston Churchill, Franklin Roosevelt, Dwight Eisenhower, George Marshall, and

* From an interview in the *Cape Times*, quoted in *Contact*, III, No. 19 (September 24, 1960), 3.
† *Op. cit.*, p. 197.

Dag Hammarskjöld. Paton, looking on himself as a representative of these Liberals who had suffered in prison and in other ways during 1960, accepted the award in their name at Freedom House, in New York City, on October 5, 1960. President Eisenhower sent a message of congratulation, and Archibald MacLeish gave the main welcoming address. (Paton's response in his Freedom Award address is included in this volume.)

In the course of his return journey to South Africa, Paton addressed meetings in England to help raise money for Defence and Aid—a fund that supplied legal aid and financial assistance for political detainees and their dependents. He also attended World Council of Churches meetings in Geneva, Switzerland. When he arrived at Jan Smuts Airport, Johannesburg, on December 5, 1960, he was met by representatives of the South African Government, who came not to congratulate him but to deprive him of his passport and thereby confine him, in future, to South Africa.

No Share in Opposition: 1961–68

Speaking in Parliament on September 18, 1958, newly elected Prime Minister Verwoerd foreshadowed the future of the Liberal Party: "When South Africa becomes a republic," he said, "there will be no place for liberal or similar parties which wish to place white and non-white on equality." South Africa became a republic on May 31, 1961. Within three or four years, the nonracial Liberal Party was decimated through the political bannings of its active leaders. It is easy to understand why the South African Government abhorred the idea of a nonracial Liberal Party. Dr. Verwoerd had stated the obvious when he said there was no place for such a party in a republic organized on the basis of racial separateness; for the Liberal Party and the Nationalist Party disagreed about the very nature of society and even, in a sense, about the nature of man; such differences are not easily negotiable. One reason, therefore, for the extreme severity of measures taken against the members of so relatively powerless an organization as the South African Liberal

Party was the felt threat to *apartheid* implicit in the party's mere existence. "A fact that must be faced by everybody," said the official Nationalist Party voice, *Die Transvaler,* "is that liberalism is one of the greatest threats to the survival of the Republic of South Africa."*

Also from the standpoint of pure political expediency, it is easy to understand why severe measures were taken against Liberals by the Nationalist Party in the period between 1961 and 1966. The time was ripe, for the will to act, a suitable political climate, and the appropriate legal machinery existed concurrently.

There could be no question about the will to act—Nationalist spokesmen had repeatedly declared that there could be no coexistence between Afrikaner nationalism and liberalism in South Africa. Mr. Vorster, then Minister of Justice, went further. He was not content to equate liberalism with Communism as his colleagues had so frequently done. He spoke of liberalism as the "greater danger," even the "prime promoter of Communism," and white South Africans readily accepted the logic of such statements as the following, which he made in Parliament, on March 6, 1964: "Communism in its essence is anti-national. Because it is anti-national and because the liberals . . . throughout the whole world reject nationalism, the *liberals . . . are wittingly or unwittingly the prime promoters of Communism.*" (Emphasis added.)

The political climate favored action against the "danger" of liberalism because of the public fear of internal subversion by those members of banned African organizations who had gone underground and formed "The Spear of the Nation" (dedicated to sabotage) and *Poqo* (dedicated to terrorism). Furthermore, the active exploitation by both Chinese and Soviet Communists of tensions and crises in the new African states lent substance to South African fears about the imminent threat of Communism.

Finally, effective machinery for silencing Liberals and liberal opinion was ready at hand. Democratic countries know no parallels

* October 30, 1962.

to two aspects of the powers granted South Africa's Minister of Justice in banning persons from public life, or in detaining or restricting them at will. These are, first, that charges made on the basis of these powers need not be proved, and the person banned or detained has no recourse to the courts, and, second, that the bans and detentions are immediately renewable on expiration. These powers derive from the 1950 Suppression of Communism Act and from the 1963 General Laws Amendment Act (popularly known as the Sabotage Act). This latter statute, which broadened the powers granted the Minister under the 1950 act, contained a clause that permitted the Minister to detain any suspected person in prison for renewable periods of ninety days. How effectively Mr. Vorster used these laws to combat liberalism under the banner of anti-Communism will be readily apparent from the essays in this volume.

In appraising the South African Government's actions toward those in opposition to its policies at this time, it should be kept in mind that a number of acts of sabotage were, in fact, committed. Between January, 1963, and May, 1965, about one thousand people, mostly former members of the banned ANC and PAC, were convicted on charges under the broad definitions of the Suppression of Communism Act and the Sabotage Act. A few men who had been members, or banned members, of the Liberal Party had participated in some of these acts of violence, with grave consequences for the Liberal Party as a whole. Paton spoke of the damage done to the Party as incomputable:

Some of these saboteurs were members and banned members of the Liberal Party of South Africa, and the damage they have done to the cause of liberalism is incomputable. They made it easier for the Government to ban other Liberals who had never contemplated sabotage, but who were actively opposed to *apartheid*. Yet they did what they did largely because they wanted to show that there were white people who were prepared to suffer for the liberation of black people.*

---

* "Alan Paton Reports on South Africa," an article that (under various titles) appeared in a number of denominational journals. Among these: *Commonweal*, LXXXII, No. 10 (May 28, 1965); *Presbyterian Life*, XVIII, No. 11 (June 1, 1965).

The year 1964 saw the climax of the campaign to discredit the Liberal Party by associating it, and its members, with the aims of Communism. Since all bans were imposed (in terms of the Suppression of Communism Act) for "furthering the aims of Communism," the steadily growing number of banned Liberals swayed many who were not already convinced of the menace of liberalism. Although Paton was not banned, there were frequent intimations that he was at least a fellow traveler. He appeared in court at the close of the Rivonia "sabotage" trial,* in June, 1964, to plead in mitigation of the sentence because he feared that Nelson Mandela and those convicted with him would be sentenced to death. The Deputy Attorney-General, Percy Yutar, chose this occasion to declare that he would "unmask" Paton and show that he had come to court to spread propaganda. Mr. Yutar introduced the worn theme of wittingly or unwittingly aiding Communism into his cross-examination by pressing Paton with such questions as "Are you a Communist?" and "Are you a fellow traveler?"

In view of the atmosphere that prevailed during 1964, the banning of Liberal Party National Chairman Peter Brown, on July 30 of that year, may be interpreted as marking the virtual end of the party as an effective political organization. The language of a resolution passed at the party's National Congress, in July, 1965, supports this conclusion. The resolution, which tended to refer to the party in the past tense, stated that the Liberal Party had been "the victim of savage, systematic and, let it be remembered, unconstitutional persecution by the Nationalist Party at present in control of the Government," and went on to say, "We have seen our country

* Nelson Mandela, a former leader of the banned ANC and a member of the Liberal Party, joined the underground offshoot of the ANC, *Umkonto We Sizwe* (The Spear of the Nation), which engaged in a planned campaign of sabotage directed against "symbols of *apartheid*"—chiefly, government buildings and installations. Spear claimed adherence to a firm policy of avoiding injury or loss of life to others in carrying out these acts. The Rivonia trial drew international attention. Those convicted and sentenced to life imprisonment (the death penalty was possible) included six Africans: Nelson Mandela, Walter Sisulu, Govan Mbeki, Elias Motsoaledi, Andrew Mlangeni, and Raymond Mahlaba; one Indian: Ahmed Kathrada; and one white: Dennis Goldberg.

flooded by a tidal wave of legislation which has eroded the values and submerged the liberties which South Africa once enjoyed, and which as Liberals we most deeply cherished." Yet, in the face of this, it added, "If through this persecution, *and in fact defeat*, any of our members or our friends are beginning to lose hope in the future of our country, we would urge them that now is the time to hold fast to our convictions and our faith."* Paton had rightly interpreted the Government's purpose when he said, in an address at Rondebosch, Cape Town, in 1960, "I do not expect them to offer us a share in government, but at least they might have left us a share in opposition. But even that they seem determined to take away. Such opposition is to them subversive, traitorous, unnational."†

In September, 1966, the Government introduced a new piece of legislation under the title "Prohibition of Improper Interference Bill." The immediate purpose of this bill was to prevent members of the existing white political parties, particularly members of the Progressive Party, from seeking nomination or election to the four parliamentary seats for Coloured representatives. This bill presumed the separate existence of four population groups—white, Coloured, Asian, and African—and made it compulsory for every political party or organization to limit its membership to persons of one racial group. The terms of this bill would obviously make the nonracial Liberal Party an illegal organization. The National Committee of the Liberal Party met and decided that, if the bill became law, the party would be dissolved from the moment the President of South Africa signed the measure. The bill passed its first reading, on September 19, 1966 (113 votes to 40), but it was referred to a "select committee" (later expanded to a "select commission"), and, at the present moment, it has yet to become law.

It follows that the Liberal Party's present role differs greatly from the role it hoped to play even as late as 1960. Liberals like

* *Natal Mercury,* July 12, 1965. (Emphasis added.) Quoted in Muriel Hornell (ed.), *Annual Survey of Race Relations in South Africa, 1965* (Johannesburg: South African Institute of Race Relations, 1966), p. 7. Henceforth cited as ASRR.

† *Contact,* III, No. 11 (June 4, 1960), p. 5.

Paton are no longer occupied with keeping a parliamentary party alive; they are trying to keep the breath of life in the liberal spirit itself. Nothing reveals this more clearly than the successive shifts in *The Long View,* from views opposing specific laws and restrictions—in such writings as "The Abuse of Power" (1963)—to concern for the liberal spirit itself—in such essays as "Ideas Never Die" (1964), "Beware of Melancholy" (1965), and even "Waiting for Robert" (1966).

The problems of the Liberal Party and the difficulties faced by friends and associates who had been placed under restriction were not Paton's sole sources of concern. Still another endeavor with which he was associated was, during 1965, coming under attack for furthering the aims of Communism. This was the Defence and Aid Fund, which had its origins in the Treason Trial Defence Fund, formed to pay for the defense of 156 people of all races (including Chief Luthuli) arrested on charges of treason in December, 1956. At the end of the preparatory examination, in December, 1957, the charges against Chief Luthuli and 60 others were dropped. During the trial, which lasted more than four years, one defendant died. When the trial ended, on March 29, 1961, the remaining defendants were all acquitted. During the trial, the Defence Fund, of which Paton was one of the patrons, collected and dispersed £200,000 to aid the defendants. At the time of the 1960 state of emergency, the purpose of this fund was broadened, and it became the Defence and Aid Fund for assisting an increasing number of political prisoners and their dependents. Defence and Aid (South Africa) received financial support from within South Africa and from the Oxford Fund for Famine Relief (Oxfam), the Rowntree Trust (a philanthropic fund established by a Quaker family), the World Council of Churches, and Defence and Aid (London). In response to a 1963 U.N. General Assembly appeal for support for victims of *apartheid,* some member countries—including Sweden, Denmark, India, Pakistan, and the Soviet Union—made their contributions through Defence and Aid (London). When the Government of the Netherlands voted £10,000 as its contribution to De-

fence and Aid (London) in 1965, the South African reaction was
an angry one. David Craighead, Transvaal Chairman of Defence
and Aid (South Africa), and other officers of the fund were banned.
The Minister for Foreign Affairs dispatched a note to the Netherlands' Government appraising it of what Defence and Aid was
"knowingly or unknowingly" doing to further the aims of Communism:

As is generally known, this organization, among others, gives financial
support to meet the court expenses of persons—some of whom are
confessed Communists or have co-operated with Communists, and have
been convicted of murder and bloodshed—persons whose aim and purpose is to overthrow the lawful government of this friendly country of
which the Netherlands is the country of origin.
  This organization has, thus, through financial support associated itself with the reckless actions of saboteurs. . . . Any form of encouragement to such saboteurs inevitably promotes, knowingly or unknowingly, the communistic ambitions in Africa.*

The Defence and Aid Fund was banned at midnight on March
18, 1966, and all Defence and Aid offices and the homes of a number of people connected with the fund were raided by security
police early the following morning. Paton was among those visited
at home by the security police that morning.

Those professing the liberal spirit have had little cause to rejoice
during the past few years. There have been some brighter moments,
including the visit by Senator Robert Kennedy, and some comfort
in the readiness of Edgar Brookes and Leo Marquard to assume the
liberal burden, but the single-minded search of the zealots for Communist influence has gone on apace. A church body in the Transvaal
was seriously calling for an investigation (for Communist influence) of three other organizations in which Paton has had a life-
long interest: the SCA, NUSAS, and the World Council of
Churches.

Although Paton himself has not been restricted by any official
ban other than the withdrawal of his passport, he is far from free

* The text of this note can be found in ASRR, 1965, p. 73.

even in his personal and social contacts. He cannot, for example, meet socially with friends like Peter Brown who are banned, and most of his friends among the Anglican clergy have either left or, like Trevor Huddleston, been transferred from South Africa, or ousted, like Bishop Reeves of Johannesburg. An Indian friend, Dr. Gangathura Naicker, who had been eleven years under ban and who had invited Paton and his wife to dinner to discuss the education of his son, was sentenced to fourteen months' imprisonment for contravening the conditions of his ban by having the Patons to dinner and for failing to give notice of change of address after he had been evicted from his home by a court order issued under the Group Areas Act.*

It will be apparent from *The Long View* that these difficulties have not swayed Paton in his commitment to a nonracial society. But they have, obviously, prevented him from undertaking the creative literary work he had looked forward to in 1948. His own reflections on an earlier "moment of sterility" may, therefore, mirror his present situation as a literary man:

> I have approached a moment of sterility
> I shall not write any more awhile
> For there is nothing more meretricious
> Than to play with words.
> Yet they are all there within me
> The great living host of them
> The gentle, the compassionate
> The bitter and the scornful
> The solemn and the sorrowful
> The words of the childhood that will not come again.
> But they do not come out for nothing
> They do not form themselves into meanings
> Unless some price has been paid for them
> Unless some deep thing is felt that runs
> Like a living flame through their shapes and forms
> So that they catch fire and fuse themselves
> Into glowing incandescences

* More complete information on the trial and sentence can be found in *Contact*, IX, No. 5 (September, 1966), 16–17; and No. 6 (October, 1966), 15.

Or if the felt thing is deep indeed,
Into conflagrations, so that the pen
Smokes in the hand, and the hand
Burns to the bone, and the paper chars
Under the heat of composition.
Therefore words, stay where you are awhile
Till I am able to call you out,
Till I am able to call you with authentic voice
So that the great living host of you
Tumble out and form immediately
Into parties, commandos, and battalions
Briefly saluting and wheeling away instantly
To waken the sleeping consciences
To call back to duty the absenting obligations
To assault again, night and day, month and year,
The fortresses and bastions of our fears.*

* *Contrast,* I, No. 4 (December, 1961), 17.

PART ONE:

Into Deep Waters, 1958-59

Editor's Introduction

ON QUESTIONS OF RACE, there is no political spectrum in South Africa; no comfortable middle ground where skeptic or dissenter might feel at ease. Those who hold power in the state seek to ensure the racial purity and perpetual supremacy of their own white group through the system known as *apartheid*. The advocates of *apartheid* equate local customs and prejudices pertaining to race with immutable, God-given laws. They feel duty-bound to obey these "laws" and to ensure that others obey them also.

In his first "Long View" essay, Alan Paton described South Africa as "a white fortress. Each day, each month, each year, the Nationalists make it stronger. They make the walls thicker; they make them higher." And he added the phrase from which the title of his series derives: "Yet, in the long view, no one believes that the fortress will endure."

The essays in *The Long View* were written by a man who believes that the fortress will not endure and, therefore, that the only political questions worth discussing in such a society are "How do we move, by sound and constructive steps, away from white supremacy? How do we avoid violence and catastrophe? How do we get white people to agree to want to share liberty, responsibility, and power?"

In taking the long view, Paton sets personal encounters and political events in the broad perspectives of human longing for freedom and justice. A number of his essays are cast as parables of the nonracial spirit—parables in which South African settings and events provide the initial invitation to self-appraisal. It is to supply an appropriate prelude to this literary method that Paton's auto-biographical vignette "A Deep Experience" is included here as pro-logue.

The essays in Part One of *The Long View* are grouped about unifying themes relevant to the South African scene in 1958–59. Since they presume that the reader has some knowledge of the framework of South African life and political problems, it may be useful to review the background here.

South Africa has a population of 18.3 million people (1966). By law (the Population Registration Act of 1950), all South Africans carry identity cards showing their classification as members of one of four racial groups: Bantu (Native Africans), 12.5 million; European (white), 3.5 million; Coloured (mixed race), 1.8 million; and Asiatic (Indian origin, except for 7,000 Chinese), 0.5 million. Only adult whites have the right to vote in ordinary parliamentary elections, and only whites participate in government. Coloured males in the Cape Province can return four white representatives to Parliament in separate elections. The major political parties are projections of historical differences within the white group. Of this group, 60 per cent are of Dutch descent and speak the South African form of Dutch called Afrikaans. Formerly known as Boers, they prefer to be called Afrikaners. The remaining 40 per cent are largely of British origin and speak English.

The original Dutch settlers came to the Cape in 1652, and their struggle with the British dates from 1806, when Britain occupied the Cape. The Anglo-Boer War, of 1899–1902, was the culminating point in this struggle. In 1910, both groups came together in a single state, the Union of South Africa and, at first, followed a policy of reconciliation. The United Party, which has both English-speaking and Afrikaans-speaking adherents, is the heir to this policy. The National Party (*die Nasionale Party*) follows a narrowly exclusive policy of Afrikaner nationalism* and is, therefore, more suitably referred to as the Nationalist Party. While the Nationalist Party is close knit and single-minded in its purposes, the United Party is a coalition of interests. It has a conservative wing, differing little from the Nationalists, and a diminishing liberal wing. Both parties differ sharply in their attitudes toward their own pasts, but they differ very little in their attitudes toward retaining power in the hands of the white group. In short, both major parties look on politics and political campaigns as an exclusive preserve of the white group. In 1948, the Nationalist Party came to power under Dr. Daniel F. Malan; it has been returned to power, with increased majorities, in all subsequent elections. The United Party lost some of its liberal wing to the Liberal Party in 1953 and perhaps even more to the Progressive Party in 1959.

The nonwhite groups are excluded from the parliamentary system of government and do not have political parties in the conventional sense. They have political movements, like the Natal Indian Congress, which is experienced in organizing passive-resistance campaigns—a technique initiated in Natal by Mahatma Gandhi at the turn of the century and, later, brought by him to India. The African National Congress (ANC), led by Chief Albert Luthuli, was the largest political organization outside Parliament in 1958, but it was banned in 1960, together with its more militant offshoot, the Pan-African Congress (PAC). The first "Long View" essays appeared in *Contact* in February, 1958, two months before the South African parliamentary election of April 16, 1958. The Liberal Party had three candidates in that election—Peter Brown, in Pietermaritzburg District; Jimmy Dey, in Orange Grove, Johannesburg; and Gerald Gordon, in Sea Point, Cape Town. They received, respectively, 6 per cent, 5 per cent, and 17 per cent of the votes cast by the white electorate. During the election campaign, Alan Paton devoted his

---

* Its own term for this exclusion of all but "true Afrikaners" is *"eiesoortig-heid,"* which translates roughly as "one's-own-sort-ness." There is no English equivalent to the term; the closest the editor can come to an equivalent term is the Gaelic *"Sinn Fein,"* meaning "we ourselves."

"Long View" essays to the Liberal Party's parliamentary program. They contrast the Liberal Party aim of a nonracial society with the white-supremacy *(baasskap)* policies of the ruling Nationalist Party, then led by Johannes G. Strijdom. (Strijdom died on August 24, 1958; his successor was Dr. Hendrik F. Verwoerd, who had laid the foundations for *apartheid* while he was Minister of Native Affairs, between 1950 and 1958). These essays find no real alternative in the program of the official opposition, the United Party, led by Sir de Villiers Graaf.

A Note on Contact

Contact was launched in February, 1958, by a newly established company, Selemela Publications, Ltd.; it was intended to serve as an independent biweekly news review. The names of both the publishing company and the news review itself symbolized aspects of the Liberal Party's program. *"Selemela"* is the Sotho (a Bantu language) word for the Pleiades, the constellation whose appearance is taken as a signal, in many African tribes, for the people to go out into the fields and start the season's work. The title *Contact,* which, since 1953, had been used for an occasional broadsheet published by the Liberal Party, had obvious implications as an antonym of *apartheid.* The first issue of *Contact* (February 8, 1958) drew attention to this significance: *"Contact* has been chosen as the name of this publication because we firmly believe that in this word lies the key to understanding, racial harmony, and material and spiritual well-being not only in South Africa but in the whole African continent and the world."

At the beginning, *Contact* insisted on the status of an independent news review and denied direct Liberal Party affiliation. "Although we have sympathy with broad liberal principles," it declared, "we are tied to no party and we refuse to have any labels tied to us." Nevertheless, *Contact* has been so invariably associated in the public mind with the Liberal Party that it now seems merely academic to insist on its independent status.

Contact began as a well-designed illustrated review, produced by a competent professional staff. At first, it attracted a substantial amount of advertising from major national business concerns such as oil companies and tobacco companies. But, as the difficulties of the Liberal Party grew, the advertisers withdrew their support, and a day came when no printer would risk printing *Contact.*

Beginning with the state of emergency (March 30 to August 31, 1960), *Contact* and its editors were almost continuously in trouble with the authorities. During April, 1960, its offices were raided three times by security police; the editor, Patrick Duncan, suspended publication for a week and assumed the sole proprietorship. In October, 1960, he was imprisoned for refusing to reveal his sources of information for an editorial on the Communist Party that ran in the issue of August 27, 1960, and, in March, 1961, he was banned. Several other editors were banned in rapid succession: Peter Hjul (February, 1963), Harold Head (August, 1964), Ann Tobias (October, 1964), Jill Jessop (ninety days' detention, November, 1964), Michael Frances (July, 1965).

A run of *Contact* assembled on library shelves mutely illustrates the fortunes of the Liberal Party between 1960 and 1966. The issues fluctuate abruptly in size and appearance, and many have very little advertising. The publication made frequent appeals for financial help, but, by February, 1964, it was reduced to appearing only once monthly. The August, 1964, issue was mimeographed, since no printer could be found willing to set it. For about a year thereafter, the monthly issues were hand-printed by the office staff. *Contact* then reverted permanently to mimeographed form. During this time, the costs incurred from court cases on charges of subverting the authority of the state and of contravening the Prisons Act by publishing the names of detainees, which was forbidden during the 1960 state of emergency, almost caused its collapse.

Contact also suffered through hooligan attacks on its offices and equipment. Beginning in July, 1964, there were sporadic assaults on people and organizations opposed to Government policy in South Africa. A bomb was thrown at the home of one Liberal Party member, and bullets were fired from passing cars into the home of another. Two night raids were made on the offices of the Liberal Party, *Contact,* and the "monthly" *The New African.** In its February, 1965, issue, *Contact* reported, "During these raids the initials K.R.A. (believed to stand for Kenya [white] Refugees Association) were smeared on the wall. Typewriters were smashed, files destroyed, windows broken and addressograph plates stolen and later used for the posting of anonymous abusive letters." Police were notified of all these incidents, and Helen Suzman, of the Progressive Party, raised questions in Parliament; yet, by February, 1965, after nearly eight months and at least seventeen incidents, no person had been arrested or charged.

In terms of the present laws regulating the press in South Africa, all publications appearing monthly or more frequently must apply to the Minister of the Interior for registration and deposit $28,000, which they forfeit if they contravene the stringent regulations laid down for them. *Contact* preserved its registration for seven and a half years but canceled it in September, 1965, "since re-registration would almost certainly cost us R20,000 [$28,000]." *Contact* also ceased to have a paid staff, moved to cheaper offices, and even gave up its telephone. It continued publication in duplicated form at irregular intervals.

Six issues of *Contact* appeared during 1966, consisting chiefly of Alan Paton's column "The Long View," which formed a kind of centerpiece amid brief accounts of new bans, restrictions, and trials, all culled from other newspapers. In this attenuated form, *Contact* is the last liberal organ still publishing in South Africa, for even the respected journal *Forum,* founded in 1938 to propagate Jan Hofmeyr's liberal views, has ceased publication for lack of support.

Alan Paton wrote three separate series of essays for *Contact's* column "The Long View." The first series ran from February, 1958, to February, 1959. After Paton completed this series, Peter

---

* *The New African,* a journal closely linked to the Liberal Party, actually appeared every five weeks in order to avoid the registration fee required of monthlies.

Brown wrote "The Long View" until his imprisonment on March 30, 1960. Paton then wrote his second series, replacing Brown until the state of emergency ended, on August 31, 1960. Thereafter, except in 1962, when *Contact* contained no "Long View" column, Brown wrote it. Paton replaced Brown in January, 1964, and began his third "Long View" series. No subsequent issue of *Contact* appeared without Paton's "Long View" essay, which ultimately became almost the sole reason for the paper's appearance. *Contact* once declared, "we shall continue to publish as long as we have one person with one typewriter and one machine left to print or duplicate what we believe must be said from inside South Africa." Paton has done his part to ensure that *Contact* kept faith.

Prologue: "A Deep Experience"*

Paton's *Cry, the Beloved Country* concludes with the words "But when that dawn will come, of our emancipation, from the fear of bondage and the bondage of fear, why, that is a secret." The nonracial attitude of which Paton speaks in the "Long View" essays is a quality of personality necessary for the realization of that emancipation. The term "nonracial," as Paton and the Liberal Party use it, describes not a passive, neutral attitude but an active disposition of mind liberated from, and capable of transcending, prejudices and preconceptions regarding race. When the Liberal Party described its goal as a nonracial society, it envisaged a pluralistic society with members of all races emancipated from "the fear of bondage and the bondage of fear." "A Deep Experience," which describes the death of Edith Rheinallt Jones, in 1944, is included here to introduce this concept of nonracialism. See Paton's *Hofmeyr* for further information about the life and work of Mrs. Jones.

THE EMANCIPATION of a white person from colour prejudice is very seldom a sudden conversion. It is rather the result of a number of experiences. Yet there is one experience that lives in my memory. Through it I knew that I was no longer primarily a white person.

* *Contrast,* I, No. 4 (December, 1961), 20–24.

I had never been militantly white, but now I became militantly non-racial. I saw a vision, there is no other word for it.

There was a white woman in Johannesburg called Edith Rheinallt Jones. She was not beautiful in the conventional sense. She was a woman in her fifties, heavily built, and she breathed heavily after any exertion. She had been told almost ten years before that her heart was finished, and that if she wanted to live, she had to give up her many activities, with the Institute of Race Relations, and the Wayfarers (a kind of Girl Guides for nonwhite children), and the Helping Hand Club (a hostel for African girls in Johannesburg), and a dozen other things too, not to mention the running of a hospitable home where any person was welcomed.

Edith Jones decided that although she did not want to die, she did not wish to live without the Institute and the Wayfarers and the Helping Hand Club and the dozen other things too. Therefore she decided to carry on as usual. Her most vigorous activity was with the Wayfarers. She went out into the most remote parts of the countryside to visit little troops of schoolgirls, and to encourage and instruct the Wayfarer leaders, who were mostly schoolteachers. When she was there, she usually visited the chief and the church people and the magistrate and the health authorities as well, so that she became, in time, the best-known white woman in the whole of South Africa, and one of the best loved too.

I was Principal of the Diepkloof Reformatory then, and Edith Jones and her husband, J. D., were great supporters of the experiments in freedom and responsibility that we were carrying out. Then came the war and everyone was working twice as hard as before. Edith Jones asked if I, when I was free from the reformatory at weekends, would drive her in her car to visit some of these Wayfarer troops in the country areas, and I agreed. So it was that I began to learn what this woman meant to hundreds and thousands of unknown people in the most remote parts of South Africa.

One of these journeys remains clearly in my mind. We set out from Johannesburg early in the morning, and took the Great North Road into the land of the Bavenda people. We left the main highway at Pietersburg and took a road into a countryside where long hills lay like tawny lions in the sun. They say this is the country where John Buchan dreamed up his story of Prester John, and even today, it has this remoteness and this mystery. After driving deeper and deeper into the tribal place, we could take the car no further, and we left it and walked down a steep and stony hill to the school. Edith Jones was not supposed to take walks like this, and her breathing was painful to hear, but she had no time for rest or self-pity. At last we could see the school, and the schoolmistress too, Mrs. Takalani, a woman as large as Edith Jones, waiting for her visitor with every sign of pleasure. Already some of the Wayfarers had come for the parade and the inspection and were peeping from behind a corner of the school building to see their chief. It had no doubt strained the family resources to make the uniforms they wore, but there they were, all eager and neatly dressed, and obviously excited by the visit of this important white woman from Johannesburg.

I did not wait to see the parade, but took a walk through the valley, saluting and being saluted by hundreds of people going to the schoolhouse for the big occasion. After an hour or two I returned, and spent some time looking round the two rooms that made up the school. There were the usual colour drawings on the walls, and clay figures of tame and wild beasts; also instruction on cleaning the teeth, washing the hands, and what to do about flies and mosquitoes. Nothing could have been simpler than the building and equipment, and nothing more evident than the atmosphere of industry and aspiration that filled these humble rooms. In a kind of kitchen next door, one of the village mothers was boiling water, and after the parade, Mrs. Jones, Mrs. Takalani and I had tea and cakes. It was clear that we were the Big Three, for no one joined us; and it was also clear that the cakes had been brought all the way from Pietersburg, such town cakes being the only ones considered fit for the consumption of such high people.

I think the parade must have gone well, and I think Mrs. Jones

must have given out high praise, for Mrs. Takalani was in a state
of spiritual intoxication.

"You must bring her again," she said to me. "When she comes
she makes things new."

She turned to Mrs. Jones. "Did you hear what I said?" she asked.
"I said when you come you make things new."

"Don't talk nonsense," said Mrs. Jones.

"Don't you say I am talking nonsense," said Mrs. Takalani. "Why
do you think all these people come here? They come here to see
you."

"That is nonsense," said Mrs. Jones. "They come here to see what
their children are learning in the Wayfarers."

As for me, I listened fascinated. I had never before heard a white
woman and a black woman talk to each other in this fashion. It
was something new for me. At that time my own relations with
black people were extremely polite, but I realised that these two
had long passed that stage.

We walked up the steep and stony hill to the car, and Edith
Jones had to stop every few paces to get her breath again.

"You should not be visiting such places," Mrs. Takalani told her.
"You should be staying at home."

One could see that Mrs. Jones was longing to say, "Nonsense,"
but had no breath to do it with. She had to content herself with
glaring at her friend.

At the top of the hill, Mrs. Takalani wept for about five seconds.
To do this she went off a few paces, and turned her back to us.
Then she blew her nose and came back.

"Thank you for bringing her," she said to me, "and bring her
again."

"Next time," she said to Mrs. Jones with authority, "we are having our inspection here, at the top of the hill."

She pointed down in the direction of the invisible school. "You
should have said goodbye to the school," she said, "for you will
not see it again."

And that came true. A month later, ten years after the doctor's warning, the brave heart gave in altogether.

They had a farewell service for her in St. George's Presbyterian Church, Johannesburg. That was my deep experience. Black man, white man, Coloured man, European and African and Asian, Jew and Christian and Hindu and Moslem, all had come to honour her memory—their hates and their fears, their prides and their prejudices, all for this moment forgotten. The lump in the throat was not only for the great woman who was dead, not only because all South Africa was reconciled under the roof of this church, but also because it was unreal as a dream, and no one knew how many years must pass and how many lives be spent and how much suffering be undergone, before it all came true. And when it all came true, only those who were steeped in the past would have any understanding of the greatness of the present.

As for me, I was overwhelmed. I was seeing a vision, which was never to leave me, illuminating the darkness of the days through which we live now. To speak in raw terms, there was some terrible pain in the pit of my stomach. I could not control it. I had a feeling of unspeakable sorrow and unspeakable joy. What life had failed to give so many of these people, this woman had given them—an assurance that their work was known and of good report, that they were not nameless or meaningless. And man has no hunger like this one. Had they all come, no church would have held them all; the vast, voiceless multitude of Africa, nameless and obscure, moving with painful ascent to that self-fulfilment no human being may with justice be denied, encouraged and sustained by this woman who withheld nothing from them, who gave her money, her comfort, her gifts, her home, and finally her life, not with the appearance of prodigality nor with fine-sounding words, but with a naturalness that concealed all evidence of the steep moral climb by which alone such eminence is attained.

In that church one was able to see, beyond any possibility of doubt, that what this woman had striven for was the highest and best kind of thing to strive for in a country like South Africa. I knew then I would never again be able to think in terms of race and nationality. I was no longer a white person but a member of the human race. I came to this, as a result of many experiences, but this one I have related to you was the deepest of them all.

I. The Nonracial Spirit

TOWARDS A NONRACIAL DEMOCRACY*

> Paton wrote this "Long View" essay for the first issue of *Contact* from Nigeria, where he was a delegate of the Anglican Church to the first All-African Church Conference at Ibadan, in January, 1958. The conference was attended by delegates from twenty-four African territories, representing all major Protestant denominations including the Dutch Reformed church.

I AM WRITING this in Nigeria from the All-Africa Church Conference. From up here one gets a clear view of the South.

South Africa is a white fortress. Each day, each month, each year, the Nationalists make it stronger. They make the walls thicker; they make them higher. Each year more and more of the white inhabitants are called from other jobs. They have to guard the fortress.

Yet, in the long view, no one believes that the fortress will endure. Sooner or later it must yield. But till then the inhabitants must all be on guard.

Is there no other way out than this? Must white South Africans

* *Contact,* I, No. 1 (February 8, 1958), 11.

live like this all their lives? This paper, *Contact,* doesn't think so. It thinks there is a better way. This paper is being published because some people believe there is a better way.

We don't think it will be an easy way. We expect it to provide some headaches and heartaches. But it offers a man something better than a fortress life, something better than to spend his life guarding the status quo.

What is our political problem? It is to move from white supremacy to nonracial democracy as quickly, as soundly, as we can. We have to do this because we ought to. But we also have to do it because we have to. The world demands it, quite gently now, more loudly tomorrow.

Slavery went, child labour went, the inferior status of women is going. *Apartheid* will go too. It has become, not merely distasteful, but downright offensive to most of the world. It has become embarassing to the rest, because it could set the world on fire.

Up here in Nigeria they are angry with Britain for abstaining from voting on *apartheid* in the United Nations Assembly.* Many told me they would not stay in a Commonwealth that regards race discrimination as a domestic affair.

Up here in Nigeria, South Africa is the most important topic in the world. They talk all the time about South Africa. Ten young student teachers from St. Paul's College in Ibadan came to see me

* In the twelfth session of the U.N. General Assembly, on November 1, 1957, the Political Committee adopted a resolution sponsored by twenty-two Afro-Asian countries, five Latin American countries, Greece, and Ireland. The resolution recommended that the General Assembly appeal once more to South Africa to revise its *apartheid* policy "in the light of the principles and purposes of the U.N. Charter and of world opinion," and it deplored the fact that South Africa had not responded to similar previous appeals. The voting on the resolution was fifty-nine in favor and five against (France, Belgium, Portugal, Australia, and Britain), with ten abstentions. The British representative announced that he would vote against the resolution, irrespective of "any opinion we may hold on the merits or demerits of the Union's policy of racial segregation," because, under Article 2 of the U.N. Charter, the matter was essentially within South Africa's domestic jurisdiction. (Where there is no indication to the contrary, all footnotes to the Paton selections have been provided by the editor.)

and to ask me what they could do to help South Africa. Everywhere we went, the Nigerians wanted to talk to the South Africans.

People up here don't think these are matters of politics. They think they are matters of justice, and therefore of religion. They think so with an intensity that must be seen to be believed.

How I wished white South Africa could have seen it! Perhaps they will one day, on television. Or perhaps they won't, because it will be declared to be racial incitement.

Even at this Church Conference, passions flared up on the question of race discrimination. They flared up once on the use of the word "Native." They flared up again on the question of segregation of the land.

This is the kind of world our children are being born into, the countries of Africa advancing everywhere to independence, first the British colonies and dependencies, then surely the Belgian and the French, ultimately the Portuguese. This is the kind of world we have to prepare ourselves and our children to live in.

That seems to me to be the only political question worth discussing in South Africa. How do we move by sound and constructive steps away from white supremacy? How do we avoid violence and catastrophe? How do we get white people to agree to want to share liberty, responsibility and power?

It seems to me that not only the Nationalist Party but also the United Party stand to maintain white supremacy—the first by force, the second "by consent."

Is this the most realistic thinking that white South Africa can produce? This paper doesn't believe it, and this paper intends to support realistic thinking.

Of course the Nationalists say that they are the realists. They say that the Liberals are kicking against the pricks of inflexible white determination to remain the *baas* [master]. But great events will change that inflexibility into flexibility.

The realism of the Nationalists is the realism of despair. And in the end it will lead, if it is not checked, to the destruction of all that Nationalism stands for, including Afrikanerdom itself.

I believe, and my Liberal Party associates believe, and this paper believes, that white South Africans must learn to see their fellows as men and women, with like fears and hopes, with like potentialities, with like willingness to do their duty, and to serve their country. We believe that anyone who wants to live in Africa must be willing to live there on the same terms as anyone else.

We believe that all men are equal, and that while it may be dangerous to give them equality, it will be fatal not to do it. We believe that every right and every responsibility should be open to all men and women. We believe that the maintaining of this belief creates confidence and gives hope for peace.

These ideas we will propagate as persuasively, as intelligently, as faithfully and as long as we are able.

LIBERALS AND THE UNITED PARTY: SIR DE VILLIERS GRAAFF*

Prior to 1953, South African liberals placed their hopes for social progress in the United Party, particularly while Jan Hofmeyr was alive and likely to succeed General Smuts as the party's leader. The United Party then had a liberal wing, which drew its support from voters in the large cities, and a conservative wing, which drew its support chiefly from Afrikaans-speaking rural districts. Sir de Villiers Graaff became leader of the United Party in 1956, a time when the party was trying to win back the rural voters who increasingly supported the Nationalist Party's racial policies. Therefore, during the 1958 election campaign, while speaking at a farm called Elandsfontein, Sir de Villiers emphasized the United Party's conservative "white leadership" views, which were hardly distinguishable from those of the Nationalists except for the tag "with justice." The United Party was decisively defeated in the general election of April, 1958, and Sir de Villiers Graaff lost the parliamentary seat he had held for years. Colonel R. D. Pilkington, the unopposed United

* *Contact*, I, No. 4 (March 22, 1958), 11.

Party member for Rondebosch (Cape), resigned his seat to permit Sir de Villiers to return to Parliament as party leader. During the period under discussion, Mr. Strijdom remained Prime Minister.

SPEAKING AT A FARM called Elandsfontein, near [the town of] Bredasdorp, Sir de Villiers Graaff is reported to have said, "If there is any danger of equality in the policy of the United Party, you will not find me in that party."

I do not wish to interpret this unfairly. But I assume it means that Sir de Villiers is rootedly opposed to race equality. I assume it means that so long as Sir de Villiers is leader of the United Party, nonwhite people may look forward to a position of unchanging subordination.

It means even more than that. It means that nonwhite people can expect to be integrated economically, and to be segregated in every other way. This policy has a strange name. Speaking at the same farm Elandsfontein, Sir de Villiers called it "white leadership with justice."

Here I find myself in complete accord with those Nationalists who find this policy unacceptable on ethical grounds. To let a man work for you, even to pay him well for it, and to deny him any kind of say over his own life and liberty, is a disgusting policy.

.   .   .   .

Sir de Villiers Graaff is a champion of the values of Western civilisation. He believes that the Nationalists have betrayed them. But what is he doing now? He is telling the nonwhite people of South Africa that, during his time of leadership, they need not look forward to any real advancement.

Sir de Villiers must know what has happened in Indonesia, India, and Ghana. He must know what is going to happen in Nigeria and Uganda. He must have read about Algeria. What is he doing to prepare the country for a period of change? Precisely nothing.

Even the extreme Nationalists believe that one cannot hold

people down for ever. But Sir de Villiers clearly hopes to hold them down for his lifetime at least. Is this the best he can do? Is this the way he prepares South Africa to take a worthy place in the changing world?

I have often said that our Prime Minister, Mr. Strijdom, in all his speeches, has never addressed one warm or affectionate word to the [12 million] nonwhite people he governs. I am beginning to think that Sir de Villiers is going the same way. The election seems to be solely concerned with whether we have one white nation or two. The only issue seems to be whether to remember the Anglo-Boer War or to forget it.

But, for nearly 12 million South Africans, the Boer War means nothing at all.

I read that Sir de Villiers Graaff will not tolerate any "economic blackmail" on the part of Africans for the redress of political grievances.

What outlet does Sir de Villiers propose for such redress? None that I can see. His [earlier] Johannesburg speech—as reported—contains warnings to the African people, but not one word of hope. His speech bears such a resemblance to the Prime Minister's that I recoil.

I admit they differ on Anglo-Afrikaner relations, but on black-white relations they hardly differ at all. Both issue warnings to the African people not to use the only outlet that [Minister of Native Affairs] Verwoerd has left them to use.

No one would suppose that either of these gentlemen bears the grave responsibility of the welfare of 12 million voteless people. They speak—in speech after speech—as though the real problems of South Africa were problems of Anglo-Afrikaner relations.

Both of them are anachronisms. It is a sobering thought that over a million voters are going to vote for these anachronisms as though they were the men of the hour.

I myself stand for the policy of race equality which Sir de Villiers Graaff, and of course Mr. Strijdom, reject so uncompromisingly. I do not know the exact sequence of events which will lead to race equality, but I do know that it must come. And meanwhile I do my best to see that it comes, in so far as I can make it, by orderly means.

That is why I take off my hat to Gerald Gordon, Peter Brown, and Jimmy Dey [the Liberal Party candidates]. They not only want to open the doors so that nonwhite people can get some fresh hope. They also want to open the windows so that white people can get some fresh air.

They are in fact the men of the hour.

Why don't we of the Liberal Party fight from within the United Party? To answer bluntly, we couldn't. We couldn't serve a party whose leader finds race equality so revolting an idea. And who supports economic integration but opposes any true advancement. And who calls this policy "white leadership with justice."

It is sometimes very uncomfortable being a Liberal outside the United Party. But we would find it much more uncomfortable within.

A CALM VIEW OF CHANGE*

> The ideal of total *apartheid* presupposes a territorial division of South Africa into white areas and black areas (commonly called "Bantustans"). The polices of the Nationalist Party are based on this ideal as a practical possibility; the Nationalists regard the existing tribal Reserves as "national homes" within which all Africans may eventually develop economically and politically. Outside these tribal Reserves, which form 13 per cent of the land and sustain less than one-third of the African population, Africans are presumed to be temporary, migrant workers with no political rights. In 1951, the Nationalist Government created the Commission for the Socio-Economic Development of the Bantu Areas Within the Union of South Africa. This commission, under the chairmanship of Professor F. R. Tomlinson, was composed

* *Contact,* I, No. 5 (April 5, 1958), 11.

of experts who favored *apartheid*. Their voluminous report submitted in 1954, indicated that, by the end of the twentieth century, the "Bantu Areas" (in which they included the then British High Commission Territories of Basutoland, Bechuanaland, and Swaziland) could sustain two-thirds of the estimated African population, provided that vast expenditures were made for rehabilitation and the purchase of new land. When Paton remarks, in the following essay, that the Tomlinson Report proves total *apartheid* is impossible, he has in mind that the remaining one-third of the African population (estimated at 7 million), which the commission presumed would continue to live in white areas, would still outnumber the white population of those areas. Furthermore, the commission's assumption that three territories not under South African rule—Basutoland (now independent Lesotho), Swaziland, and Bechuanaland (now independent Botswana)—could be included in the proposed Bantu Areas was dubious at best. An even more telling blow to the possibilities envisaged in the Tomlinson Report was struck by Dr. Verwoerd, Minister of Native Affairs, when he issued a white paper disputing the necessity both of purchasing additional land for the Reserves and of investing "white" capital to develop industry in the Reserves.

After Dr. Verwoerd became Prime Minister, he set forth his own policy on the Reserves; this policy envisaged eight separate Bantu states, which he compared to colonies, within South Africa. According to Leo Marquard, Dr. Verwoerd and his new Minister of Bantu Administration and Development, M. D. de Wet Nel, "stressed the importance of reviving that tribalism which the Tomlinson Report held to be incompatible with modern economy." (For additional background information, see Leo Marquard, *The Peoples and Policies of South Africa,* New York: Oxford University Press, 1960, pp. 30–39.)

In the two essays that follow, Paton speaks of a future South African society brought into being by changes not envisaged by proponents of total *apartheid* and the Tomlinson Report. The essays are the outgrowth of the election campaign of 1958, during which Paton solicited votes on behalf of Peter Brown, Liberal Party candidate for Pietermaritzburg District (which includes the small town of Kloof, where Paton lives). The voters in this district are mostly English-speaking whites; in 1958, they supported, for the most part, the United Party. Paton writes of the grass-roots sentiment he encountered during the campaign.

I HAVE BEEN canvassing the voters of Pietermaritzburg District. Some are *kwaai nasionalis* [hotly nationalist]; some are staunch United Party. Some point to head or heart and say, "I keep my vote here." In all these cases, in the absence of other hints, the canvasser gives polite thanks and goes.

But there is another kind of voter, the kind that understands clearly that the Anglo-Boer War and the Republic are not the real issues, that the real issue is the future relationship of black and white. These are the voters who know that technological advance is now world-wide, and is no longer dependent on the West.

These latter voters fall into three classes. The first is sympathetic, but clings to the United Party for security in a stormy age. The second votes Liberal.

The third has no hope at all; these voters see all whites driven by fear to become white nationalists, all blacks driven by hate to become black nationalists, and the two clashing head on, with the result, ultimately, that all whites will be thrown out of Africa. There might at some earlier time have been two solutions to this; one was total *apartheid,* which the Tomlinson Report has now proved impossible; the other was a common society, which white fear and black hate have now made impossible.

Most of these melancholy voters in Pietermaritzburg District will vote United Party. Why should they swop horses in midstream, when they expect to be drowned anyway?

I believe there are, besides others, purely subjective and unreliable reasons for dreading a black revenge. One is of course the guilt that so many white people—all, perhaps—feel about their treatment of nonwhite South Africans. This guilt is of two kinds, the personal guilt, and the communal guilt they feel as members of a dominating class.

Within reason, we should be able to get rid of the personal guilt altogether. That is one of the first prerequisites to a more creative and constructive attitude towards South African affairs.

It is a more difficult matter to get rid of the communal guilt. One lives in a colour-bar world, and one cannot behave in all respects as though one did not. But one must begin by challenging the customs; there can be no relief from melancholy until we do.

I add one remark from the religious and psychological points of view. Guilt can be expiated. But guilt that continues, uselessly and destructively, is wrong and unhealthy, and one ought to see someone about it.

I believe there are sound objective reasons why South Africa, though it will undoubtedly experience great and painful change, will not experience irreconcilable conflict.

Though there seems to the melancholy to be already an irreconcilable conflict between people of one colour and people of another, these people are much nearer to one another than appears. Assimilation has gone much further than we think.

There are many Africans who believe that their advancement as human beings is bound up with the economic and industrial advance of the country, and that this advance depends on fruitful white-black collaboration. There are many Africans who cherish the same values as their white counterparts, and who dread the thought of violence and upheaval. There are no stouter defenders of what is best in our civilisation.

Those of us who reject the colour bar in our private lives have experienced many times the community of interest across the colour line. White men do not all think alike, nor do black. They only appear to do so under the evil and divisive policies of *apartheid*.

In all this contemplated period of change, the urgent question will be the land. There must be an evolutionary redistribution of land, by removal of race restrictions, by unprecedented aid to hitherto excluded buyers, and by taxation of large estates.

This is of course essentially a calm view. Inflame the country and the calm view does not prevail. But it is never too late to take the calm view or the long one. When the Nazis began to rain firebombs on London, the citizens took the calm view and saved their city from untold damage.

Duty demands that we take the calm and constructive view, or at least that we support those who do.

LIBERALS AND THE NATIONALIST PARTY*

WHAT IS going to happen at the [1958] election? And what is going to happen thereafter? These are, at the time of writing, the two universal questions.

I myself expect the Nationalists to be returned with more or less the same number of seats. I expect the United Party to fare the same. It is what I might call a "hard" situation. It implies that the needle of the Nationalist–United Party barometer, after forty-eight years of fluctuation, has reached a steady position.

The reasons for this steady position are the delimitation,† the birthrate, and the growing isolation of the Afrikaner people.

I do not expect ever again to see the United Party as a government. Nor do I see it as an opposition with any future.

What will happen after the election? Will the Nationalists compose their own differences,‡ regarding no issue in the world as more important than their own solidarity? Or will they break in two, and half of them seek coalition with the United Party? I do not know, and, taking a long view, I do not think it makes much difference.

If coalition took place, would the United Party liberals be forced

---

* *Contact,* I, No. 6 (April 19, 1958), 11.

† The delimitation is the unequal proportioning of rural and urban constituencies that gives rural voters one-third more seats in Parliament than an equal number of urban voters.

‡ The reference here is to the split over the meaning of *apartheid*. As the policy of separate development—separate Native states—evolved, the meaning of *apartheid* began to undergo changes. Hence, within the Nationalist Party, some equated *apartheid* with separate development, others with the older (and simpler) idea of *baasskap*.

to leave the party? And if they did, would they form a new liberal group [or] would they join the Liberal Party?* Or would they retire, disillusioned with politics?

These are to my mind more important questions. I hope there will be no new liberal group. The country cannot afford it. I would rather see the United Party liberals retire disillusioned.

The times are so urgent, the pace so swift, the opportunities so challenging, the price of failure so great, that if there is a peaceful solution there can only be one solution.

That solution is to reject forever the policies of discrimination. What would be more foolish than a new liberal group supporting "discrimination with even greater justice?"

There is no room for a new group between the United Party and the Liberal Party.

But these are not the most important questions. The most important questions concern the nonwhite people of the country. Under our new government, whether it be Nationalist or coalition, the "traditional" policies will be followed.

There will be no restorations to the common voter's roll; there will be no political institutions for Africans except in the Reserves; the policies of *apartheid,* however much they may be adulterated for economic reasons, will be applied relentlessly in every other sphere.

The gap of ignorance that separates nonwhite from white will be widened and deepened.

Left with no legal means of expression, having no power to change the laws that determine their condition, being convinced that white authority knows neither justice nor mercy, the nonwhite people of South Africa will be compelled to use the only weapons they have left—their buying power and their labour.

Each attempt to use these weapons will be met with all the fury and determination of which race supremacists are always capable.

The postelection future is dark.

* In August, 1959, twelve United Party liberals in Parliament broke away to form a new group, the Progressive Party.

The challenge to liberalism, to party liberals and nonparty liberals, to those Olympian figures that stand aloof from the vulgarity of politics, will be exciting and demanding.

We believe with all our hearts that many of the elementary freedoms of democracy are denied to nonwhite people and that their life, if they do not struggle to amend it, will be poor and inferior forever.

Where will we be found? Counselling moderation in all things? God forbid. There can be no moderation in justice, mercy, and truth. They are what they are.

One of our clear and insistent duties, and one which we have always readily accepted in the past, is to uphold the values of decent and civilised life, and the dignity of persons. These, being values of life, must be upheld in living, not only in speeches and sermons. This is going to become harder, not easier to do.

More than one cabinet minister has said that the future fight is between nationalism and liberalism. With all my heart I hope they are right.

AN OPEN LETTER TO DR. VERWOERD*

Dr. Hendrik F. Verwoerd, chief theorist of *apartheid* (which he preferred to call "separate development"), became Prime Minister of South Africa after the death, on August 24, 1958, of Mr. Strijdom. The new Prime Minister made his first broadcast address to the nation on the evening of September 3, 1958. Alan Paton responded with the following open letter:

HONOURABLE SIR,

I listened with great attention to your first broadcast to the nation. Certain things you said were so important that I take the liberty of examining them closely.

* *Contact,* I, No. 17 (September 20, 1958), 9.

You said that the right of people who have other convictions to express their views will be maintained. This is good news and will reassure many who thought you had other intentions. It will reassure those liberals who thought that your ban on assemblies of more than ten Africans was in fact kept in existence to prevent the Liberal Party from holding meetings.*

Or it may be that you do not mind if people express their views, so long as they do it in newspapers, books, and the like. Or it may be that you do not mind if they express their views, so long as they do not attempt to persuade others. Or it may be that you do not mind their persuading others, so long as they do not try to persuade those of another race or colour.

Your views on this point are very obscure, and we would be very glad if you could be more precise. Do you in fact disapprove of interracial association? Would you like to see an end made of interracial clubs, church functions, political meetings? If so, would you put an end to them openly, or are you afraid to do that? Would you rather use legislation devised to prevent "public nuisances," or legislation devised to prevent "occupation" of one group area by members of another group? Or are you brave enough to say to the world "I do not like interracial association, and I intend to stop it."†

I suppose you remember that it was your paper *Die Transvaler* [an Afrikaans daily published in Johannesburg], when you were

---

* As a consequence of the defiance campaigns of the ANC, local and national bans on gatherings of Africans for political purposes were common during the 1950's. Though not in force at all times, such bans adversely affected meetings of the nonracial Liberal Party. Paton may have had in mind his own arrest and conviction, in June, 1957, for contravening a Durban municipal regulation requiring seventy-two hours' notice from non-Africans wishing to attend a meeting of Africans. This conviction, and that of five whites and Indians convicted with him, was set aside by the Supreme Court, in August, 1958, on the ground that the prosecution had failed to prove the meeting was for Africans only.

† At the time of his assassination, in 1966, Dr. Verwoerd was preparing to introduce a bill that would serve this purpose: The Prohibition of Improper Interference Bill. See page 40.

editor of it, which used to publish photographs of mixed platforms
and mixed meetings, with contemptuous allusions. You played your
part in encouraging young Afrikaners to regard mixed meetings as
contemptible. You and your paper encouraged the intolerance
which showed itself at the meeting where Chief Luthuli was assaulted.*

Nevertheless, if you are revising your opinions, you will find that
we Liberals will be the first to acknowledge it. We ask you merely
to leave us in no doubt.

You say that no one need doubt your aim to uphold the democratic institutions of our country. This also is good news, because
we have certainly doubted it in the past. Now we hope that you
will alleviate some of the hardships imposed by present legislation.

In a country town an African man, Mr. X, worked in a white
attorney's office, took his matriculation examination, was preparing
to be articled when the white attorney died. Mr. X could see no
future where he was, so he applied for permission to move to a city
where he could have been articled, and could have gone on with his
studies. Your department refused to let him go. Can you justify this,
Mr. Prime Minister?

You hold the doctrine that the black man is a "temporary dwel-
ler" in the white town. Surely the removal of freehold rights was
foolish as well as unjust. Property-owners are not revolutionaries,
they are conservative and law-abiding, and it is foolish to destroy
them.

Have you ever met an African man who has had his property
taken away from him and his freehold right destroyed? It is a painful experience. This may be democratic to you, Mr. Prime Minister,

---

* Chief Albert Luthuli was invited to address a political study group at the
Afrikaans University of Pretoria on August 22, 1958. A substantial part of the
audience was composed of foreign diplomats. A group of about thirty young
white men assaulted Chief Luthuli while he was on the platform making his
address. They also assaulted the white chairman and three women who tried to
protect Chief Luthuli. Six men were arrested and charged; two were found
guilty of public violence.

but to him it is a cruel injustice. He is revolted to hear that you believe you are upholding democratic institutions.*

Your own people, Mr. Prime Minister, keep alive in memory many of the injustices which were done to them by my own. But now you are busy allowing the same thing to happen all over again.

Why could you not change your mind about this one thing, and allow freehold rights in the cities? That is the way to establish a stable middle class, with no taste for revolution.

All the English-language newspapers quote you as saying, "the state after all is responsible for good government in the interests of all."

Somebody made a mistake here. The sentence should read, "the state *before all* is responsible for good government in the interests of all."

That is why the state exists, and that is why it has a Prime Minister. May you always remember it.

* For a specific instance of the removal of freehold rights under the Group Areas Act, see "The Charlestown Story," pages 116–27 below.

II. Christian Conscience in a Racial Society

VERWOERD'S CLAIM TO DIVINE GUIDANCE*

During his first address to the nation as Prime Minister, on September 3, 1958, Dr. Verwoerd said, "In accordance with His will, it was determined who should assume the leadership of the Government in this new period of the life of the people of South Africa. We firmly believe that all will be well with our country and our people because God rules."

LIKE MANY OTHER South Africans, I find the Prime Minister's constant reference to God and His will distasteful; I find it also ominous, both for Dr. Verwoerd and for ourselves.

This idea that one is a chosen instrument of God's will is highly dangerous, and highly dangerous people have played around with it. Hitler was the worst of them all; regarding himself as the instrument of Providence, he shamed and humbled Christendom by murdering 6 million Jews. The Spanish Inquisitors, believing that they alone held the true faith, felt justified in taking the lives of those who were in "error." Calvin, seeking to make the temporal state obedient to God's will, had Servetus burned alive, and the poor

* *Contact*, I, No. 19 (October 18, 1958), 9.

wretch while burning cried out his allegiance to the God of all mankind.

No matter who one is, or what faith one holds, one dare not entertain this paranoiac idea. Because of it Hitler brought down his country in ruins, and Calvin is to-day embarrassedly remembered by the city whose life and laughter—both hateful to him—he tried to confine by law and punishment.

Some Christians themselves believe that God is not only the primary cause of all creation, but also of all free acts of man; in other words, that God is omnipotent. But they do not pretend to understand it. Yet even if one is a believer in God's omnipotence, it is distasteful to believe that of all these acts done by God, some have His approval and some have not.

It has always been the Christian view, and in my opinion properly so, that God, although revealed by Christ as Father, is in one of His aspects incomprehensible. To know His will for a government or a policy is therefore to know too much. The Catholic view is that, outside of what God makes known to us by revelation and the authoritative teaching of the Church, we can have no guarantee of being right in our judgments.

There is another reason why this claim to be the instrument of God's will is distasteful. The world, the tough hard-bitten world, expects any God-directed life to be characterised by exceptional grace, love, and purity; and if the person were one of great authority, by the exercise of justice and mercy. Many of us fail to find either justice or mercy in the provisions of the Native Urban Areas Amendment Act that can order a sixteen-year-old to leave his parents in the city and return to the place of his birth; or in the Group Areas Act proclamations in Pretoria, which Professor Pistorius* described as a blot on the character of a Christian nation; or

* Professor V. L. Pistorius, of Pretoria University, resigned from the Nationalist Party in protest against the implementation of *apartheid*. His book *No Further Trek* (Johannesburg: Central News Agency, 1957) is an incisive criticism of Afrikaner Nationalist policy. His attack on the Group Areas Act proclamations (which set up the zones and timing for moving the Indian population of Pretoria) appeared in *Contact*, I, No. 12 (July 12, 1958).

in the Population Registration Act that can declare to be coloured a man who has lived all his life as white, and who has married a white girl, and who has white children who now will be coloured also.

Mercy and justice are shown towards *persons,* but these acts know no mercy, and the only justice they show is legalistic and loveless. No law is good that harms persons. No law is good that breaks up families. No law is good that spreads fear and uncertainty in the minds and lives of so many people, of the African freehold owners of northern Natal, of the white families that know they have coloured blood, of the workers in industry who do not know the day when their occupation will be reserved for others, of the country boy who is not allowed to go to the city to be articled to a lawyer. It were better, said Christ, that a stone were hanged round a man's neck and that he were drowned in the depths of the sea, than that he should harm one of these little ones.

Dr. Verwoerd is highly inconsistent. When he claims the divine approval for his appointment, and presumably for his policies, he destroys the foundations of that democracy in which he has said he believes. Are his opponents not opposing the divine will? And would he not therefore be entitled to deal sternly with them, as Calvin dealt with Servetus? Or as the Inquisitors dealt with those who were in "error"?

In my humble view, there is only one way in which a religious politician may approach the question of God's will. He will do so humbly, not claiming to know what that will is, but will try to live his life in obedience to the great and small commandments, notably those which command him to love God and his neighbour. That love will be manifested, not only in his acts, but in his spoken words, and all sorts of conditions of men and women will rejoice that he has power. He will pray, like the saints, to be made the instrument of God's love, not claim to be the instrument of His power. While he will love and cherish his own, he will not flaunt his loyalties. He will test his policies, not by what they contribute to him and his own, but by the ancient tests of truth, justice, and love, and where necessary, mercy. He will never say "of course some must suffer, but that is because of the mistakes of the past"; he will rather move heaven and earth to ensure that they do not suffer. In trying to do God's will, he will remember the words of the great prophet "learn to do well, seek judgment, relieve the oppressed, judge the fatherless, plead for the widow."

It would be difficult to overthrow the government of such a ruler; in this unhappy and chaotic world, where violence and hatred/ burst out in one place or another, a world which many of our chil⊦ dren have so obviously rejected, where goodness seems to retreat into enclaves, what hope it would give to see power once more subordinate to justice, and how willingly the people would give a ruler such power.

That indeed is the true meaning of God's will.

THE ARCHBISHOP OF CAPE TOWN VIEWS APARTHEID*

In February, 1958, four months after he became Anglican Archbishop of Cape Town, Dr. Joost de Blank wrote a condemnation of *apartheid* in the journal *Good Hope,* the official organ of the diocese of Cape Town. Besides rejecting white domination *(baasskap)* as "inhuman and unchristian," Dr. de Blank called on the Nationalist Government to repeal the laws barring the entry of nonwhite pupils to Anglican schools. Dr. de Blank's stand provided a major election issue for the Nationalist Party—much to the embarrassment of the United Party. In a statement issued from the office of Sir de Villiers Graaf on February 6, 1958, the United Party repudiated the Archbishop's stand: "The United Party . . . is against the establishment of mixed schools. Any attempt to change this practise must ignore the realities of the South African situation." In 1963, Dr. de Blank resigned his archbishopric on medical advice and returned to England as a canon of Westminster Abbey; he died there in January, 1968.

* *Contact,* I, No. 3 (March 8, 1958), 11.

THE NEW Archbishop of Cape Town doesn't like *apartheid*. I didn't think he would. But he puts us all in his debt by making up his mind so quickly about it. According to the rules he should have waited a couple of hundred years.

I certainly don't want to drag the Archbishop into political controversy. I have no wish to "use" him to further the end of *Contact* or any political party. But I want him to know that there are hundreds of thousands of South Africans who are thankful that he saw so quickly that *apartheid* is an evil thing. There are also many Christians who share this thankfulness; they would like to be proud of their religion, not ashamed of it.

The Liberal Party is not a Christian organisation, nor could it be. It is a political organisation with a strong moral motive. At the moment this seems to many white South Africans to be very odd; that is only because they are used to immoral politics. I don't mean they cheat and lie: I mean they are used to a brand of politics which aims to secure privilege and power at the expense of other people.

Now although the Liberal Party is not a Christian organisation, its policies have a great deal in common with Christian ethics, and its philosophy has been influenced by Christian theology. I shall not therefore apologise for writing something about these things.

If one is a Christian, one believes that there is a spiritual order as well as a temporal, but one also believes that the values of the spiritual order—justice, love, mercy, truth—should be the supreme values of the temporal society, and that the good state will uphold and cherish them. Further one believes that the Church, while without temporal power, has the duty of championing these values in the temporal world.

One believes also that when the state substitutes for justice, love, mercy, truth, any other value, the temporal society will decay. This is exactly what has been happening in South Africa, and especially since 1948.

The Government has made *apartheid* the supreme value. They

have done it by saying that you can only have justice, love, mercy, truth, in the framework of *apartheid*. Is that true, or is it not?

It is not true, and every Christian should know it is not. A policy that can push out the Indian traders of Johannesburg to the bare veld twenty miles away, that can separate African husband and wife and children at Windermere, that can allow petty officials without public reprimand to subject coloured persons to gross indignities in order to determine their racial classification, that can forbid friends of different races to associate in restaurant or cinema, has long since severed its connection with justice, love, mercy, and truth.

Why do so many of us white people not see this any more? Are we punch-drunk? And tired of resisting? That is too easy a supposition. We too have elevated *apartheid* until it has become the supreme value even though we should hate to admit it. That is really why we have given in.

Or shall I say we have *consented* to the elevation of *apartheid?* Half-heartedly, I agree. But what more does a tyrant want? A man like Luthuli must look at us in desperation sometimes, behind the closed doors of our shut-off world, and wonder why we cannot see that it is we and not our stars that make evolutionary change impossible. How will these doors be opened, if we do not help to open them ourselves.

While one is tinkering, and allowing other people to tinker, with these supreme values, lots of things begin to happen. The Christian religion, for example, begins to allow quite a lot of important but subordinate values to enter as absolutes, such as being nice, "moderation" in speech and action, and upholding the temporal authority.

A nice Christian woman said to me, "I have come to believe that we must have *apartheid,* but with as little brutality as possible." As we motor along the roads, some people are pickupable, and others are not. A colour-bar organisation is able to declare unctuously that its aim is to bring together people "from all the corners of the earth."

And some foolish fellow writing to the paper declares that the "vast majority" of South Africans support Mr. Louw in condemning the Declaration of Conscience.*

Here I have dealt only with the moral ideas that Christianity and liberalism have in common. That is why, while not wishing to drag the Archbishop into politics, we must record our thanks for his stand. It is for us a moral reinforcement, and the more we have of it, the better for South Africa. Up till now—with exceptions naturally and of course—the defence of Christian morality has been left too much to bodies that are not Christian at all.

We welcome the Archbishop to South Africa, and hope that nothing will happen to cut short his stay amongst us. We believe that he has already shown himself to be as true a South African as any of us, because it is clear that he understands what alone can be the foundation on which a true South Africa must be built.

CHRISTOPHER GELL: SALUTE TO THE BRAVE†

Christopher Gell was paralyzed by polio in 1945, while he was Under-Secretary to the Government of the Punjab in the Indian Civil Service. He came to Port Elizabeth, South Africa, for health reasons, in 1947. The first issue of *Contact* (February 8, 1958) announced:

* The Declaration of Conscience, issued in protest against South Africa's policy of white supremacy and sponsored by the American Committee on Africa (with Eleanor Roosevelt as Chairman), called on the people of the world to mark Human Rights Day, December 10, 1957, the ninth anniversary of the General Assembly's adoption of the Universal Declaration of Human Rights. In response, Eric Louw, South Africa's Minister of External Affairs, addressed the nation by radio on behalf of the cabinet. His speech characterized Mrs. Roosevelt as "not a stranger in American left-wing circles," and declared that the American Committee on Africa had "a decidedly pinkish tinge," and that its Executive Director, the Reverend George M. Houser, was "a known leftist." Mr. Houser described Mr. Louw's remarks as "ridiculous"; Mrs. Roosevelt said she would not bother to comment.

† *Contact,* I, No. 10 (June 14, 1958), 11.

Christopher Gell, polio victim whose prolific output of well-informed writing on the South African socio-political scene has won him a formidable reputation both in this country and overseas, is a member of the *Contact* team of correspondents. . . . Although confined to an iron lung for all but a few hours a day he has made an intensive study of South African problems and is perhaps the most authoritative writer in the country on the involved subject of the Group Areas Act.

Christopher Gell died on May 28, 1958. Alan Paton's *The People Wept* (see below) is dedicated to him, and the Christopher Gell Memorial Award, established in his memory, was first presented to Chief Albert Luthuli, in 1961.

CHRISTOPHER GELL, that bravest of all the soldiers of righteousness, is dead. Thirteen years ago he was struck down by a thunderbolt. His weapons were broken to pieces, his body left almost impotent. Slowly he raised himself from the ground; he picked up the fragments of his armour out of the dust, and pieced them painfully together. Out of them he fashioned for himself a new weapon, called the sword of the spirit. Physically helpless, he became a leader of armies, and refuted in his wasted body the lie that it is only the power of money or votes or armies that counts; for under God, and with the help of his wife, he was invincible.

It is to be expected that it would be the nonwhite people of South Africa that would most mourn his death. He was their champion and their brother. He defended them from the attacks of the rulers of South Africa, who, driven by fear, corrupted by lives of privilege, and completely pessimistic about human virtue (why, we shall not now enquire), made more and more law to control less and less liberty. I repeat, he was not only their champion, but their brother. Nothing filled him with greater anger than [that] anyone should think that it was debasing for a black man and a white man to reveal to each other their dreams and hopes and hates, and to take strength from one another, and to give strength also as equal to equal, and brother to brother. Nothing filled him with greater anger than the cruelty and rapacity of the Group Areas Act, by which a ruler, having brought men into his kingdom in the name of progress, sought to kick them out in the name of justice.

But although he rendered this great service to his nonwhite fellow countrymen, his service to white South Africa was no whit less, though it was—as it had to be—of quite another kind. He reminded white South Africa continually of the supratemporal values on which her civilisation was based, the great foundation stones of justice, mercy, and truth. He was stern in judgment on those who would love their neighbour only so long as he did not live next-door. He judged the churches sternly also, and I do not think that any man had any greater right to do it, for he judged them by nothing less than the great commandments, the implications of which he fully understood, for to these commandments, in his own way, he was fully obedient, having offered to the service of righteousness, with a generosity known only to the saints, all that he possessed, all those broken gifts that he had so painfully pieced together after he was struck down.

He was a true lover of South Africa, but unlike so many of her lovers who love only themselves, he loved all of her peoples. It is said—because he sometimes wrote angry words—that he was in fact antiwhite, and especially anti-Afrikaner. Yet I know this to be untrue, for a few months before his death he told me that he was always pondering over the difficult problem of how to be altogether anti-*apartheid,* and not at all anti-Afrikaner, a problem that the Afrikaner himself has made intensely difficult for us all.

The life of this brave and noble man has many lessons for us, but there is one that humbles me most of all. Here was a man from whom suddenly almost everything was taken away, and who out of his poverty created a new kind of riches. How often do we not feel that the obstacles that confront us are insuperable! How often do we not lose hope! Here was an example to rebuke us, and there-after to inspire us.

There is a lesson here for all who are losing hope. For if anyone should have lost hope, it should have been Christopher Gell.

There should be no foolish talk that the light of liberalism is going out, and that soon nothing but darkness will be left. On the contrary, there are more young liberals today than ever before. It is the duty of those of us who are older to be as faithful and steadfast as was Christopher Gell, so that young men and women can take courage from our example, and know that they are neither mad nor mischievous, but only steadfast.

It is one of the signs of our times that white South Africa does not know that one of the greatest and truest of her citizens is dead. Ten years ago our newspapers would have devoted columns to his life and death, our radio would have broadcast tributes to him, our churches would have preached sermons about him. But today they shut themselves up in the prison of their conformity. Strange, is it not, that it is he who walked free, not they.

I do not know the full nature of his religious faith, but I know that he called himself an Anglican, and that he revered the name of Christ. Therefore I close with the second half of the great prayer of Francis of Assisi, who like Christopher Gell, did not fear to love those whom society cast out.

Teach me, O Lord, to seek not so much to be consoled as to console; not so much to be served as to serve; not so much to be loved as to love. For it is in giving that we receive, it is in pardoning that we are pardoned, it is in dying that we are born into eternal life.

May the brave soul of him rest in peace.

MICHAEL SCOTT: WHAT KIND OF MAN WAS HE?*

The Reverend Michael Scott is a British-born Anglican clergyman known internationally, since 1947, for his repeated appearances before the U.N. Fourth (Trusteeship) Committee on behalf of the Hereros and other tribes in the former German colony of South West Africa. South West Africa has been administered by South Africa, under a

* *Contact,* I, No. 23 (December 13, 1958), 9.

League of Nations mandate, since World War I. Michael
Scott lived in South Africa between 1926 and 1929, prior
to his ordination, and, again, between 1943 and 1950. He
was barred from South Africa as a "prohibited immigrant"
in 1952. For his dedication to the cause of human rights,
Michael Scott has been regarded by some as a courageous
crusader, while others have denounced him as an agitator.

MICHAEL SCOTT'S book, *A Time to Speak,** is a kind of autobiography, even though it is not, and was not intended to be, primarily
about himself. Therefore one is entitled to ask, "What kind of man
was he?" Should one say, "was he" or "is he"?

I think that a South African could say, "was he," for he is not
likely to walk the soil of South West Africa and South Africa,
Basutoland, Swaziland, and Bechuanaland, the Rhodesias and Nyasaland, for some long time to come. And it is doubtful too if he
would be allowed in Mozambique and Angola, or in Kenya or in
the Belgian Congo.

What kind of man was he? Was he an incorrigible meddler, partial to interfering in others' affairs? Was he worse than that, an
agitator, preferring discord and agitation to peace, sowing bitter
thoughts in simple minds? When he went to prison in 1946 as
the result of a protest against the segregation measure known as
the Asiatic Land Tenure Act,† was this, to use his own words, the
"futile gesture of a rather eccentric clergyman" or "no less possibly
a piece of self-righteousness and exhibitionism"?

It says something very important about the man that he could
ask such a question about himself. He was not only humble, but had
some deep knowledge of the complicatedness of human nature. He
says that it is not impossible that he was inclined to self-righteous-

---

* New York: Doubleday, 1958.

† A restrictive law directed against the Indian population of Natal. Michael
Scott joined the Passive Resistance Movement in its campaign against this law
and, along with some 2,000 Indians, camped on restricted land in Durban. Of
this incident, Paton wrote, "The Rev. Michael Scott, whose burning passion for
justice made questions of legality seem cold to him, joined the Passive Resisters
of Durban on 13 June, and camped illegally with them on vacant land now
controlled by the Land Tenure Act." *Hofmeyr*, p. 430.

ness and exhibitionism; but his moral and spiritual greatness lay
in the fact that in spite of these possible weaknesses, he was willing
to be used as an instrument of a righteous purpose.

He was as diffident as Moses, full of self-doubting. When he left
St. Paul's College, Grahamstown, the warden said to him "You
have never been able to make up your mind, dear man, and I don't
think you ever will." Scott goes on to say of the warden, "He had
a friendly and sincere way of making the most acid comments and
rebuffs. No one ever resented them because it seemed as though he
liked us all the better for our faults and weaknesses."

What kind of man would repeat a thing like that? Certainly not
one who was self-righteous in any untoward degree. I hope that
some of those who hated and condemned Scott will read his book,
for what emerges from his story is the picture of a brave, diffident,
and humble man, with only one thing abnormal about him (if it is
abnormal), namely, a hunger and a thirst for righteousness.

I am sure that Michael Scott would prefer that we now begin
to consider his book, but it is he who forces us to wrestle with the
inescapable Christian problems of how to have peace and the sword
together, of how to be meek and bold together, of how to surrender
and be free together; and what is more, how to do these things in
South Africa.

Michael Scott does no more than state these problems. In any
event, they are solved, if they are to be solved, not in argument or
in books, but in life and action—in short, in a person. And whether
Michael Scott likes it or not, one must record that in this particular
person, these particular problems are solved in a particular way.

Indeed it has to be so, for our Lord promised that he who
hungered and thirsted after righteousness, would be filled.

Now what about the other story, of the tragic country with which
Michael Scott's name is indivisibly associated, just as were the
names of Rhodes, Kruger, Milner, Olive Schreiner, Botha, Smuts,
Hertzog, Hofmeyr, Malan, Gandhi, Dadoo, Luthuli, Khama, Mo-
shesh, Huddleston, Strijdom, Bishop Reeves, and now Verwoerd:

South Africa, endowed by God and history with a wealth of problems unfortunately not exportable, but not unknown in the United States, Algeria, Kenya, Rhodesia, Israel, Cyprus, even in Britain now. These are the problems which arise when more races than one occupy a country.

Some say they are cultural problems, some that they are class or economic problems, some that they are out and out racial problems, made still more vexatious by the complication of colour difference. I incline to the latter view, while not denying the others.

Groups, because they are different, feel themselves menaced by others; and where a group has power, as the white group has in South Africa, it entrenches its position by discriminatory laws, sometimes boldly asserting its determination to dominate, sometimes, in deference to internal conscience or to external disapproval, asserting that only by racial separation can one achieve justice and harmony.

It was this situation that confronted Michael Scott when he came to South Africa for the second time. He first, in the Campaign for Right and Justice,* concerned himself with the search for an overall solution, but later, after some disillusionment, turned himself to the task of fighting specific injustices.

So he joined the Passive Resistance Movement to resist the segregation of Indians in Natal, and went to prison for his resistance, where he experienced doubts about eccentricity and exhibitionism. He declined to pay taxes, on the grounds that the laws were unjust. He went to live in Tobruk shantytown [near Johannesburg], the only white person in an African township, thus challenging the entire body of white custom.

He next investigated the ill-treatment, resulting sometimes in death, of African labourers in the notorious farming district of Bethal; this was the most courageous action of his courageous life.

---

* In 1944, in Johannesburg, Scott formed a committee concerned with broad questions of national policy regarding race; this committee grew into the movement known as the Campaign for Right and Justice.

Then after Basutoland and its ritual murders,* Bechuanaland and its Seretse Khama† and other affairs, he espoused the cause of the Hereros, who after their brutal treatment by the Germans, found that the mandate power, South Africa, was little disposed to consider their claims to the lands of which they had been dispossessed.

This was the cause that he took to the United Nations, but when he went to New York to do it, he was confined to a small area of that great city.‡

Are these things true that he writes about? Does he give a true picture of these events and situations? Or is he simply meddling in other people's affairs, and causing disturbance where none was?

His book surely gives the answer to these questions. He was moved by a hunger for righteousness, to right injustices—in the words of the great Prophet, to "seek judgment, relieve the oppressed, judge the fatherless, plead for the widow." Those who see him as an instrument of evil and discord, are surely blind, seeing not him but only their possessions, their status, which they believed he threatened. *Apartheid* is the bulwark, the shield, the wall, against all who threaten these possessions.

The new doctrine of separate development has, for all its protestations, the same purpose. *Apartheid,* and/or separate development, has become the supreme good; the old universals—justice, love,

* Ritual murders or medicine murders: A victim is selected and killed to provide "medicine" for the failing powers of a chief. Several such murders occurred in Basutoland during 1947. For a detailed examination, see G. I. Jones, *Basutoland Medicine Murder: A Report on the Recent Outbreak of Diretlo Murders in Basutoland,* Cmd. 8209 (London: Her Majesty's Stationery Office, 1954). For a brief account, see John Gunther, *Inside Africa* (New York: Harper & Row, 1955), chap. xxviii, "Medicine Murder in Basutoland," pp. 568-84. In 1946 and 1947, Scott investigated complaints of wrongful arrest for these ritual murders.

† Seretse Khama, now President of independent Bechuanaland, was "exiled" by the British Colonial Office after his marriage to an English girl; Scott championed his return.

‡ In 1947, and again in 1952, Scott was issued a restricted U.S. visa, which allowed him only "transit" through New York to the United Nations. For some time, this amounted to restricting him to the route between his quarters and the U.N. buildings.

truth, mercy—have become subsidiaries, good only in so far as they minister to the supreme good. How could a man like Michael Scott fail to arouse the antagonism of those who believed *apartheid* to be the supreme good?

So the Church of Christ is in danger of becoming, not the upholder of revolutionary truth, but the protector of stability. So comes to life the tormenting problem of reconciling peace with reformation, order with justice, stability with change. Michael Scott ranged himself on the side of reformation, justice, and change, and made his name a byword in white South Africa.

I said I would write about the country, not about the man. But that has proved impossible. How far Scott ever solved the problem of reconciliation with those whose policies he hated is not told here. But I am satisfied that no hatred ever held sway over him except the hatred of injustice. He chose a hard road for himself and the strain of it showed in his eyes and face. I cannot write of his saintliness, only his courage, though there must be cases where one is the same as the other.

III. Peaceful Change or Cataclysmic Act?

THE ACCRA CONFERENCE*

In April, 1958, the first all-African meeting of the representatives of independent states met in Accra, Ghana. Arranged by Ghana's Prime Minister Dr. Kwame Nkrumah, this Conference of Independent African States is generally regarded as having great historical importance; prior to the Accra meeting, diplomatic conferences affecting Africans were held in European capitals. Hence, the first Accra conference symbolized the end of the colonial age. In December of the same year, Dr. Nkrumah arranged a second all-African conference in Accra. Called the All-African People's Conference, it was attended by nationalist leaders from colonial Africa, and its major concern was the liberation of the remaining colonial territories in Africa. Members of political parties—and of trade-union federations—attended, and the South African Liberal Party sent a delegation of three of its members: Jordan Ngubane (Chairman), Patrick Duncan, and Cynthia Duncan. The central theme of the conference was whether to support violent or nonviolent means of attaining liberation. It is about this conference that Alan Paton writes.

THE ACCRA CONFERENCE of African leaders is in full swing while I write this, and it would be presumptuous to comment on it. But

* *Contact,* I, No. 24 (December 27, 1958), 9.

any person with eyes in his head can see that Africa won't be the same again. The bells are tolling for the death of an age. They are tolling for the death of white supremacy.

Such tolling is painful for the close relatives of the deceased, that is to say, for white people. Therefore I am writing this week especially for white people, not to console them for the death of one who has surely had quite an innings, but rather to help them to get used to being without him. For I think it is important that they should get used to it, so that they can begin to think constructively about the future.

It might be said that I shall be writing for the converted, but that is not wholly true. I am writing especially for a fellow reader of *Contact,* a fellow member of this Liberal Party, a fellow Christian, who writes to me that he is disturbed by the fact that the party has sent delegates to Accra. Accra appears to him to be an antiwhite conference, an attempt by Ghana to interfere with the affairs of the Union. He objects to the "mooted involvement" of the party with extraterritorial movements.

My friend is not the only one who has these fears. Let us look at them more closely.

Let me say right at the outset that the party sent delegates to Accra primarily to learn more about what is happening on the continent. We need to know all that we can, if we aspire to give a lead to our own country. Our delegates can be trusted not to support racialism of any brand. As for our "mooted involvement," only the party can commit us to that.

But the fears are in fact much deeper than that. They are the white man's fears of the rising tide of African nationalism, the white man's fears of freeing the giant who may turn and rend him, the white man's fears of appearing to be a traitor to his race, culture, and civilisation.

Under the influence of these fears, words such as "liberation" and "freedom" take on a frightening quality. Even words such as "democracy," "human rights," "brotherhood" acquire a new and unpleasant meaning, so that some who once upheld them as ideals now sneer at them as delusions.

My friend even uses the word "imperialists," and puts it in inverted commas, as though in fact the imperialists were not really imperialists; as though what even Western historians have always called the "scramble for Africa" was not really a scramble for Africa, but something else.

Another word that has acquired a number of secondary meanings is "colonialism." For a growing number of African people, the word is synonymous with "exploitation." In reaction to this, some white people regard it as synonymous with "spreading of civilisation," "conferring of benefits," "improvements in health and education."

It is important that we should realise that whatever material benefits colonialism may give to dominated peoples, it gives them only on conditions that are to-day unacceptable; meanwhile it corrupts the colonisers, it emasculates their morality, it vitiates their religion, it debases their intellects (because of the need for incessant rationalisation), and it makes it necessary when one teaches children high principles, to teach them also that loyal adherence to high principles is extremism.

Mr. Leo Marquard has pointed out that in South Africa we white people have our own brand of colonialism, that in fact our nonwhite people are our colonies. That is quite true. We have been in South Africa for 300 years, and at the end of that time we are further from the nonwhite people of our country than we have ever been before. If the people at Accra should also regard the white people of South Africa as outsiders, who is to blame but ourselves?

I do not wonder that the conference at Accra should feel resentment that the lives of native Angolans are controlled and determined by decree from Lisbon, or that the lives of the Congolese should be determined by decree from Brussels. But they also feel resentment that lives of black South Africans should be determined by decree from Pretoria, based on the acts of a Parliament in which not one of them sits.

They have every right to resent it. They have the same right that the Afrikaners had to resent rule from overseas. And look what they did about it.

Now is this hatred of colonialism really hatred of injustice, or is it really hatred of the white man? Let me answer this question indirectly, and I hope constructively. The more white people resist the decline of colonialism, the more they insist on the "backwardness" of black people (a condition which colonialism has never shown great anxiety to abolish), the more they pass laws to protect white economic advantage, the more will hatred of colonialism become hatred of white people. The more white people do to hasten the end of colonialism, the more they insist on the potentialities of black people, the more they do to enable black people to develop their potentialities, the less will hatred of colonialism be synonymous with hatred of white people.

This has been well put by Professor L. J. du Plessis of the University of Potchefstroom.* He says that South Africa should lead a nonviolent revolution which would liberate and develop all the peoples of Africa. Otherwise, he says, we (that is, white South Africa) "will have to disappear from the scene."

I do not think anyone can put it more clearly than that.

I say to white South Africa, be calm and be wise. It will help nothing to draw back from people just because they say hard things about white supremacy, many of them abundantly justified. And very often, to say hard things about white supremacy means to say hard things about white people too.

I say to my fellow member of the Liberal Party, be calm and be

---

* L. J. du Plessis, Professor of Law and Politics and Dean of the Faculty at the University of Potchefstroom, was once a leading member of the Nationalist Party and a close collaborator of Dr. Verwoerd. Increasingly critical of the proposed creation of Bantu states and other related aspects of Verwoerd's policy of separate development, du Plessis was notified, on April 10, 1959, that he had been expelled from the Nationalist Party.

wise. Don't let yourself be panicked into the Nationalist fortress, for it is without exception the most dangerous refuge on the earth. Rejoice in the liberation of mankind, in the advance of Africa into a better world, where men are no longer treated as boys, where families are no longer harried by any Urban Areas Act, where the future of children is no longer determined by their race and colour.

Put aside these fears, and join whole-heartedly in the task of liberation. Then you will be able to play your part in ensuring that the new loyalty of Africa is loyalty to all mankind.

PRECEPTS OF A CABINET MINISTER*

The Liberal Party and individuals who actively seek to improve the lot of nonwhite South Africans are frequently accused of "racial incitement." In this essay, Paton asks why men in high public office—such as Dr. Albert Hertzog, whose constant theme is the irreconcilable strife between whites and nonwhites—should not be considered guilty of "racial incitement." Dr. Hertzog is the son of a former Prime Minister, General James B. M. Hertzog. Though an ardent Afrikaner nationalist and founder of the Nationalist Party, General Hertzog was opposed by an even more extremist segment of his party, which was led by Dr. Daniel Malan. No moderate on race issues, General Hertzog, nevertheless, distrusted the extreme Afrikaner nationalism of the "purified" wing led by Malan. His son is a cabinet member, Minister for Posts and Telegraphs (which includes the state-owned broadcasting system), and an active member of the *Broederbond* (Society of Brothers), which his father had, at one time, condemned. The *Broederbond,* a select and secret inner society of Afrikaner nationalists, is generally thought to have been behind Dr. Malan's rise to power; reportedly, it controls the Nationalist Party and, through it, South Africa.

* *Contact,* II, No. 1 (January 10, 1959), 9.

I MUST SAY that Dr. Verwoerd has put some queer people into his cabinet. This latest speech by Dr. Albert Hertzog at the Strand [a town near Cape Town] would have made his father turn in his grave. General Hertzog warned his son not to fool around with the *Broederbond,* or it would destroy him. The process seems to be well advanced.

In all my fifty-five years of life in South Africa, I have never read a more disgraceful speech—a compound of hate, insult, and folly. Is this the statesmanship of Afrikaner nationalism? Is this the way it responds to the challenge of emerging Africa? If it cannot produce something better than this, its end is even now in sight.

Dr. Hertzog did not, like so many of his revered leaders, say that we were fighting a second Blood River. He said the South African War had never ended; however, "the soldier is no longer the British Tommy, but the Native, the Coloured, and the Coolie."* He said that hate was "deeply embedded in the minds of non-Europeans."

I do not believe this to be so; but if it were so, whose fault would it be? I say categorically it would be the fault of Dr. Albert Hertzog, and all those who think and speak as he does, who accuse non-Europeans of being full of hate, who refer to Indians as coolies, and call on all white men to stand together for the purpose of continuing a war.

Surely this comes dangerously near racial incitement? The answer is quite simple. It is not racial incitement in South Africa to insult nonwhite people. It is racial incitement only when one challenges *baasskap.*

Why isn't this man accused of blackening the name of Africa abroad? This answer is quite simple too. The only people who

---

* Blood River was the scene, on December 16, 1838, of a battle in which the Voortrekkers (pioneer Afrikaner settlers), under Andries Pretorius, defeated the Zulu chief Dingaan. The annual commemoration of this event frequently produces emotional oratory related to the struggle for survival of the Afrikaner people. However, Dr. Hertzog, in his speech on this occasion in December, 1958, drew his analogy for the present embattled position of the Afrikaners not from the one-day battle of Blood River but from the prolonged South African War of 1899–1902 (commonly called the Boer War), between the Afrikaner Republics and the British. "Coolie" is a derogatory term for Indian.

are accused of this crime are opponents of the Government. Dr. Hertzog has listed them—the Communists, the liberalists, the capitalists, the United Party. Even the least enthusiastic opponents of the Government [that is, the United Party] do not escape his denunciation.

All decent and reasonable people, no matter to what race they belong, are shocked by this latest outburst. What sort of mind harbours these terrible thoughts? What sort of political philosophy produces them?

If it is true that hatred of the white man is mounting in South Africa, it constitutes the gravest of challenges to our statesmen, for they, after all, have the weapons of political power. Such a challenge calls for the exercise of wisdom, courage, honesty, and certainly of love. For what can cast out hate and fear but love?

There are no signs of these qualities in the speech of the Minister. If the situation is bad, he has inflamed it. If the outlook is grave, he has made it graver.

One might justifiably ask, did he want to make the situation worse and the outlook graver? One can hardly believe that he did want to do so, but that is what he has done.

It is time that this irresponsible and dangerous man was removed from his position of power.

I assume that the speeches and resolutions at Accra have something to do with this latest outburst. But this is the worst possible way in which to react to them. This is the way in which to convince other countries in Africa that the rulers of South Africa believe in eternal conflict between white and black, and that they intend the white man to be the eternal victor. What kind of response will that evoke, except the very kind that Dr. Hertzog fears?

One is compelled to reflect—with no joy, believe me—on the utter barrenness of Afrikaner nationalist policy, on its utter inability to understand the challenges of today, on its failure to evoke the cooperation of nonwhite South Africa. Dr. Verwoerd may claim that things are going swimmingly, but here is one of his lieutenants painting a picture as ugly as we have ever seen.

If the Government goes on like this, history will say of Dr. Verwoerd and his ministers that they betrayed the Afrikaner people, and that they offered them survival on terms unacceptable to the great majority of their countrymen.

The Government wants people to like them no matter what is done to them. They expect Africans to like them in spite of the Urban Areas Act; they expect Coloured people to like them in spite of the Voters Act; and they expect Indian people to like them in spite of the Group Areas Act. They expect English-speaking people to like them too, in spite of a score of studied and unstudied insults. But all they can get is the cupboard love of the stooges.

Finally, Dr. Hertzog wants all white people to join in the continuation of the South African War. Well, Doctor, in the words of Sam Goldwyn, "you can include me out."

NONRACIALISM IN A RACIAL SOCIETY*

I HAVE HAD a letter from a "sympathetic opponent" of the Liberal cause. He asks if after the experience of these [1958] elections, Liberals still think that white South Africa will accept peaceful change.

What he is asking is this—is it worth while to fight elections?

This questioner puts his finger on one of the Liberal dilemmas. Every party has them. The Nationalists have one such dilemma in regard to immigration. The United Party has such a dilemma in regard to liberalism, which it must reject on the rural *platteland* and flirt with in the cities. The African National Congress is caught between broad and narrow nationalism. The dilemma seems to be a fundamental characteristic of human activity and organisation.†

* *Contact,* I, No. 7 (May 3, 1958), 11.

† The Nationalist Party desires white immigration, which would increase the white population, but it fears such an increase could lessen the predominance of its own Afrikaans language and culture. For the United Party dilemma in regard to Liberalism, see "Liberals and the United Party," pp. 63–66. The African National Congress (now banned) was the largest and oldest organiza-

This particular Liberal dilemma arises from the fact that the Liberal Party is a nonracial organisation in a society racially organised; it is a bridge organisation in a country that is gulf-ridden. It feels that it has a duty to convert white people as well as a duty to uphold the claims and aspirations of nonwhite people.

These difficult choices present themselves, not only to organisations, but also to persons. I propose therefore to give my own views, I being the person that is best known (or so I suppose) to myself.

Do I think that white South Africa will accept peaceful change? I have never thought that white South Africa by itself will initiate change. But I am a peaceful person, and what is more, I don't want —for several reasons—to emigrate to some other country. Therefore I am committed to work for change as peaceful as it may be.

Do I think that peaceful change and bloody revolution are the sole alternatives? Do I think the only alternative to peaceful change is a single cataclysmic act? Frankly I do not.

I believe there may be a period of change in which there will be both evolutionary and revolutionary events.

In such a situation we will need nonracial thinking, devotion to liberty, a championship of individual rights. It will be the duty of Liberals—as much as anyone else—to champion these things.

Any such contribution is bound to be one of the creative factors in this evolutionary sequence. Any work honestly done now will affect the end result.

There is of course the extreme possibility that all supporters of a nonracial society will be exterminated in a cataclysmic act, and a black Verwoerd will take his revenge. All the Liberals I know are aware of such a possibility, but it does not deter them from action.

Therefore after these elections, after having wooed white voters

---

tion representing African aspirations in South Africa. Under the leadership of Albert Luthuli, it accepted allies from other racial groups in its nonviolent resistance to *apartheid*. A splinter group, which advocated a more exclusive black nationalism, broke away from the ANC in April, 1959, to form the Pan-African Congress; this was led by Robert Sobukwe.

and having been engaged in the activities of an all-white world, members of the Liberal Party will return to other equally great obligations.

One of these is clearly the obligation to the Multiracial Conference.* Another is our obligation to nonwhite organisations. I myself have been encouraged by friends in such organisations, who have expressed appreciation of our work in the elections.†

The Liberal Party has never been in any doubt that the only way to defeat the dangerous policies of nationalism is by rallying the support of all true believers in liberty, whoever they may be.

We, and all nonparty liberals, will continue to help in this, in both partisan and nonpartisan ways (if there are such categories). We shall still do what we can inside Parliament and outside Parliament.

We declare again our allegiance to the cause of a common society of freedom and opportunity for all, and our kinship with all those who stand for the same cause.

But I do not think we shall relinquish our duty to try to open the eyes of the blind, and to bring out of darkness those who sit in the prison house. After all, lots of us have relatives in there!

* The Multiracial Conference, attended by 500 delegates of all races, was held in Johannesburg, in December, 1957. In resolutions closely resembling the Liberal Party's 1956 statement of policy, the conference called for a re-examination of South Africa's policies on social equality and voting rights.

† Chief Albert Luthuli, President of the African National Congress, gave specific endorsements to the Liberal Party in the 1958 elections.

IV. Patterns of *Apartheid*

THE PEOPLE WEPT

This section of *The Long View* consists of seven essays on the situation of the Indian and African people in South Africa. The first is an excerpt from the introductory portion of Alan Paton's booklet (published under his own imprint at Kloof, Natal, 1958) *The People Wept, being a brief account of the origin, contents, and application of that unjust law of the Union of South Africa known as the Group Areas Act of 1950 (since consolidated as Act No. 77 of 1957).* Paton drew his title from Nehemiah, VIII, 9: The people wept when they heard the words of the law." He adds, "The quotation is apt but ironical, in that the children of Israel wept for joy. The Group Areas Act is quite another kind of law, having in it no element of the divine."

The body of Paton's booklet provides some background to the Group Areas Act and recounts case histories of particular persons affected by it. The Group Areas Act aims at the total separation of the four main racial groups in South Africa, not only in residential areas and in such facilities as schools and public transport but also in social, professional, commercial, and industrial pursuits and organizations. The act itself is complex. It was first made law as the Group Areas Act of 1950, incorporating a good deal of earlier legislation, including the Asiatic Land Tenure Act of 1946. The 1950 act was amended almost annually through 1957, when it was thoroughly overhauled to consolidate various amendments. (Act No. 41 of 1950, as amended by the Group Areas Amendment Act No. 65 of 1952, the Group Areas Amendment Act No. 6 of 1955, the Group Areas Further Amendment Act No. 68 of 1955, the Group Areas Amendment Act No. 29 of 1956, and the Group Areas Amendment Act No. 57 of 1957—all these provisions were consolidated in the Group Areas Act No. 77 of 1957.)

It seems wise, because of the act's complexities, not to attempt to describe it in greater detail here. In *The People Wept,* Paton himself says, "Let the reader therefore understand that we shall not spend time admiring the complexity, ingenuity, or even uniqueness of this Act," and again: "Those who disagree with me will say that I never really tried to describe the Act. That is quite true. I am like a man whose children have eaten a bitter and poisonous fruit, and who immediately orders the tree to be cut down. And in reply to those who say 'at least come first and look at the tree,' he says, 'I have no need to, I have seen the fruit.'"

Though he does not describe the act, Paton is familiar with its intricacies. This is evident in his introduction to a scholarly study of its application, *Durban: A Study in Racial Ecology,* by Leo Kuper, Hilstan Watts, and Ronald Davies (New York: Columbia University Press; London: Jonathan Cape, 1958), which should be consulted for more detailed information.

HAVING A VOICE which by God's grace can be heard beyond the confines of South Africa, I use it to speak for people who have no voice at all, to protest on their behalf and in the name of justice against that law known as the Group Areas Act of 1950 [as amended, 1957].

The Nationalist Government of the Union of South Africa considers it to be almost an act of treachery for a South African to criticise his Government abroad. I admit at once that I would be happier not to do this, but there seems to be no choice. He is a lucky man who lives in a country where his ideals and principles can be reconciled, however roughly, with the actions of his government. But, for me, the Group Areas Act cannot be reconciled with any ideal or principle of love or justice.

Sometimes it is said that by writing or speaking critically abroad one is "blackening the name" of the country. The truth is that the words "South Africa" convey different ideas to different people. The Nationalists are undoubtedly lovers of South Africa, but only so long as the practise of *apartheid* prevails. Were the practise to be struck down tomorrow, many of them would think of their country with anger and pain, as many of us non-Nationalists do now. Nor would they hesitate to "blacken its name" to those who would listen to them in Kenya, Algeria,* and Mississippi.

It is important that the outside world should know some of the main facts about the Group Areas Act. This act has the intention of dividing the whole of South Africa into thousands of areas, where racial separation will be completely achieved, social, educational, commercial, industrial, and many another kind, except that the authorities will permit the continuation of those associations considered useful by them.

This goal of almost complete separation is seen as a noble one by some white South Africans, and it is naturally in that light that it is presented to the world. When I was young I was taught that a worthy goal could only be attained by worthy means, and my experience of life has confirmed me in this belief. Now the Group Areas Act causes such suffering, and is so indifferent to the rights and happiness of persons, and inflicts such wounds upon them, that it seems to me the very instrument of evil. That some of the people who operate and approve this act think it is a good and just law, I must concede. But why they think so, I am at a total loss to explain. They can only think so by blindly cherishing the ideal of complete separation, thus shutting their eyes and ears to the injustices that result from its enforcement.

The ideal of complete racial separation is said to be theologically based. It is said to be a Christian duty to preserve the categories

* *The People Wept,* published in 1958, predates Algerian independence.

of God's creation, and to prevent its diversity from degenerating into a mongrel chaos. I hope to show in this booklet, *The People Wept,* that our Government, in seeking to perform this task of preservation, has offended against the greatest of Christian laws. The Government has in fact set the ideal of complete separation higher even than the two great commandments on which Christ taught all law depended. I hope to demonstrate this beyond the possibility of dispute.

Is this business of racial separation not perhaps our own domestic affair? I do not think so. In a civilised society it is not considered to be a man's domestic affair when he ill-treats his wife and children. Neither in a civilised world should it be considered a country's domestic affair when its government makes a law which treats human beings with harshness and injustice. Such a law is the Group Areas Act.

It will be my intention to refrain from vituperation in this booklet, in the belief that vituperation does no real service to any good cause. But I shall not refrain from using such adjectives as "cruel," "callous," "unjust," and "evil," because they alone convey precisely the true nature of the Group Areas Act.

From time to time good people write to me, and occasionally speak to me, to reproach me for increasing division in a country already bitterly divided, and to urge me to devote my talents to the tasks of reconciliation. I am myself no lover of strife, and can be made unhappy by quarrelling and altercation; I would not write booklets such as this if I did not have to. To these good people I would say that as they feel called to a ministry of reconciliation, so do I feel called to expose the inhumanities which result from any attempt to enforce *apartheid* by law. It is only when white South Africans realise what these inhumanities are that they will understand clearly the nature of the laws to which they have consented; and as for people abroad, this booklet will provide them with a true picture of what is happening.

Let me make it quite clear that there are no doubt a few non-white people who may derive some advantage from the operations of the Group Areas Act. I shall not be writing about them, but those who seek this information can find it elsewhere, for our State Information Office is always glad to publicise such cases. I myself shall be writing about those people, millions in number, whose security has been threatened, whose material possessions have been taken away or reduced in worth, and whose value as human beings, so high in the eyes of God, has been brought to nothing by this act. I proceed on the assumption that an act that can do this, even if only to one man, and even if only once in his lifetime, and even if others derive advantage, is an unjust act.

This booklet, *The People Wept,* is therefore partisan. It is written not to praise the Group Areas Act, nor to describe it dispassionately. It is written to reveal it as a callous and cruel piece of legislation, and to bring nearer the day when it will be struck from the statute book of the Union of South Africa.

.   .   .   .

Indians first came to South Africa in 1860, when labourers were brought to Natal to work on the sugar plantations; they were followed by traders, mostly from Bombay province, who established themselves in Durban, who travelled into the interior hawking and peddling goods, and who eventually set up business in the remote dorps* and villages. They rendered a service to isolated white settlers that no one else was rendering. White-haired Mrs. Fatima Bhayat, ninety-five years old, testified at the Group Areas hearing in Rustenburg that her husband had always welcomed Paul Kruger, President of the Transvaal Republic, when he visited Rustenburg, and that the President had eaten meals at their house, where they had lived since 1887. Today the Town Council proposes to move all Indians out of the town.

Some Indian traders now control large, efficient, and flourishing

---

* "Dorp" is an Afrikaans word meaning small town or village, but the word can also contain implications of remoteness, primitiveness, roughness, and even sleepiness. The dorp never achieved the wildness of the small town of the American West.—*A. P.*

businesses, which are to be found in Durban in an area in the heart of the city, and in Johannesburg, mainly in the area roughly bounded by Sauer, Commissioner, President, and Alexander streets.

It is I think a feature of commercial activity that it brings wealth to those who conduct it efficiently. These traders had money to invest, and except in the urban areas of the Orange Free State where such purchase by Indians was forbidden,* they began to invest it in land. In the Transvaal in 1885 ownership of fixed property was forbidden to Indians except in certain restricted areas. One of the results of this restriction of area was that the value of Indian property began to rise fantastically, and today is worth two, three, four, even eight times the value of similar white-owned properties. In 1891 the Free State prohibited Indian ownership or occupation throughout the whole republic. In fact Indians were not—and still are not—allowed to cross provincial boundaries without permits. It was in protest against this law that Gandhi led 2,700 Indians on foot from Natal into the Transvaal in 1913.† It was a long duel between Gandhi and Smuts, but when Gandhi finally returned to India in 1914, it was with an assurance that "existing laws" would be administered "in a just manner with due regard to vested rights."‡ Later the Class Areas Bill of 1924 and the Areas Reservation Bill of 1925 were designed to segregate Indians in Natal, but these bills

---

* The four provinces of South Africa (Cape, Natal, Orange Free State, and Transvaal) retain certain constitutional rights from the period prior to their coming together as a union in 1910. In the Boer republics of the Orange Free State and the Transvaal, tight restrictions were placed on Indians, and these restrictions remained in force when the republics became provinces of the Union of South Africa.

† Mahatma Gandhi came to South Africa, in 1893, as a lawyer representing Indian interests. He remained to initiate his technique of passive resistance, leading the Indian community in Natal. In 1906, he began a long duel with Jan Christian Smuts—at the time, Attorney General of the Transvaal Republic and, later, Prime Minister of the Union of South Africa. In 1913, Gandhi led a march across the Natal border into the Transvaal to protest the terms of a new immigration act. He and many others were imprisoned, but, in 1914, the Smuts-Gandhi Agreement was negotiated. It ameliorated some restrictive regulations but did not basically alter the discriminatory practices.

‡ As quoted in Jan Hofmeyr, *South Africa* (New York: Charles Scribner's, 1931), p. 152.—*A. P.*

were withdrawn following a round-table conference between South Africa and India. However, in the Transvaal in 1939, and in Natal in 1943, owing to white agitation against Indians who were "penetrating" white residential areas, the position was pegged, and all property transactions between whites and Indians were controlled. In 1946 the Asiatic Land Tenure Act introduced control of all Indian purchases in the Transvaal and Natal, and gave in return representation of Indians in the Senate by three white senators. The Indian community would have nothing to do with this compromise, and in 1948 one of the first acts of the new Nationalist Government was to withdraw the proposal, and to substitute for it a new policy of total racial separation the like of which the world had never seen.

One of the supreme instruments of this separation was the Group Areas Act of 1950. It was designed to separate race from race in both town and country, to separate urban residential area from urban residential area, so that members of one race would not even be able to see members of another, to control ownership and occupation and sale and lease in these areas, and to prevent even the transit of one race through the area of another except perhaps by train, which transit, being more or less sealed off, was considered the "least objectionable."*

Accompanying and aiding this act were many other acts, notably the Population Registration Act [1950], which provides for the racial classification of every person. The Bantu Education Act [1953] made possible a specific education for African children, and destroyed the missionary schools, thereby reducing the contacts between white educator and black pupil. The Native Laws Amendment Act [1957] provided machinery to forbid racial association with Africans in any club, school, hospital, or church. The Group Areas Amendment Act of 1957 provided machinery to forbid the use of the premises in one group area by persons living in another, deeming mere presence to be occupation and therefore punishable.

* So said the Technical Sub-committee appointed by the Durban City Council, in its report of June 22, 1951. [*First Report of the Technical Sub-committee on Race Zoning* (Durban: 1951), pp. 5–6.]—*A. P.*

The Government proposes to forbid the Universities of Cape Town and the Witwatersrand [Johannesburg] to admit nonwhite students, and to establish separate nonwhite colleges under direct government control. It has legislated to provide separate organisations for the nurses of different races, but the white organisation will make the decisions [Nursing Act, 1957]. A similar separation had already been achieved in the trade unions. The Transportation Board has ordered the cities of Durban and Johannesburg to apply segregation fully in their transport; and in the small town of Kloof [Natal], where I live, our only taxi-driver, who is an Indian, has been forbidden to carry white passengers, a restriction which virtually destroyed his livelihood.

But this pamphlet, *The People Wept,* concerns itself specifically with the Group Areas Act. Dr. Malan, our Prime Minister from 1948 to 1953, called it the "heart of *apartheid.*" So it is; and a fitting heart too, for in it is found all the contempt for humanity that is the mark of *apartheid. Apartheid* in its essence is something done by somebody who has power to somebody who has not. It is therefore expecting too much of human nature to expect *apartheid* to be just.

RACIAL JUGGERNAUT MOVES ON INDIANS*

The Durban City Council, representing a white population that had traditionally supported zoning restrictions against Indians in Natal, accepted the first Group Areas Act proposals, in 1950, with alacrity. It appointed a technical subcommittee to replan the city in racial zones. This subcommittee produced elaborate plans within a year. The various amendments to the Group Areas Act through 1957 changed the Durban City Council's attitude to its own costly plan. The City Council opposed the 1957 amendments to the Act as interfering with the autonomy of local authorities and im-

* *Contact,* I, No. 11, (June 28, 1958), 9.

posing on them the financial burden of carrying out the Government's own *apartheid* plans. On June 5, 1958, the City Council decided to prepare new zoning plans and re-solved to request the Minister of the Interior not to make any proclamations for Durban until the new zoning pro-posals had been submitted to the Land Tenure Board. But, on the very next day, June 6, group areas for Durban were proclaimed by the Minister in line with the City Council's earlier unrealistic proposals. In the following two essays, Alan Paton discusses the Durban situation.

THE FIRST proclamations under the Group Areas Act [as amended, 1957] have just been published in Durban. These proclamations are in line with the proposals originally put forward by the Durban City Council. But now the Council would like to reconsider the proposals. I fear the Council is too late.

All persons whose properties are affected have been given thirty days in which to fill in and submit the required forms. The City Council would like this time extended. The Group Areas Develop-ment Board has turned down this request.

I assume that the City Council is appalled, both by the vast and expensive task before it and by the fact that 25,000 properties and 100,000 persons, overwhelmingly nonwhite, will be affected.

There is a proverb that he who sups with the devil needs a long spoon.

There are Indian settlements in Durban known as Prospect Hall and Riverside. The first Indians settled there in 1865. There was no one else there. Now, ninety-three years later, they are to be moved.

There is provision for compensation, and this is what is most feared. The authorities will attach a "basic value" to the properties after hearing representations from both the owner and the Board. From this decision there is no appeal.

Was the Group Areas Act intended to cripple the Indian popu-lation? Or was it intended, as Dr. Dönges* said in the House, to

* Then Minister of the Interior; elected President of the Republic of South Africa, February 28, 1967, he died on January 10, 1968.

be carried out with justice to all? Let the facts speak for themselves.

Soon after the Nationalist Government came to power [in 1948], the Land Tenure Act Amendment Committee and the Asiatic Land Tenure Laws Amendment Committee met together to collect evidence and produce a joint report (U.G. 49 of 1950).

One of the passages of this report will never be forgotten. It read:

Before starting our recommendations we feel that reference should be made to one matter which, strictly speaking falls outside our terms of reference but which is so closely associated in the public mind with the Asiatic question that it has a determining influence on the evidence tendered to us and accordingly also on recommendations based on such evidence, and that is the possibility of repatriating the Asiatic from South Africa. There appears to be an ever-growing belief in the public mind that the only satisfactory solution of the Asiatic question is repatriation, and whatever is done by legislation should be such as not to endanger the possibility of repatriation and deprive the public of its most cherished hopes.

The fundamental theme of the evidence throughout the years has been and still is "repatriation, or, failing which, compulsory segregation." In the most recent evidence there is noticeable a distinct tendency for this theme to assume the form of repatriation and, pending which, compulsory segregation with boycott to induce repatriation.

Mr. W. A. Maree, MP, leader of the Nationalist Party in Natal, speaking at Newcastle [Natal] in 1956, said, "the Indians would be only too pleased to get out of South Africa after the effects of the Group Areas Act had been felt."

Mr. Theo Gerdener, MPC [Member of the Provincial Council], speaking at Port Elizabeth in January, 1956, anticipated the time when the Group Areas Act would restrict Indian traders to Indian trade.

Mr. V. G. Hiemstra, QC, appearing for the municipality at White River, said of Dr. G. Lowen, QC, who was appearing for the Indian community: "My learned friend has been studying the Act to find a provision stating that the Indians must be moved outside the town. Well, he will not find it inside the Act but will find it outside the Act. It lies in the fact that the Act was passed at all."

No one should have been in any doubt as to the purpose of the act. It was intended to cripple the Indian community. It was intended to cripple people who had been brought to the country to assist in its development, people who in two years' time will be celebrating the centenary of their arrival, and who have a record of industry and law-abidingness second to none.

Here is the story of Mr. J [an Indian], who served for five years in the South African forces. He fought against Hitler and all that Hitler stood for.

But unfortunately for himself, after leaving the Army in 1945, he set up a shop in K, a mixed township with a large nonwhite population. His landlord was a white man, Mr. V.

In 1954 Mr. V decided to rebuild his premises, but he gave Mr. J temporary premises nearby.

In February, 1955, the new premises were finished, and Mr. V applied for a determination from the Group Areas Board, as he was obliged to do. The reply was a bombshell. The whole of K was declared an area for white occupation. Mr. J was given twelve months to leave. He asked the group areas inspectors where he was to go, what was he to do? But they replied that that was none of their business.

When I heard this story I asked Mr. J if I could use his name.

Shame, anger, and grief struggled in his face.

"No," he said, "my boy's training for a teacher."

This is the Act which, said Dr. Dönges, was to be carried out with justice to all.

Mr. J is the man who must suffer so that greater good may come to us all.

No good will come of this, only suffering, grief, and bitterness.

There is no common good worth pursuing that allows individual persons to be broken.

Who blackens the name of South Africa abroad? Those who protest against this evil law, or those who made it?

It is a sign of our corruption that we can even debate such a question.

GROUP AREAS ACT CRUELTY TO THE INDIANS*

AT THE MOMENT I cannot get the Indian people of South Africa out of my thoughts. The group areas proclamations in Durban are so cruel that they fill all my mind. They mean the removal of 100,000 people to areas more remote from the city. Those who will suffer most are 60,000 Indians. The properties they must leave are valueless to most Europeans with their higher standard of living. It is said that the Group Areas Development Act will alleviate this hardship, but this is untrue. The Development Board appoints its own valuators, and though they hear representations, there is no appeal from this valuation.

Recently I attended the great meeting of protest and prayer held at Curries' Fountain in Durban. What a democratic people these Indians are! The meeting was orderly and dignified, a very model of good behaviour. What insensate folly to alienate such a fundamentally good and law-abiding section of our population!

Two of the speakers were white persons, Professor Hansi Pollak and myself. We received a warm welcome from the tremendous assembly. In the whole course of the meeting there was not sounded one bitter or racialistic note. It is this generosity, this warm-heartedness, this incredible tolerance, that I find one of the most astonishing qualities of the Indian people. Here is the very stuff of which true democracy is made, and we white people are busy throwing it away.

Many of us fear that the stranglehold of white nationalism will only be broken by violence and bloodshed. It may well be that in such a situation South Africa will have cause to be grateful to its Indian people, for they have that respect for persons and personality which is the foundation of any democratic society.

I do not think that there is any doubt that white Christianity in

* *Contact,* I, No. 14 (August 9, 1958), 9.

South Africa is at the crossroads, whether it is of the Afrikaner or the English kind. We white Christians, corrupted by the doctrines of race separation, are letting the great values of love and justice go by the board. We have elevated race purity (and its inevitable dark counterpart, race domination) to the level of the great commandments. We regard out-and-out opponents of race discrimination as extremists, and urge moderation in all things, even in justice. We regard Christians who take Christ seriously—people like Michael Scott and Trevor Huddleston—as agitators, even as Christ was regarded in his day. We Christian laymen have been conspicuously silent in our opposition to the Group Areas Act.

I do not think that we white Christians know what mortal (yet I hope not mortal) blows we have inflicted upon Christ's Church. For his Church is meant to be one body, not a number of separate racial units, each of which could see disaster befall its fellows and not spring to their comfort and succour.

I have said before in this column that I admire SABRA* for its determination to make its voice heard, which is the right of men in any democratic society. I admire SABRA for its decision to meet nonwhite leaders, and to talk to them about the difficult problems that confront multiracial South Africa. But I think they should be more forthright and vocal in the defence of their fellow South Africans who suffer, daily and pitifully, under the *apartheid* laws. Is it nothing to them that 60,000 Indians will lose their homes? Is it nothing to them that the Indian people of South Africa face a future of anxiety and uncertainty? Let their voice be heard.

Chief Luthuli sent a magnificent message to the meeting at Cur-

---

* The South African Bureau of Racial Affairs, a private organization with membership restricted to whites who support the policies of the Nationalist Party, of which many are also members. At the time Paton wrote this essay, a number of SABRA's leading members were endeavoring to turn SABRA into an independent study group willing to express views not in conformity with the Government's policies. These members were ousted in 1961, and SABRA leaders, thereafter, emphasized that the organization was an "Afrikaner institution" that accepted separate development as a basic point of departure and that they would study ways of making this policy acceptable to nonwhites.

ries' Fountain, assuring the Indian people that the Africans of this country accepted them as their fellow citizens. So does every white liberal in South Africa. Destiny has brought us all together, and confronted us with the tremendous problem of overcoming our racial fears and hates, and of building a new society where every man, woman, and child can look forward to a life of purpose and freedom.

That is the long view, not to waste our time in dreaming fantastic dreams of separate and independent societies, but to bend our energies to the building of a common society, with no nationalism except a common South African nationalism, with no discrimination except against all policies that make any person suffer because of his colour and race.

This is the only kind of Afrikanerdom that will ultimately survive.

THE QUALITY OF JUSTICE*

In 1914, Smuts made an agreement with Gandhi that "existing laws" would be administered in "a just manner with due regard to vested rights." Nevertheless, in the years that followed, restrictive legislation such as the Asiatic Land Tenure Act of 1946 was enacted. Dr. Ebenezer Dönges, the cabinet minister responsible for the Group Areas Act, had similarly declared—when he introduced the bill to Parliament, in 1950—that the act would be administered with justice, without discrimination, and with equal sacrifice from all groups. In the body of *The People Wept*, Paton cites specific instances of hardship that bear contrary witness. What follows is his concluding statement.

ONE DAY Dr. Dönges will stand before a much higher Authority than the South African Parliament. He will be asked to defend himself and the Group Areas Act.

* From *The People Wept*, pp. 43–44.

It is hard to know what this clever man will be able to say.

It was he who asserted that the act would be administered with justice and without discrimination. I hope I have refuted completely and finally that contention.

The Group Areas Act is an evil instrument, repugnant to all true religion and morality, and contemptuous of human rights.

It is false to religion in that it exalts the welfare of groups above the welfare of persons, and indeed treats persons as of less account, *and in many cases as of no account at all.*

It has given the advantage, almost without exception, to the ruling group in the country.

It has been cruel and merciless to the Indian people of South Africa, whose record of industry and law-abidingness is unsurpassed by any.

It has blackened the name of South Africa abroad, so that our Prime Minister is nervous to attend any overseas conference, where he would have to face the unanswerable question, "Is this how justice is done?"

It has blackened the name of white South Africa abroad, not only the name of the English-speaking group to which I belong, but still more so that of the Afrikaans-speaking group.

The act has purported to aim at racial harmony, but in fact it has done immeasurable harm to race relations. One might forgive fear, but it is hard to forgive those evil companions that exploit it—avarice, cruelty, and hypocrisy.

Lastly, the act is based on the evil doctrine that the end justifies the means. It supposes that a common good can be bought at the cost of individual harm. It supposes that one can preserve civilisation even while flouting its values. It supposes that one can carry out the divine will even when disobeying the divine commandments.

I could wish that my pen were able enough to convince the white people of South Africa that it is they who are being destroyed by the Group Areas Act, that I could write such words as would make the very paper catch fire, to burn them awake to the cruelty that is being done in their name.

Indeed I have written this booklet, *The People Wept,* with a double purpose. I have written not only for those people who have no voice; I have written also for those who have a voice, to urge them to stop consenting unto evil.

Both these people are dear to me, and the future depends on their ability and willingness to build a country together.

But God save us all from the South Africa of the Group Areas Act, which knows no reason, justice, or mercy.

THE CHARLESTOWN STORY

For more than a century, Africans acquired freehold rights to land in a number of areas outside the designated tribal Reserves through the normal process of purchase and registration of title deeds. The Group Areas Act provides administrative machinery for the removal of Africans from these so-called black spots. Charlestown, along with its neighboring districts Clavis and Clavis Extension, was designated a black spot. The following is an excerpt from Paton's *The Charlestown Story* (Pietermaritzburg: Liberal Party, 1960). Like *The People Wept,* this pamphlet was written to appraise white South Africans of the practical effects of *apartheid* on people. It also provides a valuable example of the kind of activity undertaken by the Liberal Party as an extraparliamentary duty; the party's willingness to undertake this work has attracted an increasing number of Africans to its ranks.

THIS IS THE Charlestown story, the story of Africans who bought or rented land in and around Charlestown. Those who bought land were making their sole investment; they had no money to put into shares, and very few could buy insurance. All their savings went into the pieces of land and the houses they built upon them.

They had good reasons for buying this land, of which we shall learn later. But it is important to note that they were encouraged to buy it, that they bought it openly and legally, and that they received title deeds testifying to their lawful ownership.

In 1948 the Nationalist Government came to power, with its policy of *apartheid*. One of the aims of this policy was to separate whites from nonwhites wherever possible, in offices, entrances, exits, cinemas, halls, restaurants, hotels, schools, universities, churches, in residential areas, and on the land. Therefore the presence of African freehold owners in Charlestown, already offensive to local white opinion, became now contrary to the policy of *apartheid*.

No compromise was possible; they would have to go. That is the Charlestown story.

The story will anger some defendants of *apartheid*, who will consider that it relates the bad luck of the present and tries to conceal the happy promise of the future. However, people have to live in the present, and any policy that causes present grief for the sake of future bliss must be regarded with suspicion. But when all the grief must be borne by others, it should be regarded with horror.

Charlestown is a "black spot," a place where Africans legally acquired land outside those Reserves set aside for exclusively African occupation. There are computed to be about 350 of these black spots in South Africa. In many cases some white farmer has subdivided his farm and sold it piecemeal to African buyers; in other cases a tribal community or group of African persons or even an African individual has bought a "white" farm outright. In other cases, such as Charlestown, Africans bought urban plots from white owners. All this land was held in freehold, as against the communal tenure of the Reserves, where land is distributed by the chief, and never belongs to the individual occupier.

Great value is attached to freehold land by Africans for several reasons. The Reserves offer little scope for a farmer; less than 13 per cent of the land in the Union is set aside for African occupation, although Africans comprise nearly 70 per cent of the population. African farms in the Reserves are therefore small, seldom more than a few acres. Further, they are held by favour of the chief, and many African farmers aspired to a freehold not subject to the decision of a chief. But it was not only the would-be farmer who wanted to acquire land; it was also the African labourer on the white farm, who wanted an escape for himself and his children from a futureless bondage; it was also the town worker who, not anxious to expose his family to the dangers and evils of the city, wanted a place where he could leave them, and a home to which he could return when circumstances permitted or compelled it.

These people were an evolutionary product of the modern age; in their black spots, in the absence of chief or master, they developed simple democratic institutions in order to run their community affairs, and their general record of law-abidingness was excellent; what money they could spare they invested in their simple homes, their gardens, and their farms. They built schools, churches, and shops. According to a rough survey made of nineteen communities by the Liberal Party in 1958, these communities contained 29,245 people—of whom 1,127 were land-owners owning an average of a few acres each—9,227 head of cattle, 6,689 houses, 26 schools, 55 churches, and 28 shops.

But because they were a living contradiction of the Nationalist theory that every African had a domicile in the Reserves, because their presence in a "white" area constituted an affront to some, and finally—I state this reluctantly—because they displayed an originality and initiative in escaping from the rigid pattern of *apartheid,* it was decreed that their decent, hard-won, upward-striving way of life must be destroyed.

The news that the Government had decided to expropriate all freehold land held by Africans in "white" areas fell as a bombshell on the owners of black spot land. They could not believe it. They pointed to the sacred title deed, the piece of paper that had spelt security in an uncertain world. This valuable document itself represented a large sum in the obligatory expenses of transfer duty, stamp duty, and conveyancing charges that had to be incurred in registering the title deed in the Deeds Registry at Pietermaritzburg, for the law required this to be done in order to make a person owner of his property in the eyes of the law as well as the world. They might have to suffer indignities; they might be treated as persons of no account; but this piece of paper was something that stood above all prejudice and custom. The white man, for all his superior airs and overweening regulations, had a sense of honour, and the title deed was the symbol of it.

It is almost impossible to exaggerate the shocked incredulity of the African freeholders of Charlestown. What made things worse was to know that a title deed was still a sacred document, provided it was held by a white person, and to know that the Nationalists did not regard any decision of a previous government as necessarily binding, because all previous governments had entered into contracts on the false assumption that an African had some kind of moral right to buy land in "white" areas.

It was no comfort to the African freeholders of Charlestown to know that they were to be removed to Buffalo Flats, a flat, sandy area, bare and uninviting, more than forty miles from Charlestown, where they would be able to live their African lives "along African lines"; and to run their own affairs, within the limits laid down by the Bantu Authorities Act; * and to have their own schools, within the limits laid down by the Bantu Education Act [1953]; and to occupy land, within the limits laid down by the Native Administration Act [1927] (which empowers the Chief Native Commissioner to control selling, mortgaging, leasing, and letting, to determine the value of improvements, and to permit or debar persons outside the family from occupying the property). The freeholders were being returned to a [remote] rural area after they had originally and in-

---

* The Bantu Authorities Act (1951) abolished the Natives' Representative Council (established in 1936) and appointed tribal, regional, and territorial Bantu authorities in the "Bantu homelands," or Reserves, which were under the new Department of Bantu Administration and Development, established in 1958 when the old Department of Native Affairs was split into two units: The Department of Bantu Administration and Development and the Department of Bantu Education.

tentionally moved to an urban area;* they would have to leave behind houses which would be of negligible value to any purchaser other than an African, and many of them would have to leave behind businesses and trades which would be in some cases difficult, in others impossible, to re-establish in a rural area.

One may tire, but one should not, of pointing out that once *apartheid* (or any other political doctrine, however altruistic) is made the supreme good, all moral values suffer a decline. Behind and under the title deed, buttressing and supporting it, lies the human idea of contract, of promise, of the giving of one's word. There is a growing number of Africans who begin to regard the white man's promise not as anything sacred, but as something to be kept or broken according to convenience; not as something absolute, but as something contingent; not as something permanently binding, but as something to be maintained or set aside according to the policy of the government of the day. But worse than this, there is a growing number of Africans who are beginning to believe that the white man simply does not care what happens to others, as long as his own interests are served.

This pamphlet is written, not in the hope that Africans will note that the writer is a white person, but that white people will learn what is being done in their name, and will learn the hard and reluctant lesson that injustice at Charlestown cannot be righted in isolation. It is *apartheid* itself that must be totally rejected, and by *apartheid* I mean racial segregation enforced by law. It is temporising with *apartheid* that has weakened the strength of opposition and undermined its righteousness.

.   .   .   .

Before Union [in 1910], Charlestown was the frontier town on the Natal side of the Transvaal border. It was a flourishing railhead

* The term "urban areas" includes small towns or dorps with their adjoining farmland, as well as large cities like Johannesburg (where Africans owned free-hold property in the township of Sophiatown until the implementation of the Group Areas Act). See Trevor Huddleston, *Naught for Your Comfort* (New York: Doubleday, 1956), for an account of the Sophiatown removals.

and customs post. At Union, however, customs were abolished and the railway workshops were transferred across the border to Volks-rust, three miles away. With them went the major part of the town's white population. Houses were deserted and the prospect of selling property to white buyers virtually disappeared. The Town Board saw its income vanishing with its ratepayers, and Charlestown faced the prospect of becoming a ghost town.

To remedy this situation, Mr. S. R. Higgins, a land-owner, butcher, and member of the Town Board, deliberately set out to persuade Africans to buy land in Charlestown, there being no law against it. The first recorded transfer of land to an African was to Mr. Abraham Ngwenya in 1911.* Mr. Amos Coka, who came in 1914, said that only twelve white families were living in Charles-town at that time. Other Africans followed, and once settled, were asked by Mr. Higgins to tell their African friends of the advantages of life in Charlestown. Thus were Africans persuaded to settle in Charlestown to fill the vacuum created by Union, to pay rates, and to assist the Town Board in meeting its financial obligations which were proving too great for the dwindling white community.

Nevertheless it would be a mistake to imagine that life in Charlestown was plain sailing. Although the African residents paid rates they did not have votes. As a consequence the white Town Board was insulated from its African burgesses; it was either un-aware of or indifferent to their wants, and was screened from normal democratic pressures.

In Charlestown many African residents maintain that, over the years, they have paid rates and have received virtually nothing in re-turn. Investigators from the Liberal Party were struck by the despair that the African owners of Charlestown felt about their position. They [the owners] declared that they had often approached the local authority, and that an enquiry would be promised and then nothing would happen. They often feared, not that the enquiry had been held up elsewhere, but that it had never been made. They often ex-

* See pages 271–72 for a further account of Mr. Ngwenya.

pressed the view that the Town Board not only failed to defend the interests of its African burgesses, but that, in fact, it did not care about them.

.   .   .   .

Early in 1954 it came to the notice of the newly formed Liberal Party of South Africa that most of the African residents of Charlestown, Clavis, and Clavis Extension, including many owners of freehold, were to be ejected. The exceptions would be those who actually worked in Charlestown itself, but even of these, none would be allowed to remain in Charlestown proper. There would in fact be a "white" town to which would be attached the usual "location."*

The proposed removal of the Charlestown black spot is to be effected under the notorious Group Areas Act and other statutes of *apartheid,* notably the latest Nationalist amendments of the Natives (Urban Areas) Consolidation Act of 1945, and certain provisions of [the earlier legislation on the status of Reserves] the Native Administration Act of 1927 and the Native Trust and Land Act of 1936.†

The moment the decision to remove all African freehold owners was known, one African resident, who had built a fine house valued

---

* A location is a part of a town set aside for those Africans who work in the "white" portions of the town, e.g. as domestic servants, messengers, unskilled workers, and the like in "white" homes, offices, shops, and factories. There are no freehold rights in a location [the municipality owns the land].—*A. P.*

† The original Natives Urban Areas Act was passed by the Smuts Government in 1923 and amended regularly thereafter. To make it more intelligible it was consolidated in 1945. Since then it has been amended on a further twelve occasions. The 1923 act was based on the findings of the "Stallard" Commission (Transvaal Local Government Commission) which invented the myth that all African urban dwellers were "temporary sojourners" in the "white" area. The effect of almost every amendment to the act, particularly since 1945, has been progressively to restrict the rights of urban Africans. One of the results of the operation of this act is that there are now land-owners at Charlestown holding registered title deeds, but working elsewhere, who cannot return to their own land for more than seventy-two hours without first having to obtain a permit to do so.—*A. P.*

at £750 [$2,100], was approached by a white person who offered
him £20 [$56] for it. The owner was affronted and said, "The
house is worth £750. How can you make such an offer?" The
white man laughed at him and said, "Don't take it then. But one
day I'll get it for £5."

. . . .

The Natives (Urban Areas) Consolidation Act of 1945 controls
at many points the lives of Africans who are "temporary sojourners"
in the towns and cities. This act, or rather Section 23 of it, was
applied to Charlestown as from 1st April, 1957, by Proclamation
No. 89 of 1957. As a result the Town Board was required to register
every contract of service entered into by an African man and to
cause every African man entering the area to report his arrival
and obtain a permit to remain in the area. This section of the act
further empowers the Town Board to refuse entry to an African
woman unless she can prove that her husband, or if she is unmarried,
her father, "has been resident and continuously employed in the
said area for not less than two years." Certain limited classes of
Africans are exempted.

Once an area has been proclaimed under Section 23 and the
local authority exercises these powers—as the Charlestown Town
Board does now—Section 10 of the act comes into force. This
section prohibits any African from remaining in the area for more
than seventy-two hours unless: (1) he has since birth resided there
continuously; (2) he has worked continuously in that area for the
same employer for at least ten years; (3) he has lawfully resided
in the area continuously for fifteen years, has "thereafter continued
to reside in such area and is not employed outside this area"; (4) he
or she is the wife, unmarried daughter, or son under taxpaying age
of anyone exempted under (1), (2), or (3); [or] (5) he has a
permit.

If proceedings are brought against an African under this section, the onus is on him to prove that he has not been there for more than seventy-two hours. The effect of this section of the act is to undermine the right of Africans to be in urban areas, and to place their whole lives in the hands of the registering officer. An African can have been born in Charlestown, he can have lived there for fifty years, but if he leaves Charlestown for two weeks, he has no right to return there for more than seventy-two hours. He may have lived and worked in Charlestown for fourteen years, but he has no right to stay there. He may ask his married daughter and her children to spend Christmas with him, but if she stays more than three days without getting a permit, she commits a criminal offence.

Section 10 of the Urban Areas Act already applies to Charlestown, and Section 9 may be applied any moment. Its effect is further to circumscribe the life of Africans and to emphasize their "temporary" status in towns.

The Charlestown Town Board has not hesitated to use the powers which the Urban Areas Act may give a local authority—in fact it has anticipated them. On 15th December, 1958, for instance, a number of African residents of Charlestown, who worked in Volksrust, received a notice from the Town Board calling on them to take up residence in Volksrust within thirty days. The notice purported to be issued in terms of a proclamation under Section 9 of the Urban Areas Act—a proclamation which did not exist. Confronted with this fact, by some of those on whom it had been served, the Town Board withdrew this first notice and issued a second. It did so by using the same duplicated form of 15th December, with alterations, overwritten in ink, altering the references to the Urban Areas Act to refer to Section 10. Legal opinion consulted by Charlestown residents on these and the previous notices established, in a written opinion, the following: "It is quite clear that the person who has signed the notices that were served upon Consultants has completely misdirected himself in regard to his powers under Section 10 of the Act and that the notices are invalid. They are of course also invalid in the original form as no Proclamation under Section

9 has been published in relation to Charlestown. Consultants may therefore disregard the notices."

The Charlestown Town Board was clearly so anxious to start moving its African ratepayers that it tried to use powers it did not possess to speed up their departure. In their ignorance of the law some of them complied. Over those who contested the validity of these notices hangs the certain knowledge that the Board has the potential power to move them and that it has only been prevented from doing so up to now by legal technicalities. In addition, it is interesting that no offers of compensation went out with the notice of 15th December, 1958, or any other notice, in spite of the assurances given by the Chief Native Commissioner in his correspondence with the Liberal Party. Those families which moved to Volksrust did so not knowing that they had any claims at all upon the Town Board.

I quote this brief history of its recent actions in support of the view that the Charlestown Town Board was indifferent to the interests of its African ratepayers and in case anyone should think that the threat to those who still remain is not a very real one.

Such is the potential nature of any policy based on the axiom that the African is only a "temporary sojourner" in the towns and cities of the land of his birth. Such also is the insecurity that threatens every African living in Charlestown and working elsewhere. People went there looking for security, but *apartheid* has put an end to that. Of the dreadful uncertainties of African urban life, the white person understands little, for they lie outside his world and they trouble him only if he can experience them in imagination. That is why many white people are little troubled by injustice, and confine themselves to their own affairs, contenting themselves with the belief that in matters of race relations, courtesy is an adequate substitute for justice. This isolation is intensified by traditional and obligatory *apartheid,* and by the growing difficulty of taking responsibility for what are known as "Bantu affairs." Under the Smuts dispensation a white person interested in Bantu affairs certainly had to fight apathy; now he has to fight the whole

Bantu Affairs Department, for he is in fact interfering with what has become the state's closed preserve.*

Editor's Postscript

On October 4, 1964, *Contact* reported that about 100 families had been evicted from their homes in Charlestown and sent to Duckponds location, thirty-five miles away. Duckponds, which is near a site for border industries,† had no rail service or shops at that time. The *Contact* correspondent wrote:

Charlestown . . . looks as though it had been struck by an earthquake. Throughout the village lie heaps of rubble with a few remaining houses standing out starkly amid the desolation. But this is no natural disaster: it is the systematic destruction of a community in the name of *apartheid*.

Tenants get notice, be it three months or two days, to vacate the houses they have bought or built. The labour gang comes round . . . a strong chain is attached to a tractor . . . and within minutes the home of a lifetime is just another heap of rubble in a Charlestown street. . . .

The stories of the people uprooted are tragic. . . . A Mr. Setlebe has been given a month's notice and has been threatened with prosecution if he does not leave. He has two cows and two horses which he will not be allowed to take to Duckponds. He has lived for twenty years in Charlestown.

No compensation has been arranged for the owners of the demolished houses, and in keeping with the callous attitude of the authorities there have been several "mistakes." One freehold owner, not scheduled for removal, returned after a short absence to find that his house had been demolished "by mistake." The local Squatter Inspector responsible

---

* Before 1948, under the Smuts Government, the Department of Native Affairs administered large segments of African life. Paton's point is that, however bureaucratic it may have been, it was sensitive to public opinion to some degree. Since 1951, the newly named Department for Bantu Administration and Development administers *all* aspects of African life and brooks no interference or advice from nongovernmental agencies.

† The Government's border-industries scheme offers inducements to white industrialists to establish factories in "white" areas adjacent to Reserves. The idea is that African employees will continue to live in their "homelands" while working in these factories. The industrialists are not allowed to set up factories within the Reserves.

for the removals, although promising to help rebuild the house, has done nothing. Then there was one old pensioner who had her house demolished and was left in the street together with her possessions. No alternative accommodation in Charlestown or Duckponds was arranged.

THE WAGES OF THE POOR*

Before 1958, all African males over the age of eighteen, whether wage earners or not, paid a direct head tax—known, in South Africa, as a poll tax—of £1 ($2.80) in addition to other local and state taxes (including income tax) to which all earnings were subject. The Natives Taxation and Development Act of 1958 increased the rates of this basic tax, applying a graduated scale; the act also applied the new tax to African females. No other racial group pays this direct tax, and Africans must carry their receipts for payment at all times and produce them on demand. (This receipt is one of the documents required under the Pass Laws.) In 1958, only 45,000 out of some 2.5 million African males required to pay the head tax had incomes over £180 ($504) a year. In the following essay, Paton shows his concern for the impoverished majority, particularly those in urban areas, who earned less than £180 a year.

NO SENSIBLE person objects to the taxation of African citizens of the Union. No sensible person objects to their being taxed as lightly or as heavily as anyone else. But the increase of the basic tax from £1 to £1 15s. [an increase of $2.10], on all African men earning from £0 to £180 per annum, will be a serious matter.

There may be some who consider that an increase of 15s. can hardly be a serious matter, and who consider that in any case a political writer of my views must be expected—under almost any circumstances—to belabour the Government. I hope to convince such persons that the increase in the tax will be an unendurable burden to the poor.

* *Contact,* I, No. 18 (October 4, 1958), 9.

One hundred and eighty pounds per annum is £15 [$42] per month. There are many Africans who do not reach this level, but who, as unskilled labourers, earn from £8 [$22.40] to £10 [$28] per month working for our municipalities. On the average, a man, woman, and at least two children have to live on this £10 per month. Many European householders of average means spend that amount on feeding—not extravagantly—two domestic servants. But the married labourer must in addition clothe himself, his wife, and his children; he must pay for rent and transport, and for the schooling. His children, unlike other school-children, must pay for their own school equipment (except for reading books, which are supplied).

It has been estimated that between £25 [$70] and £27 [$75.60] is the absolute living minimum for such a family, to give them enough of the right kind of food to keep them well, to keep a roof over their heads, and decent but inexpensive clothing on their bodies.

These estimates have been made by responsible persons and authorities. The Town Council of Benoni estimated £16 14s. 9d. [$46.90] as an "absolute minimum," and its Senior Welfare Officer estimated that £24 [$67.20] a month was necessary if the family "is to live and not merely exist." This Council pays almost £10 per month to its labourers, which is the approximate average for all municipalities.

The Johannesburg Council pays most so far as I know (nearly £13 [$36.40] per month) and so it should; but it is paying only half of the amount required for an austere life, with none of the luxuries enjoyed and deserved by all who work hard for a living.

It is not surprising when human nature rebels, and grasps the luxury at the cost of some essential need. Yet when it does, the gulf between income and expenditure becomes more unbridgeable, the hope of achieving a balance dies away, and liquor perhaps helps one to forget it all.

Seen against the background of these facts, the African National Congress campaign for £1 a day is absolutely justified. It is seen as a reasonable request, and an appeal that humanity should heed.

It is said of course that economics cannot justify such a wage, that production must increase and improve. All of us would agree that the standard of production should be raised. But there are two important reasons why it is difficult to raise; one is the colour bar, the other is because the worker is beaten by it all; he cannot buy enough food, he cannot buy the right food, his spirit is broken by a struggle against the odds that never get less.

Raise the wages and some will drink and gamble more—they are a loss already; but others will do what so many have done before them, eat better food, wear better clothes, keep children longer in school, take a little pride in the house, feel a little more joy in being alive.

And South African enterprises, especially the food and clothing industries, will take us another step forward in our struggle for a better life for all.

No town-dweller earning from £0 to £180 per annum should pay any tax at all. He is not able to feed and clothe his family as it is. To add another 15s. to his tax is to place on him an intolerable burden. People who are eating too little already will have to eat yet less.

One hears that the cabinet is considering ways and means of raising the wages of the very poor. May this be true.

When the wages of the poor white labourer were raised, the argument was humanity, not economics. And it worked.

Let humanity be the argument now. It will work too.

*BANTU EDUCATION: THE STATE MUST NOT
RUN THE UNIVERSITIES**

The Bantu Education Act (1954) is a key piece of legislation embodying Dr. Verwoerd's concept of *apartheid* as separate development. It transferred African schools from the

* *Contact*, I, No. 9 (May 31, 1958), 11.

Department of Education to the Department of Native Affairs. Its purpose was not merely to have separate schools but to create a separate system of education—"to keep the Bantu child a Bantu child" and not an "imitator" of whites. The principles of this act were extended to the field of higher education by the Separate University Education Bill introduced in March, 1957 and redrafted in August of that year as the Extension of University Education Bill. This bill was in the process of becoming law when Paton wrote the following article on the problem of attitudes toward measures one opposes but cannot alter. The bill was later enacted. Its provisions applied to the existing non-European University College of Fort Hare, and it set up two "tribal" colleges: University College of Zululand and University College of the North (at Turfloop), serving the Sotho, Venda, and Tsonga language groups. Later, provision was made for Cape Coloured and Indian students.

IT IS TO BE expected that the Government will establish separate university institutions for nonwhite students. We ought to oppose this, but it is going to be done. It is part of the pattern of *apartheid,* and it will be carried out.

The difficult question then arises, what should we do then? Should we make suggestions which we think would help these *apartheid* institutions to operate better? Or should we wash our hands of the whole business?

It is impossible in our *apartheid* society to wash one's hands of all *apartheid* arrangements. The South African Coloured People's Organisation demonstrated this by taking part in the [separate] Coloured elections. Its attitude was significant, because it is a militant anti-*apartheid* organisation, and because its members belong to the group most concerned.

To my mind it is important that if we are to have separate university institutions, they should be the best possible under *apartheid* policy. That means, to put it simply, they should be as like university institutions as possible.

Some people maintain that the Separate University Education Bill has precisely that intention, namely to make these institutions as like university institutions as possible. They point to Section 1, Subsection xv of the bill, which says that university education means "education of a standard equivalent to that established by Act of Parliament."

I find it impossible to accept this optimistic view. The fact that the Minister [of Native Affairs] will appoint the principal [Rector], that he will appoint the Council, that he will appoint the Senate, that no member of the Senate need be a teaching member of the university college, and that the Senate need not be represented on the Council is to my mind nothing short of ominous.*

So also is the fact that the Minister shall define the courses, control the admission of students, and exercise a rigid control over the teachers, even to the extent that they may not make adverse public comment on the policies and practise of any state department.

All these things do not make a university institution; they merely make a government department. It may be said that it will develop in due course into a freer institution, when it shows its ability to assume responsibility. I find this hard to believe. I believe that these provisions were specifically designed to control people's minds.

If I were asked what is the greatest threat to the human race, I would not say the nuclear bomb, though that is great enough; I would say that the greatest threat is the growing inclination of authority to control people's minds.

When authority wants to control people's minds, it uses first a

_____

* The bill provided that each college should have a Rector appointed by the Minister of Native Affairs, who also was to prescribe his functions and privileges. It also provided for a council of eight government nominees (of whom four would be appointed because of their special knowledge of higher education) and for a senate consisting of the Rector as chairman and such faculty members as the Minister, in consultation with the Council, should decide. The later draft (Extension of University Education Bill) proposed that, in addition to the Council, there be an advisory council—the former, initially all white; the latter, nonwhite—to which duties would gradually be transferred. It made similar arrangements for a senate and an advisory senate. Paton is discussing the first draft bill.

well-tried weapon, the fear of the common enemy. And if that does not work, it uses a second, the fear of itself.

Now authority in South Africa wants people to think that *apartheid* is the only possible solution to our problems. *Apartheid* is no longer an alternative to be accepted or rejected by the people of South Africa. It has become a policy to be accepted—or else.

The groups in South Africa that are least likely to accept *apartheid* are for the greater part nonwhite. They identify *apartheid* with *baasskap.* They identify it with a state of perpetual subordination. They identify it with an inferior life. Therefore their thinking must be controlled.

There are also white people in South Africa who reject *baasskap,* some on moral grounds, some on the grounds that it is an unstable solution, which means, briefly, that it will not and cannot work. Their thinking—and their teaching—is in danger of being controlled too.

Of course there must be authority. A society without authority would be a mess. But more and more, authority is demanding the sacrifice of individual liberties. The people who feel this least are those who support *apartheid,* because their authority is an *apartheid* authority. But what they fail to grasp is that complete subservience to authority, even when that authority does what they want, means the death of freedom, ultimately of theirs as well.

Liberals are often accused of an indifference to authority. But the truth is that in the modern world it is not the cause of authority that needs support, but the cause of the individual person.

The place of the university in the life of a nation is a proud one. It cannot expect to enjoy absolute autonomy, but it can expect to enjoy a measure of freedom equal to that of the home and the church. Each of these institutions has a function that cannot be performed by the state. And the good state will see to it that freedom to perform these functions is preserved inviolate.

The function of the university is to pursue the truth, which is as much of an absolute as there can be in this uncertain world. But to pursue that absolute under direction from the state is unthinkable for any university worthy of the name.

Therefore, if we must have racial university colleges, let them be controlled by an authority other than the state, in other words, by a university authority.

Epilogue: "The Days of White Supremacy Are Over"*

This parable of a knock on the door has many overtones, for *Contact*'s African readers in particular. For example, the Zulu song "Open Malan," sung at large gatherings during the ANC defiance campaign of 1952, began with the refrain "Open Malan we are knocking." (Repeated four times, the refrain was followed by "Wake up Luthuli, Luthuli of Africa.") And Chief Luthuli's well-known address on the occasion of his dismissal from his chieftainship, "The Road to Freedom Is via the Cross," expanded on the metaphor of knocking on a closed and barred door. Paton may have had this in mind when he wrote, in his essay on Archbishop de Blank, "A man like Luthuli must look at us in desperation sometimes, behind the closed doors of our shut-off world."

I HAVE BEEN WRITING "Long View" for a year now, and I think it is time to stop. The long view should be seen through fresh eyes, and spoken by a fresh voice. That is the way to win fresh support for sane and liberal views.

I want to try in my last article to produce some kind of summing-up. I want to try to set down some germinal ideas. The minds of white South Africans, under the twin stimulants of fear and selfishness, do not seem very fertile ground for such ideas. They have built a walled city for themselves, to defend themselves against the enemy, to keep safe and intact all that is cherished, above all to keep out the news of the changing world.

* *Contact,* II, No. 2 (January 24, 1959), 9.

A white South African is a man who hears about Leopoldville to-day and forgets about it tomorrow. Nevertheless this last column is for him, he being my brother by blood.

I went to my brother and said, "Brother, a man is knocking at the door."

My brother said, "Is he a friend or an enemy?"

"I have asked him," I said, "but he replies that you will not and can not know until you have opened the door."

The days of white supremacy are over. Every politician, whatever his creed, should keep that in mind. Any political theory based on some other assumption is a waste of time.

The days of the colour-bar society are over. The colour bars in world sport, the colour bars in American education, the colour bars in the Belgian Congo are dying or dead.

The colour bar is opposed by people like Queen Elizabeth, Nehru, Eisenhower, Khrushchev, Macmillan, Nkrumah, Adenauer, de Gaulle; Chris Chataway, Yehudi Menuhin, Sybil Thorndike, Eleanor Roosevelt; by the Pope, the Archbishop of Canterbury, and the overwhelming majority of Christian churches throughout the world.

It is supported by people like Governor Faubus, Mr. Edward Dunn, ex-Mayor Percy Osborn, Dr. Albert Hertzog; by the Ku Klux Klan, the Jeugbond, the International Arts League of Youth; and almost alone amongst the churches of the world, by the Dutch Reformed church in South Africa, though one must admit that many other churches oppose the colour bar more on principle than in practise. Lastly, the colour bar in South Africa is supported by a few Indian, Coloured, and African stooges.

Because white supremacy is dead, our politicians should be taking steps to adapt our political arrangements to meet the new situation. Dr. Verwoerd's way of doing this is to work towards a state of total separation.

There are two sound reasons for rejecting this. One is its impossibility. There is not enough land on which to found a separate self-supporting community of some 10 million people; there is not enough industry to make good the dearth of land; there is not enough money to build a self-sustaining nonwhite society. Nor can 3 million people go on providing the superior services for a developing nation of 15 million; and believe me, that is what they want to do. Why else do we have Job Reservation?*

The second reason for rejecting total separation is that it means the virtual condemnation of all nonwhite people to a perpetually inferior life. No African farmer can ever hope to be anything but perpetually inferior on the land he will get; nor any African advocate practising in the Reserves; nor any African university teacher under the Extension of University Education Act.

There is another reason for rejecting total separation. Along that road the African may travel hopefully but he will never arrive. Each year some imposing new building may be put up in a Reserve; each year some imposing new post for a nonwhite person may be created; each year some imposing new development may be announced. But all of them put together will never add up to more than a second-class society for second-class citizens.

Is there another way out? Is there still a possibility of evolutionary adaptation away from a colour-bar society?

If there is, then the responsibility falls fairly and squarely on the United Party to put forward such a policy of adaptation, and this it has never done. The blame falls largely on Sir de Villiers Graaff for having publicly expressed views that are fundamentally those of the Nationalists.

Where is the bold continental view that Sir de Villiers promised to take?

My brother said, "Is he a friend or an enemy?"

"I have asked him," I said, "but he replies that you will not and can not know until you have opened the door."

There you are, my brother. You will never know if the man outside is a friend or an enemy until you open the door. But if you do not open the door, you can be sure what he will be.

---

* Section 77 of the Industrial Conciliation Act (1956), popularly known as "Job Reservation," empowered the Minister of Labour to reserve certain kinds of employment for members of one racial group.

PART TWO

After Sharpeville, 1960

Editor's Introduction

IN CONCLUDING his first "Long View" series, in February, 1959, Paton had written, "The long view should be seen through fresh eyes, and spoken by a fresh voice. That is the way to win fresh support for sane and liberal views." The fresh eyes and fresh voice were those of Peter Brown, National Chairman of the Liberal Party, who wrote "Long View" until his imprisonment during the state of emergency proclaimed after Sharpeville, in March, 1960.

In the aftermath of the Sharpeville incident, Brown was but one of the many leaders of political organizations imprisoned; the state of emergency began on March 30, and was to remain in effect until August 31, 1960.

On March 21, 1960, the South African police fired on crowds of African demonstrators at Sharpeville location, near Vereeniging, in the Transvaal, and at Langa location, near Cape Town. The aftermath of Sharpeville was a critical period in South Africa. On March 30, the Government proclaimed a state of emergency. Hundreds of people of all races were arrested before dawn that morning. A number of those arrested were leaders of the Liberal Party. Besides National Chairman Peter Brown, these included Dr. Hans Meidner, Chairman of the party's Natal Division; Elliott Mngadi, Party Organizer for Northern Natal; Frank Bhengu, National Committee member from Ladysmith (Natal); Eric Atwell, a member of the Executive Committee of the Port Elizabeth branch (his wife, Joan, was arrested on the same day but was later released); Dr. Colin Lang, Chairman of the Pretoria branch, who, as Liberal Party candidate in the 1959 provincial elections, had drawn an amazing 1,448 votes in a Nationalist constituency; and John Lang, brother of Colin Lang, Chairman of the North East Rand branch of the party, and member of the Transvaal Executive Committee.

These arrests, on the morning of March 30, were made under Section 4 of the emergency regulations, which permitted the Minister of Justice to detain any person, without warrant, in the interest of public order. Most of those detained under Section 4, including Chief Luthuli and Robert Sobukwe, were leaders of political organizations; they totaled 95 white and 1,813 nonwhite persons. In addition, by May 6, according to the Minister of Justice, some 18,000 others had been arrested. Many of these were released after screening. But, on May 31—the day on which the fiftieth anniversary of the Union was being celebrated—Alan Paton, Mrs. Albert Luthuli, and the widow of Manilal Gandhi (Mahatma Gandhi's son, who died in 1956), joined by hundreds of Africans and Indians, led night-long fasting and prayers to draw attention to the large numbers still in prison. It was in these critical days that Paton, adding to his duties as President of the Liberal Party, again undertook the duties of acting National Chairman.

The following selections from Paton's "Long View" essays written during the state of emergency reveal that, in 1960, the Liberal Party faced a number of crises that were even more significant than the emergency itself. These crises (outlined in the introductory essay "Alan Paton and the Liberal Party") were related to a number of contemporary events including the emergence of a new liberal group that attracted a number of leading Liberals. This was the Progressive Party, constituted, in November, 1959, from the "progressive group" of MP's who made up the liberal wing of the United Party in Parliament. Shortly thereafter, the Liberal Party lost its own parliamentary representation, which had been under the able leadership of Margaret Ballinger, when the system of Natives' representatives was abolished. It seemed unlikely, therefore, that the Liberal Party would play a parliamentary role in the immediate future. Paton outlined a possible alternative role in his 1960 presidential address to the party congress, "A Nonviolent Third Force." The crisis in the Congo, with its overtones of black racism and Mr. Lumumba's demand for the withdrawal of white U.N. forces, was also a source of concern for advocates of a nonracial society in South Africa. Paton faced these critical situations with courage and honesty, for which the 1960 Freedom Award was a fitting token of recognition.

Prologue: "A Man Called Brown"*

Peter Brown, one of the younger generation of South African liberals, was born in Durban, in 1925. His forebears, who had settled in Natal a century earlier, had built up important industrial and commercial enterprises. At the age of seventeen, after completing high school, he immediately joined the South African forces then serving in World War II. After the war, he attended Cambridge University, in England, and, later, the University of Cape Town, where he studied anthropology and Bantu languages. He established the first YMCA in Natal (at Edendale) that served Africans primarily. Brown was one of the three Liberal Party candidates for Parliament in the 1958 elections. This occasioned Paton's portrait of him in *Contact* (April 5, 1958), "The Crusader on a Polo Pony," in which he summarized Brown's association with the Liberal Party: "He founded an interracial discussion group, and this was one of the four or five independently established groups which were the nucleus of the South African Liberal Association. In May, 1953, this became the Liberal Party and Brown opened the first party office in Pietermaritzburg; in 1957 he became its Deputy National Chairman." Brown became National Chairman in 1958. He was imprisoned on March 31, 1960.

I HAPPENED TO BE LOOKING through old numbers of *Contact,* and was struck by the coincidence that two years ago to the day, April

* *Contact,* III, No. 8 (April 16, 1960), 5.

5 [1958], I wrote about Peter Brown, "The Crusader on a Polo Pony." What better time than [now] to write again? A. E. Housman wrote that:

> Of my three score years and ten,
> Twenty will not come again,
>
> .   .   .   .
>
> And since to look at things in bloom
> Fifty springs are little room,
> About the woodlands I will go,
> To see the cherry hung with snow.

I am not in such a happy situation; more than fifty of my years will not come again. Therefore I must write while I can. Nor do I write of cherries hung with snow, but of another kind of beauty, namely, the honour and courage that do so adorn a man.

Brown would not thank me for writing of his honour and courage. Therefore I shall thank him instead for having them.

Courage does not prevent calamity, but it transfigures it. Although the future of our cause is dark, we in the Liberal Party can regard ourselves as fortunate that we have a leader of this mould.

Every society formed by man has its leaders and followers. They depend upon one another. An army is twice an army when its leader is resolute, and a leader is twice a leader when his followers are resolute. There is a time when a leader must, by his courage, enhearten his followers; there is a time when followers must enhearten their leaders by theirs. This second time is *now*.

We in the Liberal Party have no leader cult, and are not likely to have one, this not being our nature. We are proud of our Ballingers, our Mngadis, our Langs. We are proud of our Browns. But they need more than our pride in them, they need our courage also.

They do not need us to say: "The night is dark," for they know that already. They need us to say: "The night is dark, but this is a journey that we will at all costs continue."

My friend Brown—and his associates—have a courage with a

strangely natural quality. It is not fierce, or inexorable, or consuming, or steely. It is merely resolute, than which no adjective is stronger. Thanks be to God, in whose hands are our times, for his resoluteness.

It is quite usual in South African politics to refer to God and to be happy that one is doing his will.* We do not usually refer to ourselves in this way in the Liberal Party, but I do it on this occasion. I do not imagine ourselves to be the representatives of God, ourselves therefore of unspeakable majesty, omnipotent and all-knowing.

Nevertheless we imagine ourselves to be his servants, and will humbly do what is required of us. This is not to seek to exercise unbridled power; but to cherish justice, practise mercy, and fight for the dispossessed, whatever may be the consequences to ourselves.

I should like to add a word about Brown's wife, Phoebe, and other women. They share their husbands' qualities of honour and courage, and are an example to us all.

The key word to-day is courage. The key action is to stand as resolutely as ever for our ideal of a South Africa which shall use, without let or hindrance, the gifts and skills of all its peoples.

When a man has a cause, and calamity overtakes it, he may grieve a while. But if he stays grieving, he clearly no longer has a cause. I say to my friend Brown, wherever he may be, "We shall try to prove ourselves men and women who have honour and courage also."

* See, for example, Paton's "Verwoerd's Claim to Divine Guidance," pages 76–79.

I. A Troubled Time, A Time To Choose

A NONVIOLENT THIRD FORCE*

Alan Paton, in his dual capacity as acting National Chairman and as President of the Liberal Party, delivered this address to the sixth annual congress of the Liberal Party. The congress was held in Cape Town, May 27–30, 1960, during the state of emergency. It was attended by 150 delegates. Jordan Ngubane, Vice-President of the Liberal Party, shared the duties of leadership with Paton at this congress. This address outlines a role for the Liberal Party that was not envisaged in the essays written two years earlier, during the 1958 parliamentary election campaign.

I KNOW that a wide range of personal problems confront people like ourselves at the present time. Our rulers have declared a state of emergency, and this has brought suffering, and in many cases material hardship, to many of those who opposed openly and forthrightly the policies of *apartheid*. One always expected to pay some kind of price for one's opposition to *apartheid;* one has seen other people paying it, and one did not expect to remain immune. But now for the first time some of our own friends, some of our closest associates, have had to pay the high price of imprisonment, and of separation from their families. We must face the fact that the price

* *Contact,* III, No. 12 (June 18, 1960), 5.

is growing higher, and we must re-examine the situation. Is it expedient to belong to a nonconformist party? Some would reply that they are concerned with matters of principle, not expediency; but others would ask whether the party need be nonconformist in the particular way that it is. I hope, as your acting National Chairman, to give you some guidance on these difficult points.

Let me first say that I, as Chairman, would never agree to any action on the part of the party that would not be in accordance with the constitution and the decisions of our [annual party] congresses. I would not regard it as permissible for me to make or to allow to be made any substantial change in the nature or direction of the party without consulting the membership at a congress, nor would I allow any national committee or national executive to do such a thing. At the same time I do not regard policy as something absolutely defined, but rather as something to be adapted to meet changing situations in the spirit of our aims and principles. I do not pay lip-service to democracy—I try to live it in my life; and I can therefore understand that congress, committee, executive, and chairman have different functions, and that if these functions are exceeded, the party as party would cease to exist.

This party is openly and publicly committed to a policy of nonviolence; this means that it will oppose when its duty is to oppose, but it will oppose by nonviolent means. But it does not mean that it will cease to oppose merely because opposition has become dangerous. It means also that it will not consent to the use of violence by others, not encourage it, nor connive at it. A Liberal Party can never aid, or itself become, a terrorist organisation, nor do I think it is in any danger of doing so.

.   .   .   .

As I see it, we are entering a phase where the struggle between Afrikaner nationalism and African nationalism will be intensified. We ourselves have prophesied that the excesses of Afrikaner nationalism will provoke a strong counternationalism, and I do not think we should ever delude ourselves into believing that this strug-

gle at this stage could be converted into a struggle between nationalism and liberalism. Dr. Dönges has stated that this is the real
struggle in his view, but as one might expect, this is the opinion of
a person who thinks of the political struggle solely in white parliamentary terms.

I fully expect violence to be a feature of this struggle. What do
we do? Do we stand hopelessly by? Is our role alternately to respond to and to reject appeals for help made by other organisations?
I am sure it is not. But that is what we shall be reduced to if we
have no positive contribution to make.

What is that contribution to be? I am sure there will be millions
of people, of all races, who shrink from the prospect of an unnatural
and violent life. Some will be resolutely violent, and what can people like ourselves oppose to resolute violence but resolute nonviolence? The only other course seems to me to withdraw from the
struggle, either by leaving the country or by accepting a withdrawn
role here. This latter will be one of silent nonacceptance, accompanied by apparent acquiescence, and probably inner suffering of a
painful but useless kind. Now ladies and gentlemen, I do not think
I could live like that. Allow me to give my personal views on what
I should do.

I should like to acquaint myself more closely with the instruments of nonviolence. If I decided to use any of them, I should not
do so in the name of the party unless of course the party wished me
to do so. I am sure that there are many, many thousands of people
in South Africa who hate and fear violence and who do not wish
to play a purely passive role in its presence, but would like, if they
could, to present a spiritual and good and active alternative to what
is evil, violent, and destructive. In a clash of opposing nationalisms,
both of them always trembling on the brink of violence, we might
call this alternative the "third force." It would, in my opinion, be
this third force which, if it were not able to prevent the clash of
irreconcilable forces, would be there always present as a factor to be
reckoned with, and an alternative to them both.

We must not yield ourselves to that pessimistic theory which maintains that the history of the impending future will be that of one violent force ranged against another, and that all peaceful people will be crushed between them. Such a third force must expect to be bruised, but its survival will depend on its strength and power, and by its strength and power the future of our country will no doubt be determined.

We have all heard of the nonviolent march of African people to Caledon Square, and of how a young man marshalled them, led them, spoke for them, and counselled them to return.* A similar thing happened in Durban soon after, when the African people of Cato Manor marched into Durban and gathered in great numbers in front of the Durban gaol. This was one of those demonstrations that trembled on the brink of violence; and when the police ordered the people to disperse, they would not. Eventually the police, after some demur, allowed a young Indian man to address the crowd; he told the people that their cause was just, but he urged them to lay down their sticks and to disperse, such weapons being useless against saracens [armoured cars], and out of place in such a peaceful march. He told them that the eyes of the world were on them, and that their cause would be all the more powerful without these instruments of violence. Thereupon the people laid down their sticks and returned to their homes.†

* On March 30, 1960, 30,000 Africans protesting the arrest of their leaders (including Chief Luthuli and Robert Sobukwe) marched in a peaceable column over a mile long from the outlying African townships of Langa and Nyanga to the Caledon Square police station, in central Cape Town. When the procession arrived at Caledon Square, its leader, Philip Kgosana, asked to see the Minister of Justice. He received from the Deputy Chief of Police what he understood to be an offer to arrange for an interview with the Minister. But the Deputy Chief subsequently said that he had only agreed to convey the request. At the request of the police, Mr. Kgosana then asked the 30,000 people to disperse quietly, and they did so. Mr. Kgosana was then detained under the emergency regulations.

† On April 1, 1960, about 6,000 Africans demanding the release of their leaders marched along various routes from Cato Manor township toward the center of Durban. Some routes were blocked off, but one procession of about 1,000 people reached the central area. A senior police officer warned them that, unless they dispersed within five minutes, the police would open fire. After the Indian man urged them to remain peaceful, they dispersed quietly.

This young man came to see me, to tell me that his life was to be dedicated to this goal, namely to bring justice to South Africa by the use of nonviolent strength, and to offer this alternative to a country that might feel compelled to choose between two forces of violence, though it feared them both and expected good from neither.

At much the same time another young man, a white one, wrote to me and told me that he was intending to give up his job and to break some unjust law; but I persuaded him rather to study the philosophy and methods of nonviolence than to incur a heavy sentence for some trivial offence. Here were these three, all young, one African, one Indian, one white, all devoted to their country, all convinced that change could be brought about by the use of nonviolent power.

For a long time I had been thinking as to what could be done to exercise the right which I believe all men to possess, namely the right to resist oppression. I was thinking of that law known as the Group Areas Act, which is one of the most wicked of all the *apartheid* laws. And I was thinking how wonderful it would be if, when the first Indian citizen of Durban was to be moved from his home, 100,000 of the people of that city would gather at the place, to watch in silence the authorities perform this wicked act, or to pray, on their knees or not on their knees, to stand there or kneel there, to represent there in the presence of that tyrannical act, the forces of goodness and justice, and the moral disapproval of the world. This is a demonstration of course, and I have no horror of demonstrations, provided they are directed towards good as well as political ends. I would like to confront the users of violence —and I regard the enforcement of the Group Areas Act as nothing less than an act of violence—with an ordered and self-disciplined opposition. These would be demonstrations trembling, not on the brink of violence, but on the brink of deliverance. But they require, I am certain, discipline and preparation; one does not buy for nothing this nonviolent power. For one thing, I am sure one would have to go to such a demonstration with something more than the mere desire to bring a tyrannical government toppling to the ground; one would have to go there to offer to South Africa a visible and substantial alternative to tyranny, motivated by a love of what was good and just, and a desire to identify oneself with one's neighbour at the moment of his dispossession.

I think sometimes that our country is now so divided that one half of our energies is being put into carrying out *apartheid,* and one half into opposing it. People are rounded up and tried for treason; an army of policemen and officials is drawn off from useful work, even great men like judges and eminent lawyers are drawn off from their normal occupations; money is poured out like water to bring the trial to a conclusion favourable to the prosecution, while another army of people must collect money and organise a defence so that the trial may reach a contrary conclusion. I am a true admirer of all those who spend so much time and energy and talent on opposing the evil policies of *apartheid,* but I would like to see this opposition become a moral power that would win a victory every time it was employed and would, I believe, slowly sap the confidence of the apartheiders, not so much in the workability as in the moral soundness of their policy.

I say all this to you because I know that some of you would fear such a development if it came, so to speak, too close to the party. But I want to say something about the nature of the party, also. We all want a party that will *do* something, *achieve* something; all members of all parties do. But at the same time what we wish the party to achieve is—and we should face it—noble and ideal. This we cannot avoid—it is our nature—but it makes conventional party work more difficult for us than for others. The party has a special nature, and it gets this special nature from us, and we cannot do anything about it. I would venture to say that all, or nearly all (whichever you personally prefer), of the members of the party joined it because of their idealism, religious or humanistic. Every member, white or nonwhite, joined the party because of his or her belief in a nonracial society, a common society.

Our nature cannot be altered, I believe. One has to keep the party as sensible and practical as possible, but that is to make idealism workable, not to make it amenable. Some of us may sometimes look at the [new] Progressive Party with envy, and think how very reasonable their idealism sounds. But although they have good materialistic common-sense business motives, they have, like ourselves, a noble and idealistic motive. And I hereby predict that the presence of this second motive will soon involve them in problems of exactly the same nature as our own. Indeed, something that we foresaw from the beginning is now becoming clearer, that good business and nonracialism have more in common than was generally supposed, and that good business and *apartheid* have less.

This conflict between political practicality and political idealism cannot be avoided. We try to be sensible and practical, and we try to be true to certain ideals and principles at the same time. But we must squarely face the fact that this Government does not like these ideals and principles, that it does not like people who hold them, that this dislike turns and will always turn into hostility when the people who hold the ideals and principles are active and successful in propagating them, and that such people may then lose their freedom of movement, be arrested and detained without trial, be arrested and charged and kept on trial for long periods, or be allowed to go free on condition that they do not propagate these ideals any longer. I say this fact must be squarely faced, for it is the most obdurate fact of our immediate future; we have reached a point when if we stick to our principles, we shall face something more stern than the mere disapproval of the authorities.

At times like this it is natural to face the future soberly, with a mixture of courage and anxiety. But I say to you, let us not be too fearful. Great forces are on our side, not only the forces of good that take such a beating from men and yet are so invincible, but also great temporal forces, the disapproval of nations—both great and small—of the policies of *apartheid,* and the determination of some of them to exert pressures on our rulers to change their ways.

This places on us a duty also, that we should not forget what we came together to do, and that we should continue to do it, to go on exercising what we believe to be inalienable rights, to speak the truth, to attempt to persuade, to oppose injustice, to build bridges between people and people, to provide leadership and guidance for those millions of South African people who do not believe in violence, or who want some working alternative to it.

Is that not what Peter Brown was doing? Is he not in prison because he was being actively true to the ideals and principles of the party? Was he not speaking the truth, attempting to persuade, opposing injustice, building bridges, providing leadership and guidance, and was he not using his gifts unsparingly in that cause, with that great integrity and modesty which are characteristic of him? If there are any here who fear that the party may be tempted to take a dangerous and inexpedient direction and to neglect its duties as a political organisation, I ask them to consider whether it is not the simple doing of one's political duty that has become dangerous. Do we think that our National Chairman followed mischievously or perversely or ill-advisedly a dangerous path, or do we think that he was a man who suffered the consequences of doing his duty? I tell you that he knew quite clearly what the consequences might be, but if a man such as he is faced with the choice of doing his duty or of not doing it, he has really no choice at all. He and I, National Chairman and National President, used to joke about it. He said I should go to prison, being older and therefore less important for the future, and I said he ought to go, being younger and better able to stand it. But behind this joking was the realisation that to do one's duty and to stand for nonracial democracy might entail serious consequences, and this it has certainly done. As your acting National Chairman, I shall try to do my duty in the same tradition.

OUR RULERS' LATEST BLUNDER*

François Christiaan Erasmus became Minister of Justice in January, 1960. On April 26, 1960, during the state of emergency, he informed Parliament that, in view of the threat of Communism, South Africa should screen candidates seeking admission to the practice of law. He proposed that the selection of candidates be made by a statutory body under the chairmanship of the Secretary of Justice. There was a growing tendency in South Africa to assume that lawyers defending clients charged with political offenses were themselves suspect. (See "Defence and Aid," pages 231–34.)

THE LATEST blunder of our rulers is quite fantastic. They leave the outside world in no doubt as to what they are up to. Mr. Erasmus has now decided that prospective lawyers need screening. He obviously doesn't think that lawyers—except Nationalists—should take any interest in politics. And no doubt he is angry because there are lawyers who in his view impede the processes of justice by their persistence in trying to find out the truth in every situation. This sounds an ugly thing to say, because it is generally admitted that this is exactly what a lawyer should be doing. Nevertheless in a society which has been corrupted by the colour bar, authority not only is tempted to become impatient with, but also to become hostile towards, lawyers who intervene on behalf of the humble and dispossessed. It requires even greater courage to intervene on behalf of those who are not so humble, Africans or other nonwhite people who believe they have rights and who stand up for them, quietly or resolutely or truculently, it makes no great matter which.

Imagine what courage it requires, after a riot has taken place in which white policemen have been killed by black rioters, for a lawyer to come and demand who assaulted a certain black woman

* *Contact,* III, No. 9 (May 7, 1960), 5.

who was considered to have evidence valuable to the police, and to demand who overturned her furniture and smashed one of her cupboards to pieces.

Imagine what courage it requires, in one of the remote white farming areas, where a white farmer has been brutally murdered, for a lawyer to come and demand what has become of a suspect who has been taken to the police station for questioning, and unfortunately, in the few hours that he was detained there, has collapsed and died.

Yet such acts are the duty of any lawyer, and by performing them fearlessly, they add lustre to their profession, and strengthen the respect of society for the law. This is, however, not unequivocally so in a colour-bar society; for it is clear that Mr. Erasmus, for example, considers that such lawyers bring discredit both on their profession and on the law. The reason for this is quite simple; it is not the sanctity of law that is the supreme value for Mr. Erasmus, it is the sanctity of white supremacy.

Nevertheless Mr. Erasmus has to consider the attitude of the outside world, which for him means the Western world. Therefore he and his colleagues are quick to hint that such diligent lawyers are Communists and are interested not so much in justice and humanity as in the overthrow of Western democracy and the triumph of Russian Communism. Such propaganda is losing its potency; it may still deceive a few fools in England and America, but it leaves the rest of the world cold.

If the newspapers had asked me—which they did not—to comment on the latest stupidity of Mr. Erasmus, I should have said that I did not regret it in the least. It is actions such as these that are keeping world opinion active and observant, and that is what we want. We do not want to languish unforgotten. We want *apartheid* (for this latest stupidity is only *apartheid* in another guise) to remain in full view of the world. And how lucky we are, for we need do little ourselves. The Nationalists will do most of the work.

Will this latest folly shake the white non-Nationalists alive? Frankly I do not know. Many of them will criticise it, but if the outside world criticises it, they will rush to its defence. If they understood their own interests, they would stop this nauseating defence of their masters. For one thing is certain, that if white non-Nationalists continue to accommodate themselves to one Nationalist excess after another, they will play no part whatsoever in the creation of the new South Africa that draws nearer each day.

Let [the United Party leaders] Sir de Villiers and Mr. [Douglas] Mitchell take note. Let them consider carefully their opposition to this latest threat of Mr. Erasmus. For if they decide to defend only some rights of some lawyers, as in the past they have defended only some rights of some people, they will lose what little moral authority they have left.

THE CONGO*

The former Belgian Congo became an independent state on June 30, 1960. Within two weeks, a mutiny within the military Force Publique caused the collapse of authority, victimized the white population in a reign of terror, and provoked the secession of Katanga Province. On July 12, President Kasavubu and Prime Minister Lumumba requested the urgent dispatch of U.N. military assistance to support the central government. These events had a significant impact on white South African attitudes. They convinced many waverers that the Government's policies offered greater hope of security than the Liberal Party's nonracial aspirations. Paton wrote the following essay at the height of the turmoil in the Congo:

THE NEWS from the Congo does not make pleasant reading, and will not make things easier to put right in Angola, Kenya, Mozambique, the [Central African] Federation, and South Africa. Feelings of hatred, fear, and distrust are intensified and you will find many supremacists, both black and white, gloating over the mess—the

* *Contact*, III, No. 15 (July 30, 1960), 5.

first because white people have suffered death, rape, and loss; the second because the new black state is in chaos.

Let us try to examine the situation as calmly as possible.

It is quite clear that the Belgians were from one point of view not justified in handing over so swiftly and so completely. It is equally clear that from another point of view they had no alternative. If they had not handed over, they would have entered a period of waning authority and increasing turbulence. Belgian life would have got cheaper, and the Belgians would have had to face the accusation that they were unwilling to let go. They were in a fateful predicament.

And how did they get there? They got there because they had done so little to prepare the Congolese for the day when they would have to administer their own affairs, their own finances, their own education, their own development as a state able to take a place with the states of the modern age.

I have visited the Congo [from June through July, 1958], and while its colour bar never cast such a shadow as it does in South Africa, it was a colour-bar country all the same. The Belgians held the surely now totally discredited theory that Africans want only "bread and butter, blankets, and beer." The Belgian power was absolute, showing itself particularly in its veto of advanced education overseas for African students. The Belgians also held that other foolish theory that new ideas always come from abroad.

The Belgians tried desperately to change their course when they realised the way that the winds of change were blowing, and one must give them credit for it. But they were too late. They decided to give only when they realised that it was impossible not to give.

Those were their three mistakes. They realised the inevitable too late, and because of that they were unable to deal with it; their failure was due to the fact that they held a materialistic and incomplete theory of the nature and destiny of man.

Or to put it briefly, the colonial system, with its colour bar and its arrogance, had corrupted them, just as it had corrupted the British, the Afrikaners, the Portuguese, and the French.

The first thing that we must all get used to is that the forces freed by the ending of colonial power are going to take a long time to find a new equilibrium. Therefore we may expect in Africa to experience turbulence for a long time to come.

This turbulence is often going to be of a shocking nature, especially to white South Africans. But they must face the hard fact that the tragic events of the last few weeks do not compare with the tragic events that overcame the people of the Congo under Leopold I. If they bear these facts in mind, they may be able to examine the situation rationally rather than emotionally.

Change is going to go on, that is a certainty. We should spare ourselves the futile labour of railing against it, and attempting to prove that it will do no one any good. What we have to do about change is to adapt ourselves to it, and it to ourselves, as far as we are able. We are piloting a vessel down the rapids, and we have only a partial control over the vessel, and none at all over the rapids. Such an operation requires the highest skill and attention.

The Belgians paid too little attention to the nature of the stream, and heard too late the roar of the rapids. It looks as though the British and the French were wiser, although the period of equilibrium has by no means been reached in their colonies and ex-colonies. What the Portuguese will do is a question no one can answer optimistically. But what interests all of us is what will happen in our own country.

The Congo situation was far from identical with our own, although there are many similar elements. The contribution of white South Africans to the development of the country has been immense, and the vast majority of its white citizens look upon South Africa as home. What is more, South Africa possesses a comparatively large number of nonwhite people who would be able to make notable contributions to a nonracial society, though the number would have been far greater had it not been for the colour bar. Further, there has been, in spite of the practises of segregation and *apartheid* and *baasskap,* a greater measure of cultural assimilation than there ever was in the Congo. There is a large number of nonwhite people who want to go on living in a kind of society which will differ mainly from our own in the fact that it will have no racial barriers. The Coloured people are either Afrikaans- or English-speaking, the Indian people are to-day almost entirely English-speaking, and the urban African people are increasingly a house-renting, steady-earning, education-valuing, newspaper-reading community like any other urban group.

There is therefore hope for our future if we avoid the three dangers of the Congo. First, we must realise now that there is no future for South Africa if nonwhite people do not share fully in it. Second, we must not wait till change is forced upon us. Third, we must give up the theory that one can bribe change with bread and butter, blankets, and beer. I believe that we can, in Dr. de Kiewiet's* words, use these things to help us in "negotiating change," but we cannot substitute them for change.

However, there is one way of "negotiating change" which is now utterly useless, and that is *apartheid.* The entire world condemns it today as inhuman. It has no status as a solution any more.

I said there is hope for our future if we avoid the three dangers of the Congo. But the last hard fact of the situation is that we may not avoid them. White South Africa, too, may delay change until it is beyond its power to negotiate it.

The Belgians did not fail in the Congo because they failed to apply *apartheid.* They failed because in the crucial areas of administration and public responsibility they applied it only too well.

---

* Dr. C. W. de Kiewiet is a South African scholar. His *Anatomy of South African Misery* (London and New York: Oxford University Press, 1957) is a reasoned account of *apartheid* and Afrikaner nationalism.

II. In Faith, Not Fear

MARGARET BALLINGER*

Margaret Ballinger, née Margaret Hodgson, was elected to Parliament by African voters in 1938, in the first separate elections for Natives' representatives. Thereafter, she was re-elected continuously until 1960, the year that African representation in Parliament was abolished under the provisions of the Promotion of Bantu Self-Government Act (1959). Her husband, William Ballinger, had represented Africans in the Senate.

Margaret Ballinger was President of the Liberal Association, which had formed the Liberal Party in 1953. She led the Liberal Party until 1955, when she resigned for personal reasons. Alan Paton was then elected to succeed her. In 1960, ex-Senator William Ballinger and Mrs. Ballinger left South Africa to spend some time at Oxford University. Their departure was the occasion for this essay. By emphasizing Mrs. Ballinger's resolute, unwavering dedication to principle, untempted by momentarily fashionable solutions, Paton holds her up as an example of the true spirit of liberalism in time of crisis, the central theme of his presidential address "A Nonviolent Third Force," on pages 145–52.

In 1963, when the Liberal Party Chairman in the Cape Province was banned, Mrs. Ballinger returned to the active

* *Contact*, III, No. 10 (May 21, 1960), 5.

leadership of the party as its Cape Province Chairman. Before her marriage, Mrs. Ballinger had been on the faculty of the University of the Witwatersrand while Jan Hofmeyr was University Principal. Paton's *Hofmeyr* gives many glimpses of her both at that time and later as a liberal MP who did not always admire Hofmeyr.

I COULD, of course, have entitled this piece "A Brave Woman." Then I could have said who she was. But this title is better, because it says both these things at once. In any case, Margaret Ballinger is *resolute* rather than *brave;* one remembers not so much the occasions of courage, but rather the consistent course of one who never swerved in her devotion to truth and justice.

Readers of this nonracial paper must pardon me if I refer for a moment to famous white liberals of this century of South African history. We also have other liberals, thank God, people like Jordan Ngubane, who, although he has never enjoyed political power, has thought deeply about it, about how to use it, how to distribute it, how to tame it, how to prevent it in fact from eating people up, as it surely does when it gets into the hands of people like Hitler, Stalin, and Dr. Verwoerd.

But let us consider our white liberals for a moment, those who actually had the power, those who belonged to the ruling class even if not the ruling party, and who wanted that power to be used more constructively, more justly, more foresightedly than it was. There were some notable persons amongst these liberals. There was Paul Sauer's father, whose son shows few signs of his heredity. There was the sad but very clear-sighted Olive Schreiner. There was James Rose-Innes. There were Alfred Hoernlé and his wife, Winifred; Edith Rheinallt Jones and her husband; Edgar Brookes; and Leo Marquard. And if I had to choose the two greatest of the century, they would be J. H. Hofmeyr and Margaret Ballinger.*

---

* Paul Sauer has been chairman of the Nationalist Party commission that conceived the policy of *apartheid* in 1947; when Paton wrote this essay, Sauer was acting Nationalist Party leader, a position he held until Prime Minister Verwoerd recovered from the wounds inflicted on him in the assassination attempt of

Nothing will ever be able to take that away from her, that she was the greatest and most resolute opponent of tyranny during the hardest years of all, the years when it was least profitable and most dangerous to be so; in other words the years 1948 to 1960.

When I call her resolute, I am hoping to say something significant to my fellow Liberals. Her resolution was not contingent on immediate circumstances, and had nothing to do with her pessimism or optimism. I would never think of describing her as a pessimistic or optimistic person. She was merely resolute. She had certain principles, and she intended to go on having them, and to go on saying she had them, and to go on urging their application to our national life. Nothing ever deterred her

She could have been excused if she had shown signs of being weary of it all, of having grown deathly tired of putting forward views that no one in authority would ever listen to. She could well have wearied of speaking up for justice, she, a white woman, speaking up for the kind of justice that most other white women in South Africa have long since ceased to think of as anything worth while cherishing, the kind of justice that most white children still learn to revere in the abstract, while they observe that their elders fear it or pooh-pooh it or hate it in the real.

Whether she tired or not—and sometimes she must have—she never wavered in her resolution. She had a job to do and responsibilities to discharge towards the country and her constituents and she went on with her work to the end. Let that be an example to us all. We may not be able to radiate optimism all day, and to sleep like logs all night, and to promise that Peter Brown will be

April 9, 1960. Sauer's father, J. W. Sauer, was a leading Cape liberal at the turn of the century, the strongest advocate in the National Convention of 1910 of extending voting rights to Africans. The elder Sauer's supporters outside the convention included Olive Schreiner, author of *The Story of an African Farm*. Chief Justice James Rose-Innes resigned from his post to campaign for the same cause. The Hoernlés and Rheinallt Joneses were founders of the Institute of Race Relations (see "A Deep Experience," pages 54–59). Leo Marquard was a founder of the Liberal Party, and ex-Senator Edgar Brookes, a friend and associate of Jan Hofmeyr, joined the party in 1962, during its worst days, and is now its National Chairman.

Prime Minister one day, but we can take a lesson from Margaret Ballinger on resolution.

No one can say that her career has been fruitful or successful. By white South African standards it has been a failure. By universal standards it has been a triumph, something to be proud of, honourable and resolute. She went down like a fighting ship, with flags flying and guns firing.* She couldn't win the battle, she merely did her duty to the end. If the ship had a name, it would be "Indomitable."

Margaret Ballinger belonged to what, God forgive us, is known as an "old school." When she said "yes," she meant "yes." When she said "no," she meant "no." She committed the unpardonable white South African crime: when she spoke of justice, she meant justice for all. The idea of subordinating universal ideals of justice, mercy, and truth to something called "white supremacy" was repugnant to her. She never in her whole political life was unfaithful to her ideals.

I don't know what the Nationalists will do when she returns [from abroad]. Will they gather round her and tell her how wonderful she was, how honest, how sincere, how different from the United Party? [The Nationalists frequently accused the United Party of "insincerity."]

I wouldn't give twopence for their compliments. They didn't want her honesty and her sincerity. They wanted these virtues kicked out of Parliament, and they kicked them out.

I read that Valerie Adams, the feature writer of the *Cape Times,* asked her how she retained her popularity in spite of her determined opposition to *apartheid.* I don't think she retained her popularity. I think she retained something else. I think she retained the esteem of many people who know integrity when they see it, but don't want to be too closely associated with it. They esteemed her because

* The reference here is to her opposition to the retribalization of Africans that was envisaged in the Promotion of Bantu Self-Government Act; the same Act abolished their representation—and Mrs. Ballinger's seat—in Parliament.

they knew what was good, but they kept away from her because they knew what was better.

Her husband, William Ballinger, was equally resolute. He never wavered in his devotion to the same ideals that were cherished by his wife. But he is a generous man, and would not begrudge this tribute to his illustrious wife. His political career—as far as human eyes can see—is ended too, and for the same reasons, that he stood for a brave policy of reasonableness that was anathema to our masters.

Margaret Ballinger, we Liberals thank you for all that you did and were. Some of our more enthusiastic members sometimes exasperated you by their extremism, their unrealism, their utopianism. But they never doubted, and you never doubted, our common devotion to the cause of nonracial democracy. We all wish you well, and though we are saddened by your going, we are in much greater measure proud of our association with you, in the struggle for reason and decency in human relations, which we mean to continue.

OUR NEW BISHOP: TREVOR HUDDLESTON*

Father Trevor Huddleston, a priest of the Anglican Community of the Resurrection and a close friend of Alan Paton, worked for many years among Africans at the Rosettenville Mission House, Johannesburg. According to Horton Davies, a noted theologian, Father Huddleston provided the model for the sympathetic portrait of the white priest, Father Vincent, in Paton's *Cry, the Beloved Country: A Story of Comfort in Desolation.* The title of Father Huddleston's well-known book on African life in Johannesburg, *Naught for Your Comfort* (New York: Doubleday, 1956), appears to contain an ironic allusion to the subtitle of Paton's novel. Paton contributed a biographical sketch "Trevor Huddleston" to Melville Harcourt (ed.), *Thirteen for Christ* (New York: Sheed & Ward, 1963). The essay that follows was

* *Contact,* III, No. 17 (August 27, 1960), 5.

occasioned by Father Huddleston's appointment as Bishop
of Masasi, in Tanganyika (now Tanzania).

IF THERE IS a happy man in the world to-day, it is Trevor Huddleston, for he is coming back to Africa. When he left it he was as
miserable as a Christian may be without falling into accidie. He
would write me the most inconsolable letters, and I, believe it or
not, used to give him spiritual advice! Yet even at that time his irre-
pressible spirit used to show itself; he used to write on the back of
his letters, such absurd addresses

> Rev. O. Lution,
> Copse Watching,
> Stillfree,
> England.

> or

> Miss Sedgie Nation,
> "Piebaldings,"
> Much Mixing.

He was like a man torn from the side of his beloved—almost,
not quite, distraught. He was saved from utter misery by his obedience. Eventually he accepted his separation as one accepts a hair-
shirt. And then, almost like a miracle—perhaps an answer to im-
portunate prayer—he is told he may return! To Africa, to the
continent and the people to whom he gave so freely of his love.
Here, from 6,000 miles away, I am willing to wager that he has
laughed more this last few weeks than he has laughed the last few
years before them. He is like that; he laughs when he is happy, not
only at the best jokes but also at the feeblest, many of which latter,
I might add, are his own.

It is going to be good news to hundreds of thousands of South
Africans that Huddleston is coming back to Africa. They will feel
better just to know that he is on the same piece of land. I think it is
possible that the Bishop of Masasi may prove to be an important

person in the times that lie ahead. I do not know what kind of a mess this southern part of Africa is going to get into, but I certainly do not want to see stark black-white conflict. I do not know any person who could play a more important part in such a situation than Huddleston. And Nyerere too.* Those two should get on well together. They are both exceptional human beings, full of vitality without vanity.

There have been few white men in Africa who earned the affection and trust of African people as Huddleston did. The reasons were simple. For one thing he loved them. For another, he knew injustice when he saw it, even if it had fancy names like "industrial conciliation," "extension of education," and "autogenous development."

But I am not only glad for his sake and ours that he is coming back. I am glad for the sake of the Church. Huddleston believed strongly that it was the Church's duty to champion justice and to denounce injustice, and that means, to put it plainly, to champion *people,* especially the oppressed, the despised, the scorned. He saw, with the same clarity as Archbishop de Blank, that the Christian Church in Africa stood at the crossroads, and that her archenemy was not Islam or Communism, but pseudo-Christianity, that is, the Christian religion corrupted by power and possession and privilege. In pseudo-Christianity, order is more important than freedom, stability more important than reform, the law more important than justice, and realism more important than love.

Huddleston believed that the duty of the Church is to show forth in her own body the true fellowship of Christians triumphing over the barriers created by men. He wanted the Church to be a transforming, not a conforming, body. The arguments about language difference, cultural difference, social difference—he understood them all; but his love was urgent and triumphed over all difference. He could see clearly that white Christians were allowing these differ-

* Although December 9, 1961, was the formal date of Tanganyika's independence, Dr. Julius Nyerere was, as a result of preindependence elections, the recognized chief of state in August, 1960.

ences to exercise over their lives a sovereignty that belonged only to God.

The Christian Church has lost much ground in Africa these last twenty years, largely because she has allowed herself to become identified with the status quo instead of with righteousness. It is men like Huddleston who can restore men's faith in her. Rebellion and obedience are perfectly combined in him. If it had not been so, his recall from South Africa would have broken his heart. Huddleston can well be called a dog of the Lord. When he is jerked in, he growls and pulls, but he comes in the end to the beloved Heel. Fidelity, not self-will, is what he lives by. Behind what other heel could such a dog run?

There is another reason why I am glad that Huddleston is coming back. He is a champion of human rights, of the rights of men to freedoms which should be respected by the state. His championship is all the more trustworthy because he knows what it is to be subject to authority. No one knows better than he how to reconcile the claims of order and freedom. This reconciliation is going to be one of the most difficult problems of the new Africa, and there are many of us who hope that Tanganyika is going to set an example of a sane society to the rest of the continent. This is more likely now that Huddleston is going there.

May his ministry in Masasi bring something for our comfort after all.

Epilogue: Freedom Award Address, 1960

Alan Paton received the annual Freedom Award at Freedom House, New York, on October 5, 1960. Edward R. Murrow, recipient of the 1954 Freedom Award, presided; Archibald MacLeish delivered the address of welcome. Representatives of the literary and political worlds came in such numbers that many had to be turned away. President Eisenhower sent a message of congratulation, which read in part: "Through his brave and sensitive writings on behalf of the under-privileged, Mr. Paton has worked to remove the social and racial barriers which plague mankind. In striving to achieve for all men recognition of the dignity to which they are entitled, he stands as a fine symbol of Freedom House." On his return home, Paton was deprived of his passport for blackening South Africa's name abroad.

YOU MAY REMEMBER, Mr. Chairman, that when you received this award in 1954, you quoted Shakespeare's words "Beggar that I am, I am even poor in thanks," and expressed thus your feeling of un-worthiness. I express mine by telling you the story of a famous rabbi who, when he rose in the morning to say his prayers, would first read letters that had been written to him by those who revered him. And someone asked him, "Why do you first read these letters before you say your prayers?" And he replied, "I read these letters because in them I am called *tsadik,* a leader, a holy man, and the like. Then when I have read them, I say to the Lord 'You and I know that I do not merit those titles of honour. But since there are good men who in all sincerity believe them to be true, make me better so that they need not be put to shame.' "

Therefore, I accept this honour from you, with pride because it was offered to me, and with humility because I do not feel worthy to receive it. But one thing was always certain, I could not have refused it, for the very announcement of it brought hope and encouragement to thousands of my fellow citizens in South Africa, who were heartened to know that there were people in far-off America who were concerned for them and for their country and for their freedom, so much so that they chose one of their number to be the recipient of this award. Though you give this award to me, I feel, and many of them feel, that you are giving it to them. Many of them have had to pay for their beliefs and principles more dearly than I have been called upon to do; some of them spent a considerable part of this year in prison, arrested, detained, and released without the preferring of any charge against them. Had they lived in this country, many of them would have been sitting in this great audience here tonight; many of them would have sat, not in prison, but in positions of honour and authority. Though the nature of their offence was never revealed to them, it is well known what it was. They believed, and they said that they believed, and they worked for what they believed, namely, that freedom, status, opportunity, and the assumption of responsibility should be within the reach, within one state, of every South African citizen, without regard to his origins. You have no doubt heard South Africa called a land of fear, and in many respects this judgment is true; but it is a land of courage also, in that men and women came out of prison and without a moment's hesitation resumed the very activities which had been the cause of their being sent there.

.   .   .   .

As you all know, I come from a continent where freedom, in many languages, is the cry of the day. You all know that it was the

Westerner who, by virtue of that fantastic flowering of human genius which took place in the West, to all intents and purposes controlled the world. But such a dominance could not last, because neither human knowledge nor human aspiration can be thus contained. And it is because of the decline of this dominance that our continent experiences such turbulence; powerful forces have been released from external control, and are now seeking a new equilibrium.

This new Africa has three striking characteristics. The first is the desire, the determination, to have freedom—*uhuru,* the East African word which one now finds painted up on the walls of southern Africa—and to have it as soon as possible. The second striking characteristic is the desire, the determination, to enter fully into the modern technological, industrial world, to eliminate poverty, to educate every child, to train all the men and women required to administer, teach, and operate a modern society; but the main motive behind all this is not materialistic, it is the fierce desire to walk as equals in the company of the nations of the modern world. The third striking characteristic is the dangerous one, and that is a bitter resentment, not so much against having been ruled, but against having been ruled arrogantly. The colour bar is the extreme expression of such arrogance, and the extreme reaction to it is anti-Westernism; and this can mean (and we should face the possibility) hostility to Christianity, hostility to the churches, hostility to the white skin, hostility to Western ideas of freedom and democracy, hostility to offers of Western aid, even hostility to the United Nations. . . . It is characteristic of African rioting in southern Africa that clinics, schools, and churches are often burned down; this is often taken by white persons to be a manifestation of black ingratitude, but it is in fact a revolt against the arrogance of the colour bar, and in this revolt kindness and generosity are hated just as much as coldness and cruelty. I have no doubt whatsoever that some Africans turn to Communism, not because they are convinced by its arguments, but because they so hate the colour bar; and these are only too often the most bitter, the most implacable, the most dangerous, enemies of the West.

Luckily, however, there lies between these two extremes, the colour bar on the one hand and the hatred of the West on the other, a great deal of middle territory. One cannot help thinking at this moment of the warmth and generosity that have characterized the achievement of Nigerian independence [on October 1, 1960]; last Sunday, Westminster Abbey, the national shrine of the British nation, was filled with Nigerians and Britons giving thanks for this independence. But this should not blind one to the fact that even in England people are sometimes humiliated because they are coloured. Nor do I need to remind Americans that every race clash in America is immediately made known to the entire world, while examples of tolerance and harmony are often made to sound like excuses. Nor do I need to tell this audience how the Government of my own country, the Union of South Africa, has recklessly thrown away all its chances of leadership on the African continent, and has not only ceased to be an asset but has become a burden to the West, because of its policy of *apartheid*.

However, I do not want to dwell any longer on the sins of the West, for that is not my subject tonight. I am here both as African and as Westerner, and I want to see the countries of Africa enriched by the contributions of the West, and helped by the West on their way to that kind of nationhood that each of them so earnestly desires. I want this for two reasons: The two paramount considerations of my life are that the countries of Africa should be liberated from every vestige of subordination to other powers, and that government of the people, by the people, for the people should take deep root in these new countries. I want this so that the African people need not be subjected to new tyrannies, and so that the new African state should, in Lord Acton's words, recognize that its supreme function is to make it possible for man to lead the good life. And if anyone in this audience wants to know what I mean by the good life, let me say that I mean the same as he or she does, and if that doesn't satisfy him or her, then I mean that one is given the opportunity to do one's work and perform one's duties, and to retain, as far as possible, the belief that one is a self-determining creature, and isn't just being pushed around. I hope philosophers in the audience will forgive me this statement, but they must remember I am only a part-time philosopher.

I want to see the West, partly because of its material debt to Africa, and partly because of these sins that I spoke about and don't want to speak about any more, and partly because of its own self-interest, giving the most generous assistance to the new African countries, primarily in two ways: The first is to help these countries to develop their resources and raise their standard of living; the second is to help them to educate their children, and their young men and young women, in such a way as to make their independence real.

I welcome, as an African and a Westerner, President Eisenhower's suggestion that Africa should be spared the ravages which "chauvinism has elsewhere inflicted in the past." That means to me, plainly and bluntly, that no attempt must be made to draw Africa into the power conflicts of our age. The President also expressed the hope that Africa would be able to give the rest of the world lessons in international relations. This statement will be welcomed in Africa, and should help to clear up doubts that existed in regard to Western aid. It is my firm belief that this kind of generous economic and educational assistance given concurrently because either without the other is dangerous to freedom, given in such a way as to win men's willing friendship, given direct or through the United Nations as wisdom advises, will be a much greater bulwark for the freedom and security of the West than any series of treaties or any number of bases. No country is better able to offer this educational help than the United States. I am thinking not only of help to develop the internal educational systems of Africa, but the throwing open of the colleges and universities of this great country, on the most generous scale possible, to students from Africa. This is not only a good way to defend democratic freedom, it is not only the best way, it is the *only* way.

It is my hope that we shall soon learn details of the great United Nations scheme to give aid in Africa.* Psychologically it would be a good thing if it were done as soon as possible, so that the people of the world could have news, not of angers and passions and discords that seem perpetual, but of a concerted movement by the nations of the world to bring help to their brothers in Africa. It would help to restore man's self-respect. It would help to give him a more hopeful picture of himself than he has been able to have, say, since the world collapsed about him in 1914.

You people of Freedom House believe that freedom from war must come through a strengthened United Nations and the rule of law. So do I, with all my heart. Therefore I understand with what concern you follow these [U.N.] debates that have had no parallel in the whole history of mankind. We all know that it is not the future of the United Nations that is at stake, but the future of the race of man. I may say that I have yet another reason to hope and pray for the strengthening of the United Nations, for it may be that one day it will hold the only hope for any kind of solution of the bitter problems of South Africa. Of one thing I am satisfied, that if the present rulers of South Africa should be able to continue with their present policies of *apartheid,* we can expect increasing unrest and conflict.

I ask only one thing of you, that you should continue to concern yourselves with our country and its people and their freedom, as you have done tonight. For it is when we know that we have friends who remember us and who cherish the same values that we do that we are able to continue, and we are ready to sacrifice our own liberty rather than the principles on which liberty is based.

* This hope may have been prompted by the actions of the U.N. Economic and Social Council, on April 12, 1960, setting up an Industrial Development Committee and recommending substantially increased funds for economic programs in emerging states, particularly those in Africa. No separate scheme for aid to Africa was established outside the framework of existing U.N. agencies.

PART THREE:

With Bell, Book, and Candle, 1963–67

Editor's Introduction

JAN HOFMEYR, modern South Africa's only liberal statesman, had declared in his famous *Herrenvolk* speech, of March 16, 1946, "By way of illustration of what prejudice means in South Africa I cannot do better than refer to the growing tendency to describe as a Communist—and therefore one who should be condemned by bell, book, and candle—anyone who asks for fair play for all races." Neither Hofmeyr nor his audience could have then imagined the speedy transformation of this tendency into the overriding policy of the South African Government. The history of the South African Liberal Party since 1963 (its tenth anniversary) shows the effects of this transformation and provides a textbook example of the two-pronged threat to human freedom posed by fanatical Communism and its dark counterpart, fanatical anti-Communism.

During 1962 and 1963, the South African Minister of Justice, who already held arbitrary powers under the Suppression of Communism Act and its amendments, was given new powers to suppress subversive organizations. These powers were conferred by the General Laws Amendment Act of 1962 (popularly known as the Sabotage Act), and the General Laws Amendment Act of 1963, which contained the notorious ninety-day clause permitting suspect persons to be held in solitary confinement without trial or preferment of charges for renewable periods of ninety days. The ostensible purpose of these acts was to combat subversive activities carried out by *Umkonto We Sizwe* (The Spear of the Nation), an underground arm of the banned African National Congress, and *Poqo* (Xosa for "pure" or "alone"), a terrorist offshoot of the banned Pan-African Congress. The Minister used his new powers to crush *Umkonto* and *Poqo;* he also used them to crush the Liberal Party.

On the tenth anniversary of its founding, the South African Liberal Party posed no parliamentary threat to the ruling Nationalists. Yet, many observers agree that government agencies showed a notable vindictiveness in suppressing and harrassing its members, its organized meetings, and its publications. Commenting on the banning and restriction of Liberal Party members during 1963, *Liberal Opinion,* the official journal of the Liberty Party in Natal, pointed out:

To their free use of their powers under the law the police have added continuing attempts to intimidate [Liberal] Party members. This intimidation takes the form of visiting and questioning members and [of] trying to persuade their employers to sack them. Unfortunately this last technique is too often successful, especially where employers are dependent on Government permits to remain in business.*

In March, 1963, the Johannesburg *Star* predicted:

It cannot be long before the [Liberal] Party is declared illegal. The Ministerial and Press campaign against it is an unfailing indication of things to come. If nothing else, this may prove a contribution to political honesty. For too long the Government has sheltered behind a mask of anti-Communism in suppressing movements contrary to the interests of White rule. If they suppress the Liberals it will no doubt be on the same pretext, but the explanation will carry no conviction. For the fact is that the issue never has been Communism but racial equality.

During the ensuing year, the momentum of the government drive against the party increased. On July 29, 1964, the London *Times* reported: "House searchings, arrests, and detentions under the 90-

---

* *Liberal Opinion,* III, No. 1 (September, 1963), 5.

day law continue steadily . . . those who have been announced are almost all either officials of the Liberal Party or young lecturers or former students of Cape Town, Witwatersrand, and Rhodes universities." The October, 1964, issue of *Liberal Opinion* reported, under the heading "Hard Times, Getting Harder," that the campaign of intimidation and arbitrary action against Liberal Party members had gained great impetus since the beginning of July: "During July and early August between twenty and thirty Party members disappeared into the silent terrors which lie behind the 90-day clause. Some of them, after being held for weeks, have been released without there being any suggestion that they had ever committed any offence." Several leading party members, including National Chairman Peter Brown, were banned for five years. The same issue of *Liberal Opinion* reported that the banning of Peter Brown was followed by a systematic police attempt to wreck the party in Natal: "One part-time Party worker was raided twelve times in a month, many members have been threatened with detention, banning, or banishment. Every effort has been made to terrorise the families of active members. Police have visited ordinary members, one at a time, and told them that now that Peter Brown was banned, they needn't expect to hold any more meetings in their areas."

The Liberal Party was not declared a banned organization, but it was reduced to relative impotence through the banning of leading members under the Suppression of Communism Act. In all, about forty members of the Liberal Party were banned; almost all of these were holders of national or regional office in the party. (For a full list of banned Liberals, see Appendix A.) Like all other banned persons in South Africa, Liberals were banned from engaging, in the words of the act, in "activities furthering the cause of Communism," even though the Liberal Party, in the personal attitudes of those attracted to it as well as in its declared policy, is strongly opposed to Communism and all other forms of totalitarian government.

A few banned Liberals, in the bitterness of their political frustration, abandoned the party's policy of nonviolence. Patrick Duncan came to the conclusion that a policy of nonviolence would never change the policies of the Nationalist Party. He flouted his ban and took refuge in Basutoland. Randolph Vigne was allegedly associated with the underground African Resistance Movement. Only four banned Liberals were ever brought to court and charged with subversive activities of any kind. During 1964, Eddie Daniels and David Evans were convicted of sabotage, and Fred Prager was charged but acquitted. John Harris was sentenced to death for murder—the charge having arisen from a bomb incident at the Johannesburg railway station. Nevertheless, the great majority of Liberal Party office-holders and ordinary members were banned not for unlawful or violent opposition but for courageous refusal to conform in their thinking and its expression to official theories of what was permissible in human relationships. Those few members of the party who did, in fact, transgress the laws played into the hands of an administration determined to associate Liberals with Communist subversion and underground revolutionary activity. It was this campaign to vilify the Liberal Party that Alan Paton had in mind when he presented his presidential address "The Abuse of Power," on the occasion of the party's tenth anniversary, in May of 1963.*

* It should be stressed at this point that none of the men mentioned were members of the Liberal Party at the time they broke—or were accused of breaking—the law. Each had been banned, and banning automatically precludes organized political activity such as membership in a legal political party. It is indicative of the impact of the bannings that most of these men had, before the order, held a responsible position within the party: Duncan had been a member of the National Executive (and the editor of *Contact*) until his banning in March, 1961; Vigne had been National Deputy Chairman before he was banned in February, 1963; Daniels, a member of the Cape Executive before his banning in May, 1964; Evans had sat on the Natal Provincial Committee until he was banned in August, 1963; Prager had been a member from Transvaal until banned in March, 1965; and Harris, a member of the Transvaal Provincial Committee until banned in February, 1964. The frustrations engendered by the prohibition of political activity led some of these men into extremes of violence.

Prologue: "The Abuse of Power"*

Paton delivered this address to the Liberal Party National Congress on the tenth anniversary of its founding. In the face of the increasing stringency of government policies and the new outbreaks of violence, Paton used the address to renew the party's commitment to nonviolent dissent and to the building of a nonracial society. In his opening remarks, he refers to an earlier meeting. At that meeting, held at the Claremont Civic Center, in Cape Town, on February 20, 1963, Paton, Margaret Ballinger, and Leo Marquard spoke in protest against the bans imposed on Liberal Party members, including Peter Hjul, Cape Chairman and *Contact* editor, and Randolph Vigne, National Deputy Chairman of the party.

The address also includes references to two instances of violence that occurred in 1962 and 1963, and to the subsequent investigations. The background of the Paarl Commission and the Bashee River murders is as follows: From November 20 to November 22, 1962, serious riots that broke out in the city of Paarl (near Cape Town) caused seven known deaths. Five of the dead had been members of a party of migrant African workers who had marched to the town and attacked the police station, the jail, and other buildings. The remaining dead were two young white inhabitants of Paarl. Four months later, in March, 1963, five whites were murdered in the vicinity of the Bashee River in the Transkei. In both

* *Liberal Opinion*, III, No. 1 (September, 1963), 5–9.

instances, the Government placed the responsibility on the underground African terrorist movement *Poqo*. In a series of police raids, several thousand alleged members of *Poqo* were arrested; some were later executed for sabotage. Justice J. H. Snyman, a judge of the Transvaal Division of the Supreme Court, was appointed as the sole member of a commission of inquiry that was set up to investigate the cause of the Paarl riots. Witnesses at this inquiry, as well as those who testified in the Bashee River murders investigation, are reported to have made frequent mention of "liberals" as involved in incitement of rioters. During the course of the Paarl inquiry, Justice Snyman became alarmed at the extent of the *Poqo* activities; he submitted an interim report urging the Government to take swift action and recommending that retrospective legislation linking *Poqo* with the banned PAC be introduced. Shortly afterward, the Government introduced the General Law Amendment Act of 1963, which went far beyond the suggestions made by Justice Snyman.

THE LAST TIME I was here was when we held a meeting to protest against the banning of Peter Hjul. On that same evening Randolph Vigne received his banning order. This National Congress of the Liberal Party sends them both, their wives, and their families our warm and affectionate greetings. We also send our affectionate greetings to our National Vice-President, Jordan Ngubane, who has since been banned, and his wife and family.

We also had another anxiety on our minds—for the first time a newspaper of repute, reporting the hearings of the Paarl Commission, came out and reported, by means of a headline, the identification of liberals with the murders at Bashee River. The name of the Liberal Party was also mentioned, in an oblique way, so that while no direct accusation was made, the smear was left. We reacted so strongly that Mr. Justice Snyman protested that Mr. Advocate Steyn (representing the South African police and others before the commission) had been wounded at the very root of his honour. The Judge was not in the least concerned that we had been wounded at the very root of our honour, and in a much graver way.

Mr. Justice Snyman has now made a kind of retraction. He says the Liberal Party was not implicated "as such" in the Bashee River murders. As far as we are concerned he can keep his retraction.

Judge Snyman ought to answer an important question in the public interest. He says that white persons were concerned with the violence in the Transkei. He says—I quote—"Some of them have been described by witnesses as members of the Liberal Party. Some were described merely as liberals." *But who were they?* I am astonished at this. The judge tells us what witnesses say—but not one scrap of evidence has been adduced to show that these witnesses spoke a word of truth. This is what I can only call astonishing behaviour.

Mr. de Wet Nel [Minister of Bantu Administration and Development] has acted similarly. He also has evidence but it is not in the "public interest" to say what it is. One can hardly credit such a situation. A leading [Government] minister has evidence relating to murder, but he cannot reveal it. Many people conclude—and many say that they conclude—that whatever evidence the Minister has, it would not bear testing in a court of law.

We, as Liberals, must defend ourselves. The days have passed when the civil liberties of all are defended by all.

A leading newspaper can smear us in a bold headline, and yet give little prominence to any reply. A judge can say there was evidence, and never test that evidence to see if it was true or false. A minister can say there is evidence relating to murder, and regret that he cannot reveal it. A member of Parliament can make charges against the Liberal Party "as such," and take good care not to repeat these charges outside the House.

These are signs of the times. You can say pretty hot things about the Black Sash, NUSAS,* and the Progressives, or the [English medium] Universities of Cape Town and Witwatersrand and get

* The Black Sash is a women's organization committed to opposing the South African Government's racial policies. At first limited to white women, the organization opened its membership to women of all races in October, 1963. Its members symbolize their protest by standing in silence outside Parliament or in the presence of government officials, wearing black sashes as signs of mourning. NUSAS is the liberal National Union of South African Students.

away with it. You can say pretty well what you like about anybody, provided you are on the side of power. These people who say these things—and here I exclude the judge and the prosecutor for sound reasons—would not have the courage to say them if they were not on the side of power. What is more, many of these same people, if there was a marked shift in power, would be the first to come to the Hjuls and the Vignes and the Ngubanes, and say: "You are right, what can we do to help you?" And some of them would be impudent enough to add: "We knew you were right all the time."

If I am ever a member of a government, I give you my word it will be the government of a state in which those who have power will have no greater civil liberty than those who have no power at all.

While I am speaking about power, let me say one more thing. Some opponents of the Government lose heart because everything seems to go right for the Nationalists. This is a pure illusion, maintained by power. Things are not going right. Things aren't going right when Dr. Dönges includes 1.5 million Coloured people and .5 million Indian people with 3 million white people, and talks of 5 million hearts beating as one. Ten years ago Dr. Dönges' party wanted all the Indians sent back to India.* Why should all our hearts now beat as one? As we gather here, the Indian citizens of Johannesburg are being squeezed out of the heart of that great city, and forced into the veld twenty miles away. Indian traders in Durban are facing the same calamity. Here in Cape Town, Coloured people are being forced out of homes in which they have lived for generations. Both Coloured and Indian people live in the shadow of the Group Areas Act and the Job Reservation and Population Registration acts.

Why should they suddenly want to stand shoulder to shoulder with the makers of these cruel laws? Why should Dr. Dönges utter such an absurdity? Is it because he feels so certain and secure? Why should Mr. Fouche [Minister of Defence] think that Africans will

* See "The People Wept," pages 101–8.

suddenly want to defend our common country? Why in God's name should they want to fight for the Urban Areas Act and the Job Reservation Act and the removal of freehold rights in hundreds of areas?

Let me tell Dr. Dönges one thing, that there are tens of thousands of Coloured and Indian people who have no intention of being used as tools against the African population.

I can imagine with what contempt the Nationalists of old would have regarded an Afrikaner who allowed himself to be used as a tool for maintaining Afrikaners in a subordinate position. And that is what Dr. Dönges wants to use Coloured and Indian people for, is it not? Hasn't he made it clear that they must fight for the "traditional way of life"?

On an occasion such as this, one must take stock. We have been in existence for ten years. When we began, we knew we had set out on an unpopular and perhaps dangerous course. We knew that we were dealing with a government for whom such things as freedom of speech and assembly and association were nonsense. Habeas-corpus is now nonsense too. And the reservation of penal action to the courts. Well, we've run into the dangers that we foresaw.

It takes courage to set out on a dangerous course, but it takes even more courage to continue on it when the actual dangers are met. One gets tired and frustrated, and sometimes ostracism and political loneliness are harder to endure than one foresaw.

Did we go wrong? Was it perhaps wrong or foolish to condemn tremendous schemes of national reconstruction like the Group Areas Act and Bantu Authorities? Was it perhaps wrong to organise people and make them more militant, only to find that the more militant they became, the more ruthlessly they were punished for their militancy? Are we not perhaps living in a crisis of law and order, and shouldn't we support the forces of law and order until the crisis has passed? And lastly, isn't *apartheid* perhaps good after all; not absolutely good, but the best you can get in an imperfect world? Isn't it true, perhaps, that races just can't live together, and that the best thing to do is for them to live separately?

If I, as your National [Party] President, as a man who is, as Angus Wilson once described him, a private man pushed into public life, can make it again clear why we founded the Liberal Party, and can reaffirm our beliefs and principles and policies, then I am glad to do so.

Let me talk to you just a few minutes as a writer rather than a politician, and talk to you about plucking the flower Safety from the nettle Danger. They talk about the diversity of the Cape flora, but the nettle Danger is all I see growing around here. And I can't promise to pluck the flower Safety from it. What you have to do is to pluck some kind of life from it, some kind of meaning for yourselves and your children.

Ten years ago we thought that the only way to do it was to work for a nonracial society; people said it was impossible, and we said *apartheid* was even more impossible. We still say so. We see no future for *apartheid* at all. We see an illusion of a future, but that's only because the Government has power. We see not only ourselves in this country, and people like-minded, but also we see the whole world turning against *apartheid* with a massiveness of revulsion that has not been equalled before now. We know it would be more immediately comfortable to believe in *apartheid,* but we know that at that moment of surrender it would be our reason and our integrity that surrendered.

If Vigne and Hjul and Ngubane had surrendered to a belief in *apartheid,* they could be sitting pretty, writing textbooks for Bantu education. Sobukwe wouldn't be out on Robben Island [Prison], and [Nelson] Mandela wouldn't be in gaol for five years, and Luthuli would be getting a big job in Zulustan. I myself would get a splendid job on the Publications Control Board,* and you'd hear me on the SABC [South African Broadcasting Corporation], talking on such topics as "Who Says Our News Is Slanted?" and

---

* The Publications Control Board is a board of censors established by the Publications and Entertainments Act of 1963 to judge all local and imported films, plays, books, and magazines.

"Who Wants These Forty-eight Playwrights, Anyway?"* and "The Greatness of Portugal." And, in my bravest moments, you'd hear me on the subject "The English Press Is Not 100 Per Cent Bad."

All these things could happen if we were allied with power. But what a petty, blind, arrogant, local power it is.

Dr. Verwoerd's foreign policy is in ashes, and he himself admits that he would embarrass the nations of the West by visiting them. I don't blame [Foreign Minister] Eric Louw for this. He merely took a bad policy and made it look worse. Dr. Verwoerd and Eric Louw have never understood that you can't have a foreign policy with *apartheid* in it. You can't have relations with people abroad when you reject their brothers at home. Eric Louw has had only one debating argument in his whole life, and that is: "You say I'm bad, and now I'll prove you're bad too."

I am astonished when I read and hear of all the reasons for our dangerous isolation. It was once due to agitators and Communists. Then the Liberals and, to a lesser extent, the Progressives were blamed. Then the Pan-African Congress and *Poqo* took the centre of the stage, and that gave Mr. Vorster his new and colossal powers. Now the searchlight has switched back to the African National Congress. I am most astonished when the United Party is blamed for our isolation. But, of course, one expects the Black Sash, NUSAS, and the English press to have their turns. Even that impeccable organisation the Rotary Club has been accused of subversive work.

One thing it seems the Government will not see—and it will not see because it does not want to see—that it is *apartheid,* segregation, Job Reservation, group areas, the discrimination of the powerful against the weak, the holding of a man back because he is not white, the suggestion that white and Coloured people and Indians are all in varying degrees superior to Africans; it is this that has isolated us from the rest of the world.

* In June, 1963, forty-eight British and American playwrights signed a declaration to the effect that a clause in all their future contracts would prohibit performance of their works in theaters where there was discrimination among audiences on the grounds of color. Signers included Daphne du Maurier, Graham Greene, Arthur Miller, John Osborne, C. P. Snow, and Angus Wilson.

The Government, which looks upon itself as so practical, ful-
minates against Africans and African states as short-sighted, nasty-
minded ranters, who are biting off their noses to spite their faces.
What effect do such arguments have? Precisely nothing. Whatever
may be the faults of Africans, one thing is certain: they hate
apartheid with all their hearts, and long only to destroy it. That is
the cardinal fact.

The crisis of South Africa today is not one of law and order. It
is said to be, because thus many lovers of law and order are seduced,
and give their moral support to the regime.

The crisis of today is fundamentally the crisis of *apartheid,* and of
apartheid in its worst aspect, namely *baasskap.* It takes courage to
say so in these times, but that is what we have to do. Dr. Dönges
is appealing to Coloured and Indian people to support white
supremacy, for the sake of a few scraps.

Is *apartheid* in its other aspect, namely, separate development,
worth dying for? It certainly is not. There is one charge that
apartheid has never been able to meet, and that is: how can a thing
be good if it can be achieved only by cruel laws? How else can one
describe the Group Areas Act? And Job Reservation? And the
Urban Areas Law? And the removal of the black spots?

We are told that such steps bring peace, but how can they bring
peace when they leave people with such a memory of hurt and injustice? Is this the way to bring about harmony? People die, but do
their children forget such a dispossession? Did Afrikaner children
forget? I have noted that South African supporters of *apartheid*
abroad are excellent in their speeches, and resentful, and often
angry, in the face of questions. The reason is simple; the speech
deals with separate development, but the questions deal with
baasskap.

Let us not be tempted by the laager.* I promise you this, that

* "Laager" originally meant the defensive circle of wagons the Voortrekkers
set up for protection against the Zulus; *apartheid* has often been referred to as
"white laager," meaning a defensive posture on the part of whites to keep out
the nonwhite peoples.

once all the white people go into the laager they will never come out of it again.

No, the values enshrined in our policies on May 9, 1953, were right beyond all doubt. In those liberties we believe now, as strongly as we believed then. That *apartheid* will come to an end, no sensible man can have a doubt. The Afrikaner nationalist always believed that his passion was stronger than economics. The passion of liberated Africa will prove the same.

I do not doubt that at Paarl Judge Snyman looked into the pit. He saw Paarl partly in the conventional white way of agitators, plotters, and Communists. But he also looked into the abyss and saw it as a crisis of race relations. He saw a vision that had been seen by others before. But he was right in what he saw. Unless race relations are improved, our future is dark.

I ask Judge Snyman: how does he think race relations can be improved so long as black men are regarded as chattels, so long as Mrs. Mapheele can be thrown out of Paarl and separated from her husband, so long as [Government] ministers take offence because a woman invokes her rights under the law?

I tell him, and the Liberal Party tells him, that there is no hope whatsoever of any improvement in race relations so long as there are these cruel laws.

Our way is dangerous because all life is dangerous. The way of *apartheid,* call it *baasskap* or separate development, is the way of certain death. Hofmeyr was ten times the politician I am, but he expressed the truth in very unpolitical language. He said it was a choice between faith and fear. It still is.

This faith we have expressed in our policies, which are as sensible a blueprint for the future as a party could produce. It is not only a universal suffrage which we regard as the inevitable future; it is a drastic revisal of our whole system of possession and privilege.

I agree with our National Chairman [Brown] that our task is not easy. It is to continue the work we have begun, to win support for a nonracial society in which there is opportunity for all, and from which the grossest economic disparities will be removed.

Our policies, and our sanity, may be needed sooner than we believe possible to-day.

Editor's Postscript

The case of Mrs. Mapheele provides an instance of the plight of families whose individual circumstances do not fit the rigid requirements of the machinery of *apartheid*. Since much of the extra-parliamentary activity of the Liberal Party consisted of investigating and publicizing such cases of individual hardship, Paton's audience was familiar with Mrs. Mapheele's case—that of a married woman separated by administrative edict from her husband and child. The following account of the case is adapted from an article in *Contact* of October 18, 1963, under the heading "Political Divorce":

Mr. and Mrs. Jackson Mapheele, an African couple, were married by Christian rites in the Anglican church at Herschel, a little Cape farming town. Mr. Mapheele had worked in Paarl for more than ten years and was, thus, qualified to reside in the "proclaimed area" of Paarl, where he had been staying in the "bachelor quarter" of the African location. As he was unable to find accommodations for his wife, they settled the problem by arranging that Mrs. Mapheele should board with a "Coloured" family in the town, while he remained a resident of the African "bachelor quarter." Then, without any warning, Mrs. Mapheele was ordered out of Paarl by the Bantu Affairs Administration because, they said, she did not qualify to reside in the "proclaimed area." She did not leave and was subsequently charged in the Paarl Magistrate's Court with being in the area "illegally."

She was convicted, but she appealed against the order. In passing sentence, the Supreme Court judges who heard her appeal said that they gave her all their sympathy but that the law had to take its course. They made an appeal from the bench that her case should be considered by the appropriate authorities.

An appeal was, therefore, lodged with the Minister of Bantu

Administration and Development, de Wet Nel, who, in denying the application, described Mrs. Mapheele's appeal to the courts as a "provocative action taken in respect of the laws of the country." The Minister's reprimand to Mrs. Mapheele for exercising her right to appeal to the courts for a ruling on whether she could remain with her husband and child drew widespread comment. As *Contact* put it: "To Mr. Nel, the law of *apartheid* had decreed that she could not live with her husband and child and that was that."

After nearly a year of appeals and court action, Mrs. Mapheele was separated from her husband and child and sent back to Herschel. Yet, the Minister was not altogether unmoved. He offered Mr. Mapheele employment in the Bantu Development Corporation in Herschel, where his wife was entitled to live, only to discover that existing *apartheid* regulations (as outlined in "The Charlestown Story," pages 122–26) invalidated such humanitarian gestures; for, if Mr. Mapheele accepted the offered employment and stayed away from Paarl for more than a year, he would lose his legal right to return there. If he then gave up or lost the employment at Herschel, he would have no legal right to live *anywhere in South Africa* for more than seventy-two hours. As Dr. Oscar Wolheim pointed out (*Cape Times,* November 11, 1963): "Mr. Mapheele is, in point of fact, being asked by the Minister to stay in Paarl without his family, or to live in Herschel with his family as a virtually 'stateless person.'"

I. Dispensing Justice

A TOAST TO THE END OF THE COLOUR BAR*

Alan Paton, replacing Peter Brown, began his third series of
"Long View" essays in the January 24, 1964, issue of *Contact*. This is his response to Dr. Verwoerd's New Year message.

MOST OF MY READERS will have heard or read Dr. Verwoerd's New
Year message to the nation. This is the antidote. The Prime Minister warned us that the attack in 1964 would be on the nation's
mind, customs, and way of life. It is high time some of these things
were attacked. They do no credit to the nation. It is high time that
the colour bar was swept away in sports, the arts, and religion.
The sports colour bar is certainly not sportsmanlike, and the arts
colour bar is certainly not artistic. As for the religious colour bar,
it is condemned by all but a handful of churches, and those churches
—let it be noted—are composed of white people living in colour-
bar countries.

The Prime Minister considers that white South Africa is a bastion of Christianity. This is a very dubious proposition. What are
the Verwoerds and the Vorsters really trying to maintain? Are they
trying to maintain Christianity? Or are they trying to maintain
Job Reservation, the Group Areas Act, and ninety days' detention?
Or do they imagine they are all synonymous?

* *Contact*, VII, No. 2 (January 24, 1964), 2.

Is white governmental Christianity worth preserving? The answer is emphatically, "No." It is almost impossible for any non-Nationalist to find any connection between the teachings of Christ and the expulsion of Mrs. Mapheele from Paarl, or the threat to replace all Indian barmen by whites [under the Job Reservation Act], or the disgraceful [black spot] removals at Besterspruit in Natal.*

Dr. Verwoerd is a strange man, so realistic and hard-bitten in some respects, so naïve in others. He considers the Afro-Asian nations to be hypocritical, and the Western nations to be weak and opportunistic, while the South African nation is honest and upright. Surely a psychologist should know that to see only vice in others and only virtue in oneself is morbid.

At the risk of being called a traitor to South Africa by all the new [white] immigrants from Kenya [since self-government began, in May, 1963], I say that white South Africa's satisfaction with herself and her achievements is nauseating. It is true that white people have as good a material life as any people in the world, and it is also true that it is based on the low standard of so many of their fellow citizens. White South Africans are no more virtuous than the people of any other nation. If in some things they are more vicious, it is because they have been corrupted by the kind of colour-bar society that Dr. Verwoerd wants them to maintain.

Dr. Verwoerd plays the old tune of separate and just develop-

---

* At the beginning of 1963, some 3,553 Africans and a few whites and Coloureds lived in an area on the outskirts of Vryheid, Natal, called Besterspruit. About 400 African families owned land there, some with titles dating back to 1909. Under the Group Areas Act, Besterspruit was declared a black spot (see "The Charlestown Story," pages 116–26). In February, 1963, the Government decided to move the people at once, although no alternative housing was available. Landowners were offered half-acre plots in Mondhlo Reserve, twenty-five miles away. The Government paid compensation to property owners, gave a bag of maize to families who had unharvested crops, and provided transport. The 1,590 Africans the Government moved to Mondhlo were expected to build their own homes, for which the Government provided only poles to serve as framework for walls and thatched roofs. Meanwhile, they lived in tents. Another 1,963 people were moved to Vryheid township (an African location), where they also lived in tents until prefabricated huts could be provided. Some observers saw no reason for the hastiness of these removals.

ment. No one has exposed the hollowness of this better than Peter Brown in *Contact*. If Natal, with all her agricultural and industrial wealth, her splendid harbour, her abundant labour and water, did not dare to seek independence [when South Africa became a republic, in 1961], what hope has the Transkei of achieving it? Or Zululand? Or any other place? Even if no one interfered with us for fifty years, the Transkei at the end of that time would still be a poor pastoral and agricultural country, with second-rate cities, second-rate roads, second-rate industries.

Let us drink a toast to the end of the colour bar, on every sports field, in every theatre, in every church, in every university, in every hotel, in every post office. Let us drink a toast to the end of the colour bar in Parliament. Let us drink a toast to the final doom of *apartheid* enforced by law. Let us drink a toast to the final downfall of every white supremacist.

Let us pledge ourselves to continue the fight against any kind of racial supremacy, any kind of morbid pride in race, any kind of pride indeed in any special colour or culture or cussedness which prevents the growth of the only kind of pride that matters, namely of belonging to and serving our country, South Africa.

1964 may not bring these blessings. But I promise you one thing —it will bring them one year nearer.

A DUBIOUS VIRGIN*

Dr. Verwoerd was the first Nationalist Prime Minister to reject the terms *apartheid* and *baasskap* as descriptive of his party's policies of racial separation. He insisted on the term "separate development" or "separate freedoms."

UNDER THE influence of sixteen years of strong-arm government, many white South Africans who formerly believed *apartheid* to be unchristian and unjust have come to see its virtues. It is now many

* *Contact*, VII, No. 4 (March 13, 1964), 2.

times more difficult to see the vices of *apartheid* than it was sixteen
years ago.

Dr. Verwoerd, on the one hand, and Mr. Vorster, on the other,
are largely responsible for this transformation. It is Dr. Verwoerd
who has taken the trollop *apartheid,* put a clean white dress over her
dirty undergarments, renamed her "separate development," and persuaded many intellectuals and churchmen (not merely Dutch Reformed churchmen either) that the girl is a virgin. It is Mr. Vorster
who has made people afraid to doubt the virginity, and afraid to
see the dirty undergarments. He has identified such disbelief with
treason to the state.

It has suited Dr. Verwoerd to become the champion of all that is
sweet and holy in separate development. It has equally suited Mr.
Vorster to become the champion of white supremacy and almost
total state power (except over certain trivial freedoms). Dr. Verwoerd and Mr. Vorster use each other skilfully. Dr. Verwoerd is
the smiling and benign benefactor; Mr. Vorster is the unsmiling
totalitarian who carries out the benefactions. The duality of these
two men, with these two irreconcilable images—the one promising,
the other foreboding—is indeed the duality of white nationalism
itself.

There could be no better example of this duality than the
Odendaal Report on South West Africa, and its speedy successor
the Bantu Laws Amendment Bill.* No sooner has this Govern-

---

* In 1963, the South African Odendaal Commission of Enquiry into the
welfare and progress of the inhabitants of South West Africa introduced a
development plan modeled on Dr. Verwoerd's "Bantustan" plan for self-governing "homelands" for Africans (using the Transkei pattern). It was presumed
that this development plan, which included schemes to provide water and elec-
tricity for economic progress, would help to placate world opinion. The Bantu
Laws Amendment bills (1963 and 1964) consolidated and extended existing
legislation (for example, the Urban Areas Act). On the presumption that
Africans lived by right only in tribal "homelands," they detailed increased
controls over the movement, residence, employment, and even family life of all
Africans outside the Reserves. Strong opposition to these bills was voiced by
the United Party, the Progressive Party, most churches, and the Institute of
Race Relations, as well as the Liberal Party. By 1964, most of the measures outlined in these bills had been enacted.

ment made this gesture to the world than it shows the cruel counterpart. It cannot help it. As in a surrealist film, the smiling face and the shining teeth turn to fangs and horror.

This is quite inevitable. One cannot combine noble unselfishness and self-centred love into one durable philosophy. No sooner has the Government promised substantial aid to South West Africa than it reveals how black men will be treated in the white areas of that country. The dubious virgin, whose white dress has been designed to charm all Western lovers, even perhaps to cause a flutter in some Eastern hearts, cannot help lifting it to show her dirty undergarments. And what is more, this sluttish action, while repelling some, excites others—notably, visiting business men.

Let me say of the Bantu Laws Amendment Bill that it is evil. I can understand that white South Africans want security. But I cannot understand that they should consent to buy it at the cost of the security and family life of 6 or 7 million African people. [United Party Chairman] Douglas Mitchell, who has often reproved the Government for doing too much for Africans, is outraged at the thought that an old farm worker of ninety can be forced to return to his "homeland" when he can work no longer. He is right to be outraged. It would be an utterly evil act.

I tell white South Africans once again that *apartheid* is an evil and cruel thing, no matter how it is dressed up. It is quite contemptuous of the rights of others. It professes to benefit all impartially, and to exact the cost from all impartially, but that is a lying profession. It declares that black men have no rights in "white" areas, when those same black men have helped to build those same "white" areas. It puts restraints on black people, on their freedom of possession and movement, that white people would find intolerable. What white person would tolerate having to seek permission from some white commissioner for his aged father and mother to come and live with him?

I am afraid some of this language is rather strong. I shall probably—after having regained a slight respectability [during the time that] Peter Brown wrote "The Long View"—be relegated again to the ranks of the irreconcilable. But I have no wish to be reconciled with such legislation as the Bantu Laws Amendment Bill, nor with those who make such laws.

I am not a good man. I am far from practising all I believe in. But I would rather be harried by Mr. Vorster and his security police, I would rather be hanged by them, officially or unofficially, than state any other opinion than that the [Bantu Laws] Amendment Bill is an evil law, and a disgrace to any state that calls itself Christian.

THE NINETY DAYS*

Section 17 of the General Laws Amendment Act of 1963, known as the Ninety-Day Law, stated that a commissioned police officer could arrest, without warrant, any person whom he suspected had committed or *intended to commit* any offense under the Suppression of Communism Act or the Unlawful Organisations Act, had committed or intended to commit sabotage (as defined in another section of the 1963 act), or, in the police officer's opinion, possessed information relating to such offenses. Detainees under this clause were held incommunicado, usually in solitary confinement, for periods limited to ninety days, but renewable. The Ninety-Day Law, in effect from May 1, 1963, was suspended (but not abolished) on January 11, 1965. That same year, the Criminal Procedure Amendment Act of 1965 introduced a 180-day detention clause for putative witnesses (broadly defined) in government trials. Of the 1,095 persons detained under the Ninety-Day Law, 575 were charged with specific offenses; of this group, 210 were convicted. Of those against whom no charges were laid, 241 gave evidence for the state.

MR. VORSTER'S suspension of the ninety-day clause is welcome news. Some people will hail it as a proof that the back of sabotage is broken. Others, like myself, will be grateful that a grave threat

* *Contact,* VII, No. 14 (December, 1964), 4.

to the liberty of the ordinary citizen has been removed. For it is certain that a ninety-day clause is a temptation to any government and any police force to use unwarranted power against the citizens of the state.

Some other things are certain also. The ninety-day clause is a temptation to torture human beings, to smash their jaws, to break their limbs, and to bring some of them to the point where they would rather jump to death than face torture any longer.

These things are bad enough. But the most abhorrent thing about the ninety-day detention is that it can be used, by itself or with supplementary cruelties, to destroy or maim or change the human personality, so that decent men and women can be persuaded to betray their friends for the sake of themselves or their children, or their own liberty.

There are of course many people who regard the infliction of physical or mental injury as a bagatelle compared with the inestimable advantage that the safety of the state has been preserved. There are also opponents of the Government who in their turn would also use such methods, and would like nothing better than to give Mr. Vorster a taste of ninety days. This may be a pleasant thought, but it is pleasant only to the baser side of our natures, indeed to that base side of human nature that in the first instance consented to such a corruption of the law. It is not a thought for any true liberal to entertain. If we entertain it, then we too have been debased, and by the very power which we profess to abhor.

This problem of the reconciliation of power with justice, of authority with liberty, of the state with its citizens, is as old as human society itself. It is never fully or permanently solved. But the continuing attempt to solve it is one of the unmistakable marks and supreme aims of good government.

Dr. Verwoerd's Government does not pass this essential test. It is mainly concerned with the preservation of the safety of the state, and with the preservation of an existing order. It argues that the safety of the state is essential for the well-being of the individual. Yet it can be just as cogently argued that the liberty of the individual is essential for the well-being of the state and of society, that no society is worth preserving if its people are not free.

The Liberal view is clear and unequivocal. It says with Lord Acton that the primary function of the state is to make it possible for man to lead the good life. The state in fact is a means not an end. The state is not the master of the people, it *is* the people. It must have power, but never absolute power. Its power to punish and detain it delegates to the courts, and under no circumstances must it take back that power. Judged by these standards, the ninety-day clause is indefensible.

While I welcome Mr. Vorster's suspension of the clause, I condemn his reasoning. He says that it is no longer required and he says he will not hesitate to reintroduce it if he thinks it necessary. It is clear that in his view the state has a right to detain without charge or trial, and to bring about fundamental changes in human personality. To a liberal this view is intolerable.

I should like to make again one point that I have made before. This is not fundamentally a crisis of law and order. It is the crisis of a kind of law and order that many white South Africans like, not because it is lawful, not because it is orderly, but because it preserves their power and privilege.

Fundamentally that is what the ninety-day clause is for.

It is futile to suppose that one can preserve the law by going outside the law. The ninety-day clause should be abolished.

A PLEA FOR THE FREEDOM OF MONKEYS*

This is Paton's "modest proposal" for extending the benefits of separate development (particularly Job Reservation) to some inhabitants of remote "homelands." The book embargo to which he refers came about when, during 1964, customs officials decided to seize all books and periodicals arriving by sea or through the post office, to examine them, and to

* *Contact,* VII, No. 13 (November 27, 1964), 2, 6.

submit doubtful ones to the Publications Control Board. Shipments were placed under embargo on arrival until cleared by the Board. The Board, however, could not handle the flood of material submitted to it. Booksellers described the situation as chaotic.

THE CITY OF Durban has taken very calmly the decision of the Minister of Railways and Harbours to employ forty Indian shunters on the South African Railways. It is only the Nationalists that are perturbed. Yet they need not be, because shunting is not really a traditional white occupation. Van Riebeck [leader of the first Cape settlement, 1652] knew nothing about shunting. In fact, railways are not really South African. They are only one hundred years old, about the same age as the first British settlers would now be, and though their locomotives may blow and whistle, they are not really part of the South African scene.

A much more serious crisis is the book embargo. Here are all these books lying about, and no one to censor them. The solution is simple. Hand over the South African Railways to the Indians, and transfer all the railwaymen to the Publications Board, so that they can read the backlog of books, so that we can read them too.* Indians however will not be allowed to drive the White Train,* and rightly too, because this is quite outside their tradition.

Another crisis will soon arise in the nursing profession. Soon there will be no white girls available, because they are needed in managerial capacities. Here again there is a solution to hand. Let white people be nursed by Coloured nurses, Coloured people by Indian nurses, Indian people by African nurses. This sews the whole thing up.

Flogging may have to be abolished. It is a white occupation, but it is getting harder and harder to get white floggers. One cannot obviously apply the nursing solution to flogging, because it leaves the question wide open, who will flog the Bantu? Furthermore one

---

* South Africa has dual capitals, Cape Town and Pretoria. The White Train moves the executive arm of the Government between them twice annually.

somehow cannot quite get used to the idea of Coloured floggers for white people; it is not in the tradition of either of these proud people.

The business of postmen is very tricky. Here, at Kloof, we first had African postmen, but now we have Indian postmen. I must confess I don't like it. I would rather see Coloured postmen here, and send all the Indian postmen to Coloured areas, and all the African postmen to Indian areas. That would again sew the whole thing up nicely, and would show, I think, the immense adaptability of the theory of separate development.

Is it not fascinating to see how adaptable the policy of Job Reservation is also. There is no fear that it will collapse. Heaven will collapse just as soon. That is because Christianity and Job Reservation are really the same thing. There is only one possible justification for kicking a man out of his job, and that is if it is done in a Christian spirit. The same is true about kicking a man out of his home under the Group Areas Act. I apologise for appearing to bring religion into politics, but I am not really doing so. Here, by a miracle, they are one and the same thing.

Some people say Job Reservation is finished. They say it is impossible for white South Africa to supply the engineers, architects, telephonists, clerks, barmen, for the entire country. This is only Communist propaganda. In fact there is still a great source of labour untapped. I refer to our monkeys and baboons. Surely many of us have heard Oscar Wolheim's [a founder of the Liberal Party] famous story of the farmer who trained baboons for agriculture. They were highly efficient and would do anything except the most menial labour.

It is not pleasant to speak disparagingly of our monkeys and baboons, because they are truly South African. But the fact is that they have done too little for their country. They eat the fruit, and leave the pips for white South Africa. In the Kruger National Park they are degenerating, and sit on the roadside begging food from those endeavouring to enjoy their hard-earned holidays.

If these animals could be trained—and a problem like that should be child's play for those who in sixteen years have solved the racial problems of South Africa—many more white South Africans would be freed for managerial positions. It would not surprise me if our monkeys became the best-fed and happiest monkeys in all Africa. The tide of Communism would be halted, and the world would come to see the excellence of our policies.

One thing would have to be made quite clear however. Monkeys would not become part of the nation. They could work in our industries and on our farms, but they would remain citizens of the *kloofs* and *krantzes*.* No true South African would wish to disturb the freedom of their care-free lives. Nor, I am sure, would our monkeys wish it otherwise.

* Literally, ravines and hills. Actually, a reference to Verwoerd's "homelands" plan.

II. The Cost of Dissent

*CHIEF ALBERT LUTHULI: HIS CRIME IS LOYALTY**

Chief Albert Luthuli, President of the African National Congress, was awarded the Nobel Peace Prize for 1960. He was a friend of Alan Paton and supported the idea of a nonracial state. Luthuli was subjected to a long series of arbitrary bans. In 1953, having already been deprived of his chieftainship, he was banned from all political activities and from all South African towns and cities for one year. The day the ban expired, he flew to Johannesburg to address a meeting at Sophiatown [a Native township]. He was arrested at the Johannesburg airport and served with a second ban for two years. This ban expired in July, 1956. He was arrested again in December, 1956, and detained during the extended preliminary "treason trial" hearings. The charges against him were dropped in December, 1957, but he was recalled for extended periods as a witness. He was comparatively free only during 1958—a time when large crowds of all races flocked to hear him speak in major South African cities. In May, 1959, he was served with his third ban, this time for five years. While under this ban, he spent five months in prison during the state of emergency, in 1960. On the expiration of this third ban, in May, 1964, Mr. Vorster immediately served a further, and more severe, five-year ban on Luthuli, confining him to his home in Groutville, in the Umvoti Reserve, near Stanger, Natal, and forbidding him to

* *Contact,* VII, No. 7 (June 5, 1964), 2.

attend any gathering or to publish, broadcast, or reproduce any statement for public attention. On July 21, 1967, Luthuli died of injuries received when he was struck by a train near his Groutville home. Alan Paton paid tribute to him in an address delivered to some 7,000 mourners at his funeral. See "In Memoriam," pp. 265–67.

THE MINISTER of Justice has imposed a new ban—the fourth—on Chief Luthuli. This ban imposes a new restriction, in that it forbids the Chief to go to the small neighbouring town of Stanger. So he is now virtually under house arrest.

Therefore, for some thirteen years of his life—if there is no change in our situation—Luthuli will have been condemned to a seclusion which has grown more restrictive as he has grown older. It is a stupendous punishment which has no parallel in those Western countries which find in us, according to Dr. Verwoerd, their staunchest ally.

What is Luthuli being punished for? In one sense, this is impossible to say. He has never been found guilty of high treason. He was charged with high treason, but the state eventually dropped the charge against him.

Yet in another sense it is easy to say why Luthuli has been punished. He has been punished because he refuses to accept the ideology of *apartheid,* separate development, and Bantustans. He claims that all South Africa is his country, as much as it is Dr. Verwoerd's. The idea that he and his people can be relegated to separate pieces of land distributed throughout South Africa, he regards as absurd, quite apart from its injustice. The idea that separate development can bring liberty and self-fulfilment to African people, he regards as preposterous. He believes—as many of us believe—that these separate territories will remain forever poor.

Luthuli not only held these views, he went out and associated himself with those who held them. In particular, he associated with them in the African National Congress. His Congress made repeated representations and requests to the government of the day. It made demands too, as any self-respecting political organisation will do.

But it was like knocking on a closed door. Luthuli went over to passive resistance. He was banned. He was tried for treason. He was banned again, and yet again.

From a political point of view—and from other points of view —Luthuli has led a brave, honourable, and tolerant life. His political struggle has many parallels with the struggle of [Afrikaner leaders] Hertzog, Malan, and Strijdom. Yet it was harder, for Luthuli's people had no voting franchise, nor the hope that an enfranchised majority would eventually put their leader into power. Afrikaner nationalists sneer at him, but he compares in stature with any of their own heroes. His crime is not treachery, but loyalty. And his loyalty, while having much in common with that of the nationalists, is more inclusive, less intolerant.

History will say—and unequivocally—that Luthuli's aims were just and reasonable. History will say—unequivocally—that some of Luthuli's people turned to sabotage because there was nothing else to do. History will say—unequivocally—that Afrikaner nationalism's treatment of African patriots was cruel, unjust, and foolish. And history will not hesitate to place much of the blame on the shoulders of the Prime Minister and his Minister of Justice, who think they can hold back destiny with the aid of lightweights like Matanzima.*

AN EXAMPLE FOR US ALL: ELLIOTT MNGADI†

Elliott Mngadi—"a little man of enormous energy who always wears a huge grey homburg"—was a Liberal Party organizer for Northern Natal who had been imprisoned with Peter Brown and other Liberals during the 1960 emergency period. In perhaps his best-known contribution to the

* Chief Kaizer Matanzima supports separate development and is Chief Minister of the "self-governing" Transkei, where his government has limited local authority. Such areas are popularly called "Bantustans" by opponents of the Promotion of Bantu Self-Government Act (1959), which established them and, at the same time, abolished African representation in Parliament.

† *Contact*, VII, No. 5 (April 10, 1964), 2.

liberal cause, he organized the Ratepayer's Association to assist African freehold property owners deprived of their land under the Group Areas Act.

IN MARCH, 1964, Mr. Balthazar John Vorster, Minister of Justice, using the tremendous powers given to him under the Suppression of Communism Act, placed Mr. Elliott Mngadi, organiser of the Liberal Party in Natal, under a banning order. This means that Mr. Mngadi may not attend meetings, and is confined to a restricted area around his Ladysmith home.

Mr. Mngadi was banned because, in the Minister's opinion, he was furthering the aims of Communism. Let us have a closer look at this man. Let us put down all the known facts about his activities. We can do that because we know even more facts about him than the security police. We can say more than that—the security police do not know one single important fact about Mr. Mngadi which is not known to us.

If anyone lived an open life—and an honourable one—it was Elliott Mngadi. He organised the Liberal Party. He was also Secretary of the Northern Natal African Landowners' Association, a body that was formed to fight expropriation of the black spots, and to resist being pushed back under "Bantu" control. This work he also did openly.

In September, 1963, he organised a meeting of prayer and protest at Roosboom, near Ladysmith, attended by many hundreds of landowners. It began with divine service and ended with a protest meeting and a signing of a petition. Some Church leaders disapproved of the combining of prayer with protest; that such a thing was wrong never entered the mind of Elliott Mngadi.

Though one of the consequences of his Christian belief is that he is a strict teetotaller, he arranged for *utshwala* [African beer] to be supplied to those who felt thirsty after the prayer and protest. If some Christians felt that it was right to drink *utshwaia* after prayer, that was good enough for him. He is the soul of tolerance. If I wished to learn about tolerance and understanding, I should go to him, not to Mr. Vorster. He knows more about Christian civilisation than the Minister who has banned him.

Mngadi does not eat pork, but he does not regard as unclean those who do. If he is told that some meat dish he is eating contains pork, he will be seriously taken aback, but when he sees that he is being teased, his face will break into a smile which cannot be surpassed in Africa, even in the newly independent countries. In many ways his nature is childlike, but his courage is that of a man who knows all the wickedness—and the goodness—of the world.

Life didn't come easy to Mngadi; it doesn't come easy now. He started life in domestic service, broke into the commercial world, then became a messenger of the court. He wore a tremendous hat with the crown undented, big moustaches, and leather leggings, which gave him a fierce appearance. Yet his nature is gentle. If he were a member of a government, it would be one that would have every regard for the personality of men, even its enemies. This is not because he is sentimental, but because he is good. He understands things of which Mr. Vorster has no comprehension.

He might have gone far if he had stuck to being a messenger of the court. But instead of that, he joined the Liberal Party and embarked on a course of which he knew all the dangers. If he could have been intimidated, he would have been by his imprisonment during the emergency of 1960, along with [Liberal Party leaders] Peter Brown, Hans Meidner, Frank Bhengu, and Derick Marsh. If further warnings were needed, he received them when his home was searched on several occasions. Never did he think of changing his course. One of his most striking characteristics is his cheerfulness, but it is the cheerfulness of a man who has had to endure more than most of us. In this he is Elliott the Exemplar.

I would be tempted to say of him what Tennyson said of Galahad, that his strength is as the strength of ten, because his heart is pure. But he wouldn't like it. So I won't say it.

To those Liberals who are feeling dispirited, I would recommend that they should study Elliott the Exemplar. He is an example for us all.

INTIMIDATION*

The National Union of South African Students (NUSAS) was founded in 1924 by Leo Marquard, who, in 1953, helped found the Liberal Party. The student bodies of the English-medium (that is, the language of instruction is English) universities—Cape Town, Witwatersrand, Rhodes, and Natal—were NUSAS affiliates. Afrikaans-medium (instruction is in Afrikaans) universities had a separate organization. During and after 1963, NUSAS, which strongly opposed university *apartheid,* was increasingly denounced as leftist and even subversive. Particularly strong denunciation came from Minister of Justice Vorster, who called NUSAS "the mouthpiece of leftists and liberalists . . . tainted with Communism . . . for many years." It was NUSAS that, in 1966, invited Senator Robert Kennedy to South Africa.

LEO MARQUARD made a fine speech at the opening of the NUSAS conference in Pietermaritzburg [on July 15, 1964]. At a time when many people thought the students should beat a retreat, Marquard told them not to let themselves be intimidated, and to defend what they believed to be right. It was a good thing to hear this sane, steady voice at a time of indecision.

Another sane voice spoke at about the same time. Ben Marais† said, in effect, that the greatest thing to fear was not intimidation but the state of being intimidated; for, once a people become afraid of exercising their liberty, their liberty is gone.

In Ben Marais' article in the *Rand Daily Mail*‡ of July 10, he made the following statement: "I know of no person in South Africa condemned only because he or she made use of the right to express

---

* *Contact,* VII, No. 9 (July 31, 1964), 2.

† Professor of Theology at Pretoria University and a leading Dutch Reformed–church theologian; he opposes *apartheid.*

‡ An important, large-circulation English-language daily, published in Johannesburg.

a point of view or give expression to an inner conviction." I am using this month's "Long View" to examine this statement. I do this with no intention of detracting from my praise of Ben Marais. I do it because I believe that the statement is misleading, and that Ben Marais was not fully informed, and it is important to me that a person of his stature should be informed.

If Ben Marais meant that no person has been sentenced in a court for expressing a point of view, he may be literally correct. But if he means that no person has been punished for expressing a point of view or giving expression to an inner conviction, he is quite misinformed.

Mrs. Adelain Hain,* of Pretoria, has been banned for precisely that, and one of the consequences of her ban has been that she is no longer able to attend the birthday parties of her own children.

Mr. Elliott Mngadi, of Roosboom, has been banned for the same reason. He was an organiser of the Liberal Party, and he organised the African landowners of the black spots in Natal to resist by all lawful means the attempt to remove them. For this he was banned, and his livelihood taken away.

This list I could lengthen considerably. But I can remember punishments in quite another category. I remember that Peter Brown was kept in prison for three months in 1960 because he had given expression to an inner conviction; he was only one of many.

In any event, the word "condemn" has lost its original meaning. We no longer live under British or Roman-Dutch law [the common law of South Africa]. We live in a new dispensation, and a person can be shut away for ninety and more days, and can be released without a stain on his character, except that he may have lost his job and his friends and his reputation.

I should like to combat strongly the view that if you are a law-abiding person, you have nothing to fear. It simply is not true. It is a smoke screen, behind which many people can hide who are uneasy in their consciences.

* Secretary of the Pretoria Liberal Party until she was banned in October, 1963.

Not long ago a leading member of the Liberal Party died in Northern Natal. At his funeral another leading member was taken away for questioning. He had broken no law. He could have been taken away on any other occasion. But he was taken away on this particular occasion, so that as many people as possible could see that it was dangerous to belong to the Liberal Party.

In March, Mr. Christopher Shabalala was travelling by train in the Underberg district, on legitimate Liberal Party business. The police stopped the train in the middle of nowhere, and removed him in the sight of all the passengers. No charge was ever laid against him.

In April, a lorry conveying members to the Natal Provincial Conference was stopped at Mooi River. The driver, after questioning, decided not to proceed further. The names and addresses of all passengers were taken, and many were later visited and questioned. No charges were ever laid against them.

It may be true that no person has been condemned for expressing a point of view or giving expression to an inner conviction, but it is also true that many persons have been punished, inconvenienced, harried, humiliated for precisely that reason.

Let no one believe that the terrible powers of the state are meant to frighten only the law-breakers. They are meant to frighten us all.

SOMETHING TO BE PROUD OF*

In the following essay, Paton concerns himself with the rank-and-file Liberal Party members who did not waver in their support of the party in the critical days of 1964, when the Government intensified its campaign against party members, police detentions became frequent, and the list of the banned grew steadily longer. As Paton points out, it was heartening to the Liberals that former Senator Edgar

* *Contact,* VII, No. 12 (October 23, 1964), 2.

Brookes, a man of unimpeachable reputation, accepted the post of National Chairman when Peter Brown was banned on July 30, 1964.

IT HAS NO doubt come as a great shock to many members of the Liberal Party to find that a number of their colleagues and ex-colleagues have been charged with sabotage and conspiracy. Some of the more innocent among us imagined that recent police detentions were solely motivated by the wish to intimidate the party, and it has come as a shock to realise that many (or all, who knows?) of these detentions were made for a more serious purpose.

I think by now enough has been said of the actions of members of the party who commit or conspire to commit sabotage. I should, however, like to point out, as I did at our annual conference in Johannesburg, that many Afrikaner patriots would have reacted in the same way had they been subjected to humiliating racial laws by their British conquerors. There is no essential difference between the patriotism of a Robert Sobukwe [imprisoned leader of the Pan-African Congress] and a Daniel François Malan [Afrikaner nationalist, former Prime Minister, 1948–54], except that the first was fighting white supremacy and the second only British supremacy, and, what is more, a British supremacy that was losing belief in itself.

But that is not my subject today. My theme is a much more heartening one, and that is the way in which the party itself has reacted to this crisis. Some of its members have shown a courage and a charity towards others which are in a way beyond praise, because when one contemplates them one would rather be silent, as an audience is when a work is too sublime for applause. The Liberal Party is not a religious party, but such charity is worthy of the highest religion.

A few people have defected from the party in this crisis, and this in spite of the statements issued by Edgar Brookes and myself. Of their action I have little to say, being in the mood to extol courage rather than other qualities. All I have to say to these defectors is that they may now be able to join a more successful party (though this I think doubtful in the highest degree) but they will not be able to join a more courageous one. But perhaps in politics courage is a dubious virtue.

I want also to pay a tribute to Edgar Brookes. He could hardly have taken over the chairmanship at a more critical moment, nor at one less advantageous to himself. He has actually assumed responsibilities that he did not himself incur. His public image—that disgusting phrase—has certainly not been improved, and he has more of a reputation to lose than most. He has proved a tower of strength to us all. With his name I couple that of Leo Marquard, who has become one of our vice-presidents. Lucky we are to have two men who understand so deeply the real meaning of the present scene.

There is another heartening thing to be commented upon, and that is the courageous conduct of our African members, who though subject to intimidation and interference on an ever increasing scale, remain loyal, and openly loyal, to the Liberal Party.

Let me say a word to the membership at large. Whatever kind of political party we are, it is not an orthodox one. Whatever anxieties burn us, let us remember that we belong to a party which, when it is facing danger and crisis, does not indulge in fears and recriminations, but bears itself with a humanity of which any society can be proud.

PETER BROWN*

Liberal Party National Chairman Peter Brown was banned for five years on July 30, 1964. His ban prohibited, among other things, attendance at any political or social gathering and compiling or publishing of any document. An issue of

* *Contact*, VII, No. 10 (August 28, 1964), 2.

Contact printed that day had to appear with a statement by Brown inked out. Further restrictions were imposed on Brown in 1966. See also "A Man Called Brown," pages 142–44.

I ONCE SAID, at a meeting held in the Pietermaritzburg City Hall during the emergency of 1960, that in another country Peter Brown would be sitting, not in prison, but in a seat of high authority.

One can say in 1964 that in another country Brown's influence would not be restricted, but would be growing and expanding, to the benefit of his country and its people.

Was Brown planning violence? Was he preaching violence? Was he condoning the preaching of violence by others? He was not banned for any of these things.

Brown was banned—in my view—not only because he was our National Chairman, but also because of his close links with moderate African opinion. He exercised a great influence over it, not because he is white, but because he is trusted and respected, and I might add, loved. Many of our members are not rich in this world's goods. I shall always think that one of the finest tributes that can be paid to Peter Brown, and to his wife, Phoebe, is that these members felt no constraint in that big house on the hill, because they knew they were welcome and wanted. One cannot say that for many places in white South Africa.

How often are Liberals condemned for their disloyalty to what is loosely called "South Africa"? How can one feel any loyalty to a ruling caste that does not know what to do with the honesty and sanity of a Peter Brown except to shut him up for five years? How can one feel loyalty to a clique that has decided that if a man believes in building bridges across the gulfs that separate race from race, he must at all costs be prevented? For that is the truth, is it not? Is it not true that if you are a trusted Nationalist, pledged to racial separation, you may have as many interracial contacts as you like, but that if you are a believer in racial integration, your every effort will be watched by the security police, and, if necessary, you will be banned.

Is it not true that you can speak about racial cooperation at all-white Rotary luncheons, and all-white congresses, but that if you speak about it at mixed luncheons and mixed congresses, you are heading for trouble?

The Liberal Party is living through difficult times. They are likely to become more difficult if it can be shown that some of its members have engaged in activity contrary to the policies of the party. It will be said—with anger and hatred by some—that despite our protestations, we are seen to be a party of violence.

In such a time we shall greatly miss the steady hand of Peter Brown. He would have inspired confidence by that extraordinary sanity of his. He would have condemned the use of violence, not only as wrong but as senseless; but he would also, in that astonishing way of his, have made it clear and incontrovertible that ordinary decent people do not turn to violence unless they have reached some point of despair. And he would have laid a great share of the blame at the door of this country's Government, which, in sixteen years, by passing a series of provocative and often cruel laws, has created a situation unlike anything that was known before, where the papers are daily full of news of sabotage, detentions, refugees, torture, and allegations of torture.

How easy it is for white South Africa to blame China, the English Press, NUSAS, Communism, and the Liberal Party for all its troubles, and by so doing hide from itself its own direct and indubitable responsibility!

Edgar Brookes and I have already issued a statement which says that we, though not possessing Peter Brown's gifts (we have gifts of our own of course) or his advantages, will endeavour to emulate his wisdom and sanity. This we shall certainly try to do. Now on behalf of the party I extend our heartfelt thanks to Edgar Brookes for stepping into the breach and taking on the acting national chairmanship. We are all the more grateful because he could not have done it at a more difficult time, and because he is what is called a "retired man"!

If I may repeat yet another clever saying of my own, let me remind our acting National Chairman that I once said of him at a public meeting (he had spoken for some time, I must admit), "men may come and men may go, but Brookes goes on forever."

JOHN HARRIS*

> John Harris was a schoolteacher and a member of the Transvaal Executive of the Liberal Party until he was banned in February, 1964. He also belonged to a small, mainly white, group of young intellectuals called the African Resistance Movement (ARM). On July 24, 1964, he planted a bomb in the concourse of the Johannesburg railroad terminal. Numbers of people including children were seriously injured in the explosion, and one woman died. He telephoned the police and newspapers a few minutes before the explosion, expecting the concourse to be cleared; he said he was the sole member of ARM not in prison at the time and that he intended a spectacular demonstration as a means of bringing about a change of government. On November 6, 1964, he was sentenced to death. After appeals and petitions for clemency had failed, he was executed on April 1, 1965.

THE EXECUTION of John Harris on Thursday, April 1, brings to a close one of the saddest episodes in South African history. A young man of promise caused the death of one person and inflicted injuries on others, lost his own life, and brought unhappiness to many people, without advancing his own cause in any way whatsoever. On the contrary, he did it incomputable harm.

By temperament and principle I am opposed to the use of violence. By intellectual conviction I am opposed to its use in South Africa, believing that it will not achieve its declared purpose of mak-

* *Contact,* VIII, No. 4 (April, 1965), 2–3.

ing this country happier and better. It is on this second premise—
the intellectual rather than the moral—that I wish to base this
article.

The use of violence by John Harris was regarded by many with
the utmost horror, and by many with the utmost fury. Yet, in fact,
the use of violence is a commonplace in history. If violence is used
in a revolution, and the revolution succeeds, the users of violence
become heroes. One forgets the dead and injured. I have pondered
over the question as to whether John Harris thought he was acting
in a revolutionary situation where great changes were imminent.
If so, he paid a very heavy price for his miscalculation. So did those
who are now serving long prison sentences for sabotage.

If we are not in a revolutionary situation—and I believe we are
not—then the use of violence, quite apart from any moral consideration, is futile. Our racial problems are difficult enough. The
use of violence would only make them more difficult. Mutual fear
is bad enough, but mutual hatred is worse. That mutual hatred
already exists is doubtless true, but to increase it would be intolerable. And the best way for us to increase it is to use violence
against one another. This is a lesson for both rulers and subjects
to learn.

These views that I am expressing were unpalatable to some of the
younger generation. They desired with all their hearts to reform
the South African society, and they were right. But they chose a
method which had no hope of success.

John Harris had a burning wish to remove the injustices and
cruelties of *apartheid.* He made a notable contribution to the cause
of nonracialism in sport. He was militant in his crusade, and was
finally banned. One can only guess at the depth of the frustration
that could cause an intelligent young man to think that he could
change the heart and mind of this Government by doing what
he did.

Many of those who were enraged by Harris' act have convenient
memories. Many of them supported actively or passively the *Osse-*

wabrandwag, which would have overthrown the Government by violence, and would have plunged the country into bloodshed and civil war if it had had a chance of success.* One of its members, a certain van Blerk, exploded a bomb in the Benoni post office, and killed a bystander. For this he was sentenced to death, but the Governor-General [Sir Patrick Duncan] commuted this to a life sentence, presumably at the instance of Smuts. When Malan came to power, van Blerk was released. The clemency which Smuts, and later Malan, showed to van Blerk could well have been shown by this Government to John Harris. Mercy is an attribute not of weakness but of strength.

There are redeeming elements in this tragic story. One is the courage and dignity with which Ann Harris conducted herself throughout her long ordeal. Those who read her account of her life with her husband will not easily forget it. It is a noble and moving document.

Nor will one easily forget the courage and generosity of the Hain family.† They made a home for Ann Harris and her infant son the moment the arrest became known, and were her comfort and support throughout those terrible months. One need not say what construction cruel people put upon this act. The Hains disregarded such malice; they saw a job to be done, they thought it right to do it, and they did it well. These words apply equally well to Ruth

---

* The *Ossewabrandwag* (Ox-Wagon Fire Watch) was a pro-Nazi paramilitary organization of Afrikaner nationalists whose "storm troopers" carried out planned acts of sabotage directed against the South African war effort, particularly during 1942. The present Prime Minister, B. J. Vorster, and several present cabinet ministers were members of the *Ossewabrandwag.* In February, 1942, one of its storm troopers, van Blerk, exploded a bomb in the post office at Benoni (Transvaal), which killed a woman bystander. His death sentence was commuted to life imprisonment on appeal. He was released immediately after the Nationalist election victory of 1948, and his story was featured in the popular Afrikaans-language magazine *Dagbreek* "not as one of violence and sabotage, but as one of Afrikaner patriotism."

† Adelain Hain had been Secretary of the Pretoria Liberal Party until she was banned in October, 1963; Walter Hain had been its Chairman until his banning in September, 1964.

Hayman,* who applied herself to her tasks with characteristic un-selfishness and zeal.

In this crisis, and in the other crises of 1964, the Liberal Party behaved itself in a way that it can be proud of. It condemned the deeds, and it forgave the doers. One cannot do better than that.

* Transvaal Vice-Chairman, banned in April, 1966.

III. In the Face of Adversity

*LIBERALS REJECT VIOLENCE**

In this presidential address to the national congress of the Liberal Party, held in Johannesburg in October, 1964, Alan Paton assesses the effects of the banning and detention of Liberals, the attempt to discredit liberalism by associating it with sabotage, and the fear and hatred of liberalism that prompted "such savage steps" to be taken against an organization with so little power. This national congress elected former Senator Edgar Brookes as National Chairman to replace Peter Brown, who had been banned in July.

WE MEET, as you all know, at a critical time in the life of the Liberal Party and liberalism. And we meet at a critical time in the history of white South Africa, and these two crises cannot be separated.

Liberalism is in crisis, but it is only in crisis because white South Africa is in crisis. This is a tremendous subject, but it is the subject I have chosen to deal with tonight. I have not come all the way to Johannesburg to avoid the most crucial issues. I have not come all this way to pretend that the bannings of Peter Brown and others are the only cruel blows that have fallen on us. I am going to dis-

* *Liberal Opinion*, III, No. 4 (October, 1964), 1–4.

cuss these other matters in so far as it is proper to do so. I have always recognised in the past that a member of a party, even if it is a party that champions liberty and individualism, is not free to do or say anything in a purely individual capacity. Still less is a president. But a president also has other duties. He is not merely a mouthpiece of his party; he is also out there in front, whether he likes it or not, whether he merits it or not. So on this occasion I am going to speak openly and freely. Some of you may not like everything I am going to say. But whatever I say is said as a party president whose first responsibility is to his party.

Any person who, while a member of the party, plans to use violence against things or persons is not only guilty of an offence against the law, he is also guilty of grave disloyalty to the Party. Above all, any person who calls himself a liberal and who plans violence against persons is not really a liberal at all. He may burn against injustices to others, and burn to set them right. He may be a zealot. He may be dedicated to his cause. But he is not a liberal. And what is more, if he persists in his plans, he is likely to do grave damage to the whole cause of liberalism; how great such damage might be is at the moment impossible to predict.

If I stopped there, if I said no more, I should be failing in my duty as a liberal and a president of a liberal party. It may comfort shallow and fearful people if they place the whole blame for violence on those who commit it. It is comforting to believe that *apartheid* would have been a glorious success if only people had not opposed it. And it is doubly comforting when those people are believed to be wicked persons, whereas oneself is almost without sin. One is able to see oneself as the great defender of good against evil. And this is the comfort that many a white South African lays to his soul. Yet it is utterly false. It bears no relation to the facts at all. The primary cause of sabotage is not the saboteur. The primary cause of sabotage in South Africa is the policy of *apartheid*, whether it is called by its old name of *baasskap,* or its new name of separate development. When persons who would normally have led law-abiding lives are tempted to resort to violence, especially when they themselves are temperamentally unsuited to use violence, and when they risk the destruction of their careers, the end or the virtual end of their lives as husbands and wives and parents, then one realises the depth and strength of the compulsions that are at work. A good government does not force its citizens to such extremes.

I do not presume to speak about the inner stresses and strains that go on in the minds of saboteurs. But I can speak with authority about the external causes. What self-respecting Afrikaner nationalist would have consented to a job-reservation law that debarred Afrikaners from certain occupations? What self-respecting Transvaal or Free State Afrikaner would have consented to a law which controlled his movements into Natal and the Cape Province? What would Afrikaner nationalists have done if the Nationalist Party had been banned? What would they have done if they had suffered the detentions, the banishments, the bannings, which they have inflicted on others? There have been many trials in this country of people who have carried on the work of banned organisations, but the Afrikaner nationalist would have done the same. There is no essential difference between a Sobukwe and a Malan, except that one succeeded and one did not. While I condemn the use of violence in this country, I understand why some people are under a compulsion to commit it. And I ask myself, what would I have done if I had been thirty years younger. Would I have been a Leibbrandt or a van Blerk?* I do not know. And because I do not know, I can but guess at what lies behind the terrible decision to

---

* Leibbrandt was an Afrikaner nationalist, a boxer, and a member of the South African police who joined the German Nazi Party in the late 1930's. He was landed in South Africa by submarine as a saboteur during World War II, captured, and convicted of treason. His death sentence was commuted to life imprisonment; within hours after Dr. Malan's 1948 election victory, he was released and restored, with higher rank, to the police force. For the van Blerk story, see "John Harris," pages 213–16.

risk the destruction of one's life, one's career, one's home, one's happiness, and the happiness of one's wife and children. And I can but say, "Thank God it didn't happen to me."

There is one thing of which the Liberal Party can be proud, that in these recent years of bannings and intimidations, and in these recent anxious months of detentions and arrests and charges, there have been no defections. I recall with pride tonight the actions of the Liberals who showed such concern for those who were in desperate need, not forgetting the wives and children of those who were detained and arrested. I shan't go into detail about this, but you will know what I am talking about. And I am proud of those African members who are here tonight, in spite of all the bannings.

There is another point I want to make quite clear tonight. Sabotage may still be used to discredit liberalism. Yet the fear and hatred of liberalism must be distinguished from the fear of sabotage. Peter Brown was not banned because he encouraged and countenanced sabotage. He was banned because he believed in and propagated an idea which is dangerous to *baasskap,* the idea that South Africa has only one destiny, the idea that South Africa is one society, and the idea that every South African should participate in the government of his country, and that so long as he does not, he will continue to suffer the cruelties of Job Reservation, of race classification, of influx control. Why does liberalism arouse such hatred in the nationalist heart? Is it because it threatens civilisation, or because it threatens *baasskap?* Why are such savage steps taken against a relatively powerless organisation? It is because it holds a powerful idea, a powerful idea that will in the end bring crashing down the whole structure of *baasskap,* with its gross inequalities of wealth and privilege. And it ought to be brought down too. It is no doubt true that the standard of living has risen for all in South Africa, but the shocking disparity between white and nonwhite income remains. There can be no lasting peace for this country until an active programme is launched to distribute more equitably the wealth of our country.

It may be true that many of our African citizens enjoy a higher standard of living than is enjoyed by many citizens of other African countries. The aim of the Liberal Party is not to keep ahead of other African countries; its aim is to ensure the more equitable distribution of wealth and privilege here at home. And we think it can be done. We believe that the rate of economic expansion in South Africa, spectacular as it is, could be made even more spectacular if the racial and economic barriers were removed, that we could have an industrial revolution here that would, without totalitarian control and interference in the lives of citizens, strike a death blow at poverty.

This present crisis, of which Liberals are most intensely aware, is in fact a crisis of us all, a crisis of freedom. It is not only liberalism that faces a crisis, but every kind of nonconformity, whether of politics, religion, or literature. Every kind of opposition is facing the crisis. Take the most recent example. The Nationalists, disliking the idea of being on the same electoral roll as Coloured people, ordered them to be put on a separate roll; but the Nationalists, disliking equally the idea of sitting in the same Parliament as Coloured people, ordered them to be represented by white persons. Now comes along the Progressive Party, prepared to use this form of representation created by the Nationalists. But Dr. Verwoerd is outraged; he warns the Progressive Party not to "interfere" in nonwhite politics.* How then may a white person solicit the support of Coloured voters? There is only one answer. He must be a Nationalist.

I give the reply of the Liberal Party to Dr. Verwoerd's warning. We have no intention whatever of heeding it. We are not a "white" party, and we do not recognise "nonwhite" politics. We recognise only one politics, and that is the politics of South Africa, and that means how to create a society out of our diversity of peoples. We intend to pursue this course as long as we are able.

It is time white South Africans awakened to the direction in which Dr. Verwoerd, this benevolent and smiling man, is leading

* See "No *Genade* at Genadendal," pages 237–40.

them. He is promising them security at the expense of everything that makes life worth living. He tells us that the race question is disappearing from the scene, and this in a country where Sobukwe is jailed indefinitely,* where Mandela is jailed for life, where Luthuli is confined, where hundreds are in prison for continuing political activities, where Matanzima is fêted on the very reef where not one of his own people has any real liberty,† where Indian barmen are thrown out of their jobs because their occupation has been reserved [restricted to whites], where a white person who is reclassified as Coloured has no grounds of appeal unless he does it in thirty days.

Where are we going? We have recently witnessed the unedifying spectacle of leading Rotarians assuring the Prime Minister that they stand foursquare behind the Government. What business is it of Rotary to support any government? These leaders have degraded the ideal of Rotary, and their motto should be "subservience before self."‡ In any case, Rotary itself suffers from a lie in the soul, because it is a colour-bar society in an international organisation, like the International Arts League of Youth, which is a colour-bar society with an international name.

I not only ask where we are going. I ask where Dr. Verwoerd is going. Is he losing his grip on himself? Is it not a fantastic thing that Dr. Verwoerd, when he is so anxious to unite white people, should write to the Methodist church in such insulting language? And why does he do it? Because he is beside himself to think that after sixteen years of Nationalist rule, the Methodist church of

---

* In 1960, Robert Sobukwe was sentenced to three years in Robben Island Prison. Since the expiration of the sentence imposed by the court, he has been kept in prison under powers conferred on the Minister of Justice by the General Laws Amendment Act of 1963. Parliament has concurred in yearly extensions of these powers, and, since Mr. Sobukwe is the only person so detained, this special legislation is known as the Sobukwe Law.

† Chief Kaizer Matanzima, who supports separate development, is Chief Minister of the Transkei, the self-governing Bantu "homeland" for the Xhosa ethnic group. He paid an official visit to his Xhosa constituents in the industrial and mining centers surrounding Johannesburg (the gold-bearing reef) in September, 1964. See "The Ndamse Affair," pages 240–43.

‡ The Rotary motto is "Service Above Self."

South Africa should dare to elect an African as its President.* But the Methodist church is in crisis itself, as indeed all Christian churches are in South Africa. Congratulations to the Diocese of Pretoria on its decision to do away with racial discrimination in stipends [for its clergy]. But the other dioceses, and the other churches, as well as the Methodist church, have a long way to go. When people stand aside and pity or execrate the Liberal Party, let them remember that their own crisis is no less grave. What could be graver than the crisis of the Dutch Reformed church, which, though a Christian church, affirms the colour bar, not merely within society but within the church? The Prime Minister levels the charge of hypocrisy against the Methodists. The truth is that the charge can be levelled against all humanity, and not least against the Prime Minister himself. The important thing is not whether people and organisations are hypocritical, but whether they know they are and try to be less so. The Liberal crisis is merely the white spot that indicates the presence of a monstrous suppuration throughout the whole body politic. This is not primarily a crisis of law and order caused by saboteurs; it is primarily a crisis of freedom caused by *apartheid*.

I quote from the *Christian Recorder* of today:

If this noble spirit of liberal thinking and liberal living passes from the South African scene, we have harmed the future, almost beyond repair. We will have educated and shaped a generation, perhaps two, without any knowledge of the liberal spirit in their education and growth. That means that in 10 or 15 years' time, we will have a crop of adults who have no knowledge of the proper relation between freedom and responsibility, so important for the happiness of a nation and its people.

These are important words. The editorial goes on, "we look to the churches to maintain that high religion which causes the liberal spirit to flower." Well, that is a challenge, because sometimes

---

* The Methodist church, which is the denomination having the largest following among Africans in South Africa, elected the Reverend Seth M. Mokitimi as its President in 1964.

churches try to maintain the "high religion," but they don't want "the liberal spirit to flower." I am reminded of Samuel Butler, who said it was the greatest wish of English parents that their children would learn Christian principles, and their greatest fear that they would live by them. We don't need lip-service to the liberal spirit; we need people who will live by it.

That's what we need, men and women who will live by the liberal spirit. The days are dark, and I think Dr. Verwoerd and Mr. Vorster will make them yet darker. But I think it is a good sign that the Prime Minister is provoked into insolence by the presence of nonconformity. It shows—whatever the omens may appear to be—that liberalism is a powerful force, much more powerful than its proponents. Never forget that. The ideas don't die, and they live in you. And while they live in you, there's hope for our people and our country.

IDEAS NEVER DIE*

The year 1964 was a critical one for the Liberal Party. Many of its younger leaders were banned, and about thirty-five others were imprisoned under the Ninety-Day Law. Some young banned members, in frustration, resorted to violence and, in so doing, aided the Government's drive to associate liberalism with subversion. In his New Year message for 1965, Alan Paton reminds Liberals that "the very vehemence of these [Government] attacks is to me a proof that the Nationalists fear something that exists even within themselves."

PEOPLE, IN MY circles at least, have become self-conscious about wishing their friends a happy New Year. They qualify their wishes. Some wish their friends a "happier New Year." Some say wistfully, "May the New Year be happier for us all." Some say nothing at all.

* *Contact,* VIII, No. 1 (January, 1965), 2.

I used to think that it was the older people who felt this reluctance, because the griefs of the world weighed more heavily upon them, because the excitements of falling in love and having children and making a career saved younger people from other preoccupations. But after 1964 I can no longer believe it. The events of last year were catastrophic for many young people, and that was largely because of their concern for justice.

I should like, therefore, not to wish my readers a conventional happy New Year but to write about those things that will be as true in the New Year as ever they have been, ideas that will be as valid in the New Year as in the Old, however much this may appear to be untrue.

There is a saying that ideas are powerful, that some indeed are invincible, beyond all control of rulers. I believe this is true. I know that the lazy and the timid can shelter behind this belief, and leave all progress to be brought about by the ideas themselves. I know that the impatient want to boost the ideas along, by means ranging from persuasion to revolution. It is largely when persuasion appears to fail that the impatient turn to revolution.

In the first place I want to say that the ideas and values for which the new liberalism has stood in South Africa are as valid in 1965 as they were in 1964. There is only one foundation on which the new South Africa can be built, and that is the equal participation and recognition of all South Africans. That means the abolition of the colour bar, the death of *apartheid,* and political and economic equality.

Nothing that happened in 1964 can alter these truths, and nothing that happens in 1965 can do so either. They are the very fundamentals of liberal belief; they are embodied in the policies of the Liberal Party; they are inseparably associated with *Contact.*

These truths and ideas live in people. They have no independent being of their own. *They live in us.* And they live in a lot of other people, some known, some not known to us. While they go on living in us, they are transmissible. It is only if they cease to live in us, and to inform our lives, that they will be in danger of dying out.

Under the circumstances in which we live, it happens often that we despair of the power and durability of these ideas and values. We have a low opinion of ourselves, of our failure to win public support. Often to us it seems that liberalism and liberals are in continuous and ignominious defeat.

There are two reasons for believing this not to be so. One is the fact that many people abroad think that we are performing the only duty open to us, by steadfastly refusing to make our truths and values conform to those of our rulers, in spite of threats and intimidations.

I have a second reason for believing in the power of these ideas, and that is the fear that the Government has of them. We are at the moment fighting a desperate rear-guard action, many of our members have been silenced, and intimidation is rife. Nothing could seem weaker in some eyes than liberalism. Yet the Government calls repeatedly on its supporters to be on their guard against this insidious foe. The very vehemence of these attacks is to me a proof that the Nationalists fear something that exists even within themselves.

And if anything has strengthened these forces, if anything has called some of them out to show themselves openly, it has been the work and witness of the Liberal Party of South Africa.

LIBERALISM AND COMMUNISM*

The following essay was occasioned by a brief editorial, "*Contact* and Communism," in *Contact* of June 5, 1964. This editorial, after drawing attention to an account of *Contact* in the *Swiss Press Review and News Report,* which had stated that *Contact* was uncompromisingly anti-*apart-*

* *Contact,* VII, No. 8 (July 3, 1964), 2.

heid and also anti-Communist, went on to speak of the common aims of Communism and *Contact* in trying to bring about the end of *apartheid*. The Liberal Party officially dissociated itself from the views expressed in the editorial. The next issue of *Contact* contained a repudiation by Peter Brown as well as this one by Alan Paton.

THIS SEEMS the time to say something about liberalism and Communism, their common elements and their differences.

What is Communism? Like all words that become charged with emotion, it has become a dangerous word to use from the semantic point of view. In one aspect Communism believes in the elimination of gross inequalities, of hunger, of poverty, and privilege. In another it believes that this can be done only under the dictatorship of the proletariat, and that this dictatorship can only be achieved by a relentless class war. In another sense Communism believes in the exercise by the state of totalitarian power, the ruthless elimination of opposition, the employment of any means to achieve the desired end. In yet another sense, Communism—before it comes to power—is, in the eyes of the state, and certainly in the eyes of many conservatives and liberals, a destructive subversive force that is willing to destroy in order to build, and will, in the pursuit of its goal, destroy many things that conservatives and liberals and even some Communists, I believe, do not wish to be destroyed.

This account is both brief and inadequate, yet I go further in pursuit of brevity, and pick out two features of Communism which concern liberals most. These are, first, the socialist idealism of Communism and, second, its belief in the use of totalitarian power (until, of course, the state withers away). The first of these attracts many liberals. The second repels all liberals, except the most frustrated and desperate.

There is one other important fact to be noted. South African Communism has another strong element, and that is its detestation of race discrimination. It is this element, more than any other, and the courage with which discrimination has been fought that have evoked admiration and affection from many liberals, and above all have led them to treat with contempt the rabid anti-Communism which in this country is barely distinguishable from rabid white supremacy.

We should keep all these facts clearly before us. We should recognise the idealism in Communism and respect it, but we should not delude ourselves into believing that liberalism can have anything in common with Communism in its totalitarian aspect. We are pledged to cherish liberty and to bring about material betterment at the same time. To do so will be difficult, it will subject us to painful choices, but that is what liberalism means.

I believe that *Contact* fell last month into a semantic trap when it wrote, "both communism and this newspaper believe in universal franchise and majority rule." If *Contact* was writing of totalitarian Communism, it is very wide of the mark, for universal franchise and majority rule mean totally different things to a liberal and to a Communist (and they mean totally different things to *Contact* and to, say, Joseph Stalin). Can one really believe that Stalin's regime was majority rule? Nothing is gained by ignoring these differences.

I know that some people—not all of them Communists—deplore the fact that Liberals affirm a viewpoint that lies between Afrikaner nationalism and Communism. They call the Liberal Party "blunting the edge of revolution."

Such critics do not understand the relationship between politics and temperament. We cannot all become something else just to avoid division. In fact—for a liberal—the being of oneself is in the last resort more important than avoidance of division. Some people don't like such a truth, especially in critical times, but there it is.

And indeed one might say—in a somewhat high-flown kind of way admittedly—that the aim of a liberal state is to help people to be themselves, and not the tools of state or party.

MARQUARD ON LIBERALISM*

Leo Marquard, Vice-President of the Liberal Party, is a his-torian who has written a number of detached and balanced accounts of present-day South Africa including *The Peoples and Policies of South Africa* (3d ed.; New York and Lon-don: Oxford University Press, 1962). Paton's essay is a review of Marquard's pamphlet *Liberalism in South Africa* (1965), published by the South African Institute of Race Relations.

THEY SAY YOU can't get much for forty cents nowadays, but you can get fifty pages of Marquard for it. For less than one cent a page, you can get as sane and sensible stuff as anyone in South Africa can write. Mr. Marquard has a steady and steadfast mind, and to read him is to undergo a steadying experience. This is help-ful in times when so many South Africans, and in particular white South Africans, begin to doubt, amidst the blare of propaganda and, more importantly, amidst the threats which are made unceas-ingly against nonconformity, whether the things they believed in were really good things after all.

Mr. Marquard writes: "It is said that young Germans to-day, born after the fall of Hitler, who listen to records of his speeches, find it impossible to believe that their parents could have accepted his ranting irrationalities."

Mr. Marquard points out that this is because these young Ger-mans know freedom in a way that their parents had ceased to know it. Once freedom is lost, one can believe nothing. Therefore, even while one has freedom, one must be eternally vigilant to preserve it. Once freedom is lost, whether because one has pre-ferred security to it or whether because one has let it go because of one's fear of the state, the belief that suffers most is the belief in freedom itself.

* *Contact*, VIII, No. 8 (September, 1965), 5–7.

The new Afrikaner nationalists will of course declare that separate development means freedom for all, but when they are challenged with the bannings and banishments and ninety-day detentions, they will shift their grounds and declare that only Communists need fear the state. If they are then challenged with Peter
Brown, they will declare that Communism and liberalism are much
the same thing. Or they will shift their ground altogether, and say
that freedom is all very fine, but you cannot have freedom without
law and order, and to enjoy really exceptional freedom you must
have really exceptional law and order.

Professor van Selms* tells of a member of the French resistance
movement during the last war who shouted to the firing squad who
were about to execute him, "You fools! Don't you understand that
I am dying also for you?" Professor van Selms said of this man,
"Though fettered, he was the only free man present there."

Mr. Marquard is very clear and unequivocal when he writes about
the conflict between security and freedom. It is a very real conflict.
It is possible to believe that security is the prime essential, because
without it one cannot have freedom. It is also possible to believe
that freedom is the prime essential, because without it one cannot
have that psychological security which is essential to free life. Mr.
Marquard comes down heavily on the side of the second proposition.

Mr. Marquard is also very clear about the individual and the
state. Acton believed that the prime function of the state was to
make it possible for a man to live the good life. A person like
myself believes that one of the prime duties of the state is to protect its citizens against the powers of the state, as it does, for
example, when it appoints an ombudsman. But many white South
Africans think this is nonsense. The reason is that most of them

---

* Dr. A. van Selms, Professor of Theology at Pretoria University, is one of
the leading Dutch Reformed churchmen opposed to *apartheid* and a contributor
to the manifesto *Delayed Action,* in which eleven Dutch Reformed ministers
called on white South Africa to abandon its present social policy.

have no cause to fear material harm. Of the spiritual harm that is being done to them they unfortunately know nothing.

Are Mr. Marquard's ideas outmoded? Do they belong to the days when British gunboats kept the peace of the world? Is Mr. Marquard a square, while Mr. Vorster is very much with it, and unfortunately very much with us too? If this is true, then it is not only liberalism that has failed, but all belief in human reason, all belief in freedom, all belief in man. And that to me is not possible.

Why are the nationalists so cruel to their opponents? Why does Mrs. Verwoerd fear for the Afrikaans language?* Why this almost desperate fear of liberals and liberalism, when the Government exercises almost a totalitarian power? And why is this fear mentioned day by day, when this is obviously not psychologically sound?

The answer is simple. Whatever liberals and liberalism may be enduring now, and whatever they may have to endure in the future, the belief of liberalism in freedom, in individuality, in rationality is indestructible, because these are fundamental to the establishment of any reasonable society, and fundamental to any concept of the dignity of man. Any lesser belief, therefore, has need to be afraid.

DEFENCE AND AID†

The South African Defence and Aid Fund was established during the emergency period in 1960, to assist in the defense of persons charged with political offenses and to provide relief for their families when necessary. It was an outgrowth of the Treason Trial Defence Fund, of which Alan Paton was one of the sponsors. Defence and Aid grew into a national organization with offices in several cities. It published

---

* Afrikaner nationalists frequently express the fear that the purity of their mother tongue may be sullied by an infusion of "foreign" words or expressions. Mrs. Verwoerd's expressed fear that Afrikaans was endangered by a too liberal acceptance of "foreign" terms appears to Paton to be related to an irrational dread of liberalism.

† *Contact,* VIII, No. 6 (June, 1965), 2–3.

a monthly newsletter called *D and A*. It was not a branch of the Liberal Party, although many of its volunteer workers such as David Craighead and John Blundell were also members of the Liberal Party. Defence and Aid was banned, without trial, under the Suppression of Communism Act (Proclamation 77 of 1966), on March 18, 1966.

THE BANNING of Mr. David Craighead, the deportation with ten days' notice of Mr. John Blundell, and the decision of the Dutch Government to donate R20,000 [$28,000] to Defence and Aid have focused attention on this organisation. This is the time to remind people what Defence and Aid is, and what it stands for, but before I do that let me thank David Craighead and John Blundell for their work on behalf of justice and political prisoners, and wish the Blundells, on behalf of the Liberal Party, and many other people also, all good things for the future.

Luckily it is not my duty to attack or defend the Dutch Government. But one can derive a little pleasure from the fury of *Die Burger* and *Die Transvaler* [Afrikaans newspapers]. Let them writhe.

Is it true, as these and other papers allege, that the Dutch Government and Defence and Aid want to see subversive action, and that they encourage it by providing defence? I consider the allegation quite laughable.

Do people commit sabotage, and go abroad for military training, and continue political activity after their organisations have been banned, because they have a hope that they will be defended in the courts? I cannot believe it. They do these things for far deeper reasons, over which a Defence and Aid Committee has no control at all.

Is Defence and Aid committing an offence by defending political prisoners? Legally, no. Is it perhaps committing a moral offence? Some people say, "yes." These are the people who do not want a man defended if the offence with which he is charged is repugnant to them. They say that if a man is charged with sabotage, then simply let him not be defended. One cannot pay attention to the views of such people.

I have been closely connected with Defence and Aid for many years. It so happens that all Defence and Aid committees have been overwhelmingly composed of people to the right of those charged with offences. (This was almost 100 per cent true until 1964, when some members of the Liberal Party were charged with sabotage.) This fact is interesting, and there are profound psychological reasons for it, into which I cannot enter now. But it caused hysterical newspapers and hysterical persons to call the Defence and Aid committees cat's-paws of the Communists, and fellow travellers, and "unwitting" dupes, and a good deal else. Therefore I ask the question why Defence and Aid does the work it does, and why people came forward to do it, and what their attitude is towards these hysterical accusations. Of course I can only answer the question for myself.

I went into Defence and Aid for two simple reasons. The first is that, whatever else has been eaten away in South Africa, I should like to preserve the administration of justice from erosion as much as possible. I am a layman, but it appears to me that a prosecutor presses the charge, and that a defending counsel endeavors to rebut it, and that the judge is there, aided by these two officers of the court, to come to a just conclusion as to the guilt and degree of culpability of the accused person. It seems to me that this, what I call majestic, conception of justice is brought to nothing if the defence is absent or inadequate. It is to me a duty owing not only to the accused person, not only to the judge, but supremely to our society, that adequate defence should be secured in a society where passions are so intense, and where many white South Africans regard security as far more important than justice.

My second reason for going into Defence and Aid is also simple. Though I myself am not temperamentally attracted to sabotage and violence, and though I do not believe they will make our problems simpler, yet I understand why some people feel it their duty to act thus under the present circumstances. Furthermore, I regard the

Government and its laws as the primary cause of such action. There-fore, there is to me a strong desire to see that such persons are as justly—and as mercifully—dealt with as possible. I do not find such a desire reprehensible.

It is my recurrent thought that the political struggle of these South Africans bears a strong resemblance to that of the Afrikaner nationalists. If there is more violence today, it is because Vorster is in charge, not Smuts. Vorster can thank his lucky stars that he was detained under Smuts, not under Vorster. Now and then he alludes darkly to his sufferings, but he was never subjected to ninety days or kept standing for many hours on end, or compelled to rat on his friends. It is to preserve the pre-Vorsterian kind of justice that Defence and Aid exists, and it will carry out that task as long as it is able.*

* After Defence and Aid was declared a banned organization, on March 16, 1966, Dr. Raymond Hoffenberg, senior physician at the University of Cape Town Medical School and Chairman of the Defence and Aid Fund, applied to the higher courts for an order setting the proclamation aside. The Cape Ap-pelate Division and, later, a full bench of the Supreme Court in Cape Town dismissed the appeal. In August, 1967, one of the severest personal bans on record (described by an opposition MP as "civil death") was imposed on Dr. Hoffenberg. The Netherlands Government's gift of $28,000, mentioned at the beginning of this essay, was later transferred to the U.N. Trust for assisting persons charged under discriminatory legislation in South Africa and for relief of their dependents. Dr. Hoffenberg has, of late, become better known for his heart-transplant work at the Groote Schuur Hospital in Cape Town than for his political activities.

IV. Separate Freedoms

SOLVING OUR PROBLEMS*

"We must solve our own problems" is the commonplace South African response to any external criticism of that nation's policies. Repetition has given this phrase the status of an axiom. Nevertheless, criticism of South Africa has increasingly occupied U.N. attention. Since 1960, both the General Assembly and the Security Council have adopted a number of resolutions condemning *apartheid*. On December 4, 1963, the Security Council unanimously adopted a Norwegian resolution asking for an arms embargo and the establishment of a group of experts to consider what part the United Nations might play in "resolving the present situation" in South Africa. This group, under the chairmanship of Alva Myrdal, published its report in April, 1964. The report recommended, among other things, the calling of a fully representative national convention in South Africa as a first step toward devising more democratic institutions.

IT HAS GROWN expedient of late for white South Africans to say that we must be left alone to solve our problems in our own way. Any white person who suggests anything else is a near-traitor. I propose to put down my views on this proposition. I know it troubles quite a few people.

In the first place let me say that as far as love of country is

* *Contact,* VII, No. 6 (May 8, 1964), 2.

concerned, my love is for South Africa. I do not yearn to live in Bucks., Notts., Staffs., Yorks., Conn., Penn., or Mo. or Me., not even Miss. I don't want Nkrumah for my President, or Mao to control my destiny. I don't like living under Verwoerd, but I'd rather live under him than Mao, because I think Mao would kill me and Verwoerd wouldn't.

Can we solve our problems in our own way? I must honestly write that I see at this moment no likelihood of that whatsoever. There is only one proposition that white South Africa will consider today, and that is a policy of racial separation and authoritarian rule. I see no future for that either. If anything makes it impossible for us to solve things in our own way, it is *apartheid. Apartheid* is the one guarantee that the outside world will not let us alone.

If the outside world leaves us alone, will we solve our problems? I see no hope of that whatsoever. All I can see is more ninety days, more banning, more intimidation, more trials. It is a ghastly prospect. It appeals only to the trigger-happy nationalist who confuses cruelty with strength.

Do I see white South Africa undergoing a change of heart? I certainly do not, not until the threat of the outside world is inescapable.

Do I see white South Africans standing backs to the wall, and dying to the last man? I certainly do not. But I see them declaring their intention to do so until the very last moment—like a lot of ostriches playing a game of chicken.

Afrikaner zealots say that God made the Afrikaner nation, and that if it is His will, He will destroy it. Are there many of these zealots? My answer is, not so many as people think.

So that's the situation. The outside world—a big part of it—is determined to make white South Africans give a better life to their fellow citizens, and white South Africans are determined—and I write this with a full understanding of what I am doing—to give no more than they need to. It looks like an impasse. And so it is for the moment.

What happens next? There is one thing that will not happen,

and that is that white South Africa will get stronger and the out-side pressure weak. There is one thing that will happen, and that is that outside pressures will get strong and South African resistance weaker. The only real question is "How long will it be before this changing strength ratio begins to alter our whole situation?" I don't know the answer to that.

If one believes, as I do, that these changes are inevitable, then it is one's responsible duty to consider how one adapts oneself to them. I do not think it is sensible or loyal to continue along a path which Dr. Verwoerd believes leads to life and I believe leads to suicide.

I don't want to see the outside world enter South Africa by force and impose a solution on us by force. That I believe would be suicidal. It would let loose a flood of hatred and make responsible adaptation impossible.

I declare myself in favour of examining fully the proposals of the United Nations for a new national convention.

I declare my belief—and I do not expect all Liberals or liberals to agree with me—that the change-over from white supremacy to nonracial democracy may well get beyond our powers to engineer safely and that we will need help to bring it about. This help can come only from the United Nations.

Many people are appalled by the idea of a national convention, by the idea that centuries-old patterns of life will have to change, by the idea that the wealth of South Africa will have to be differently distributed. Let these people rather be appalled by the idea of revolution. Let them rather be appalled by the possible imposition of a solution in which they have had no say.

NO GENADE AT GENADENDAL*

Genadendal is a Coloured Reserve in the South Cape dis-trict where Coloured voters can elect whites to represent them in the Provincial Council and in Parliament. *Genade* is

* *Contact,* VII, No. 11 (September 25, 1964), 2–3.

the Afrikaans word for mercy or compassion, and Genadendal means Vale of Mercies. During 1964, the Progressive
Party decided to put up a candidate in this constituency for
the provincial elections. On September 8, 1964, Dr. Verwoerd informed the Transvaal Congress of the Nationalist
Party, "We cannot allow that white parties meddle in the
Politics of the Bantu, Coloured, and Indians." Dr. Oscar
Wolheim, one of the founders of the Liberal Party (1953),
who later joined the Progressive Party (1959), was the
latter party's candidate in the separate Coloured elections.
He sought permission from Minister of Coloured Affairs
P. W. Botha to address a meeting at Genadendal on September 12. Permission was refused in a letter informing him
of the Government's policy that the separate Coloured elections should be held "without interference from white-con-
trolled political parties."

DR. VERWOERD'S recent warning to the Progressive Party to keep
out of nonwhite politics must be regarded as an important mile-
stone in our social and political history. It is quite clear that the
Nationalists have now reached the point when they think no one
else but themselves must be allowed to have any relations with
nonwhite people. We always knew that they disapproved of such
relations, but now it appears that they are prepared to forbid them.
The whole thing is grotesque. It was the Nationalists themselves
who removed the Coloured people from the common voter's roll
and gave them a roll of their own and laid it down that Coloured
voters could elect representatives to Parliament provided they were
white; yet now the Progressive Party is being warned against using
the very instrument created by the Nationalists.

It is now being argued, in Nationalist circles in the north at
least,* that the establishment of a Coloured Affairs Board makes
"white" meddling in "Coloured" politics undesirable. The meaning
of this is clear. Parliamentary representation of Coloured people is

* Nationalist Party members from the northern provinces—the former Boer
republics of the Transvaal and the Orange Free State—traditionally favored more
stringent application of *apartheid* than their colleagues from the Cape Province,
usually known as the "Cape Nationalists."

on the way out and the Coloured Affairs Board will replace it. At long last Dr. Verwoerd is going to have his way. He never liked Coloured representation in Parliament. He is going to abolish it, and the Cape Nationalists, including Dr. Dönges, are going to give sickly grins and like it.

It is a logical step after all. It is the inevitable corollary of the Group Areas Act.

The Liberal Party has always rejected the notion of separate politics. This rejection follows immediately on its recognition of all South Africans as citizens of the one common country whose historic task it is, despite all omens, to work out a common destiny—something quite different in kind from a collection of so-called independent racial communities, all under the watchful eye of Big Brother.

It is because we rejected racial separation that we have been subjected to bannings, restrictions, and intimidations, but the Government hesitates to apply these methods fully to the Progressive Party. Furthermore, the Government is angry that the Progressive Party should have persisted in its policy of nondiscrimination after it had seen what had been done to the Liberal Party. There is no doubt whatever that the Government is angered by South Africans who now, after sixteen years, still do not accept the policy of racial separation. If the Government, therefore, is afraid to ban people like Jan Steytler, Helen Suzman, Donald Molteno, and Ray Swart,* it has only one recourse left and that is to restrict nonracial political activity by legislation. I have no hesitation in predicting that if the Progressive Party persists in its chosen courses, such legislation will be passed.

It is quite clear—and indeed it has always been clear—that the Government, and by that I mean the Nationalist Party, is determined that no white person save a Nationalist shall have any important relationships with any nonwhite person, but up till now it

---

* Leaders of the Progressive Party. Of the twelve members of Parliament who formed the Progressive Party in 1959, Mrs. Suzman has been the only one to retain her seat (Houghton, Johannesburg) in subsequent elections.

has not felt strong enough to legislate against it. Now it feels strong enough, largely because of the disorganisation of the African states, the weakness of the United Nations, and the entry of Red China onto the international stage, which has revived the flagging pro-South Africanism of the Western powers. Some think the Government makes such threats as this latest out of weakness. That is an oversimplified view. Such threats are made out of both strength and weakness.

I trust the Progressive Party will not be deflected one inch from its course. I may say of Coloured representation that it was an instrument that the Liberal Party decided long ago not to use [because it was an *apartheid* measure], but the Progressive Party has decided to use it and it must not be deterred by any threats; nor must it be deterred from taking an active interest in the affairs of the Transkei. Why should it not do so? Is not the Transkei part of our country, and is not its destiny intimately connected with our own?

It would be calamitous if the Government were to legislate against all nonracial political activity,* but it would be worse if South Africans were to desist from such activity because Big Brother has spoken.

THE NDAMSE AFFAIR†

Dr. Verwoerd's policy of separate development presumed that such ethnic groups as the Zulu, Tswana, Sotho, and Xhosa would develop as separate national entities in self-governing homelands (Bantustans). The Transkei is the home of the Xhosa people. It was granted limited self-government in 1963, with Chief Kaizer Matanzima, a supporter of separate development and Xhosa ethnic nationalism, as head of state. All Xhosa-speaking people throughout South Africa are presumed to be citizens of the Transkei. The

---

* Just prior to his assassination, Dr. Verwoerd prepared a bill for this purpose, the Prohibition of Improper Interference Bill.

† *Contact*, IX, No. 1 (January, 1966), 7–9.

constitution grants the Transkei Government independent control of agriculture, education, and welfare, but not of external affairs or national services. Many observers were skeptical of the degree of autonomy that would prevail under the terms of the Promotion of Bantu Self-Government Act.

It is not likely that Chief Minister Matanzima of the Transkei would want my advice or welcome my opinions. He regards Liberals as troublemakers, rogues, and even murderers. He and I are quite different in one fundamental respect—he is a Xhosa and I am a South African; and, of course, he is a powerful man and I am not.

Nevertheless I am going to proffer my advice and give my opinions, and this will be in regard to the appointment or rejection of Mr. Curnick Ndamse as Professional Assistant in the Transkei Department of Education.

Mr. Ndamse is a man of courage and strong opinions. While he was on the staff of Fort Hare University College,* he made certain criticisms, as he thought he was entitled to do, on the whole question of Bantu education. As a result of this action he was dismissed by the Council of the College, on the grounds that he was insubordinate and was guilty of academically reprehensible conduct. This incident reveals clearly the nature of academic freedom at Fort Hare.

Chief Minister Matanzima then decided that he would use Mr. Ndamse's gifts for the benefit of the Transkei, and he first appointed him to a post at the Jongilizwe College for the sons of chiefs, and later appointed him, or contemplated doing so, to the post of Professional Assistant. I do not know the full truth, but it is suggested that the Chief Minister did so against the wishes of the Commissioner-General, Mr. Hans Abraham, and against the wishes of white education officials, as he was fully entitled to do. This appointment was regarded as an affront to the Republic Government, which had already been antagonised by the Transkei Parliament's decision to

* A non-European institution located in the eastern section of the Cape Province.

discard Bantu Education and to introduce the official languages
[English and Afrikaans, in place of Xhosa] at an earlier stage in the
primary schools, so that ultimately most instruction, certainly that
in mathematics and science, should be given through the medium
of one of these languages if parents so desired. The schools welcomed this change, and voted overwhelmingly in favour of the use
of English. This decision naturally did not commend itself strongly
to a government and a party that is overwhelmingly Afrikaans-
speaking. The Republic Government then decided to take what can
only be described as an extreme step. The Republic Minister of
Justice, using the Suppression of Communism Act, served a banning
order on Mr. Ndamse, and this order, like most of its kind, forbade
Mr. Ndamse to enter any educational institution. In other words,
Mr. Vorster virtually made it impossible for Chief Minister Matanzima to appoint Mr. Ndamse as chief educational officer in the
Transkei.

Now under the Transkei constitution, the Transkei Government
has full control of education, while the Republic Government has
full control of internal security. It is now quite clear that this com-
partmentalisation has broken down, and indeed the entire constitution is full of these irreconcilabilities, as this paper and others
pointed out at the time. However I am not at pains to rewrite the
constitution. I merely ask the question "What should the Chief
Minister do now?"

Mr. Vorster's step was blatantly intended to make it impossible
for the Chief Minister to have Mr. Ndamse as Professional Assistant. We have no evidence that this action was contemplated before the appointment, and we have no evidence—in fact we never
do in such cases—that Mr. Ndamse was furthering the aims of
Communism. If he had been, the Chief Minister would never have
thought of appointing him.

Mr. Vorster's action is a direct and calculated challenge by the
Republic Government to the Transkei Government. The Republic
Government is virtually saying to the Chief Minister, "You are a
self-governing state, and amongst other things you are in complete

control of education, but we cannot allow you to appoint persons to educational posts who are unacceptable to us."

What is Chief Matanzima to do? He can of course insist on Mr. Ndamse's appointment, and intimate to the Republic Government that he would find the position intolerable if the banning order was not rescinded.

Failing that, there is surely only one course to take. It is to secure the unanimous support of the opposition party for a complete withdrawal from all legislative and administrative duties allotted by the constitution, and to allow the territory to revert to white control.

It is my belief that this would be regarded throughout the world as the act of a self-respecting people who were told they could govern themselves, and then found that they could not. It is my hope—though I do not expect this to be shared by the Chief Minister—that it would expose the sham of the Bantustan policy, and shake even the unshakable Dr. Verwoerd.

Out of such an action only advance could ultimately come. And it would be real.*

RHODESIA†

> Southern Rhodesia, technically a self-governing British colony, has a population of some 4 million, of whom 3.4 million are African, 250,000 are white, and the rest are Coloured or Indian. Although Africans have some representation, the white minority rules.
>
> At the time of the breakup of the Central African Federation (December 31, 1963), Britain was prepared to grant Rhodesia independence, but only on the basis of a new con-

---

* Seven months later, as a result of negotiations between the Transkei Government and the Republic Government, the ban on Mr. Ndamse was relaxed sufficiently to allow him to accept the post.

† *Contact*, VIII, No. 9 (October, 1965), 7–8.

stitution that bestowed real power on the African majority. The Rhodesian Front Party, led by Ian Smith, opposed this and campaigned for a unilateral declaration of independence (commonly called, in Rhodesia, UDI) unless Britain were willing to grant independence under the existing conditions of white domination. In the following essay, Paton uses South Africa's experience as his point of departure: In 1910, the British Parliament had accepted proposals for establishing the Union of South Africa that postponed the question of extending voting rights to Africans until after formation of the Union.

In 1910 Britain virtually gave independence to the new Union of South Africa. Although this independence was to become more complete with the passage of time, it was in 1910 that the crucial step was taken. By this act the Liberal Government in Britain put the destiny of the nonwhite people of South Africa into the hands of an all-white Parliament, and prepared the way for the destruction of the franchise and for the policies of separate development.

How then could it be expected that Britain would in 1965 give independence to Rhodesia? She made a tragic mistake in 1910, and she is determined not to repeat it. In this she will have the support of the liberals of South Africa.

What would happen if Rhodesia gained independence this year, either by seizing it or being given it? Mr. Wilson thinks there would be chaos, and he might well be right. But there is another possibility, just as unpleasant, and that is that the Government of Rhodesia would then follow the same course as was followed by South Africa; this course is not new to the Government, because it has already embarked on it. Already it has adopted the practise of detaining its most militant opponents. It has imposed on Mr. Garfield Todd (a former Prime Minister) what amounts to house arrest. It has deported some of its critics. Many white Rhodesians to-day believe that the World Council of Churches is Communist, that missionaries are Communist, that the Liberals are Communist; or if these groups are not Communist, they are furthering, wittingly or unwittingly, the aims of Communism. How familiar all this sounds!

If there is a UDI, the pace will be quickened. Individual liberties will be curtailed as in war, and this war will last as long as this naked white supremacy (for that is what it is) is able to endure. Opposition to the "will of the people" will become more costly. The methods of the South African security police will be more closely copied. Greater and greater inroads will be made into the rule of law.

The "liberal" attitude of white Rhodesia towards racial problems will also undergo change. This will be more difficult because white Rhodesia has, officially at least, expressed its rejection of *apartheid*. But back towards *apartheid* it certainly will move. It has already given the hint to the private schools, and has reacted strongly to the proposal for a nonracial hospital. It has tried to restore the authority of the tribal chiefs, and has refused to amend the Land Apportionment Act, a law which is not unlike our own Group Areas Act.

In fact, if Rhodesia is given time, it will not be very long before she is a second South Africa, but with several important differences. Her white population is only 5 per cent of the total population [as opposed to 20 per cent in South Africa], and the task of maintaining the essential services and at the same time of maintaining law and order is all the heavier. Furthermore, she has received grave warnings from great Western powers, something which has not happened to us as yet.

There is another great difference between the two situations. The percentage of white Rhodesians who would accept a lower standard of living is much smaller than the corresponding percentage of white South Africans. The inevitable economic recession will send white Rhodesians streaming from the country, and the tasks of maintenance will become impossible.

Mr. Smith will find independence a bitter fruit.

IN THE BLOSSOM-LAND*

> On November 11, 1965, Ian Smith proclaimed Rhodesia's unilateral declaration of independence (UDI). His move was strongly supported in South Africa. Although Prime Minister Verwoerd did not take the step of granting the new regime official recognition, he made it clear that South Africa would maintain close friendly relations with the Rhodesian Government. Sir de Villiers Graaf, leader of the United Party, urged the Government to recognize the new regime "to indicate the sympathy we feel for them."

I WROTE IN the [October, 1965] issue of *Contact* that Mr. Smith would find independence a bitter fruit. Apparently, however, when one first sinks one's teeth into it, the taste is pleasant. How else can one account for the state of euphoria in which, if newspapers are to be believed, white Rhodesians are living?

The white Rhodesians seem to believe that when the "nine days' wonder" comes to an end, Rhodesia will then proceed peacefully on its independent course, that new markets will be found, and that, after a period of tightening one's belt, prosperity will return.

It seems to me that white Rhodesia has no conception of the modern world. Mr. Smith has unleashed political forces of incalculable strength. It does not help for Dr. Banda to say that one white mercenary can take on a thousand Africans.† He also misunderstands the times.

Here in white South Africa the majority of opinion is pro-Smith and anti-Wilson. This is to be expected. Any Nationalist or United Party supporter is bound to be pro-Smith. But what both Nationalists and United Party supporters fail to understand is that Mr. Wilson is not merely a Labour man who is trying to hold on to power. He is the British Prime Minister, and the fate of Britain and the

---

* *Contact*, VIII, No. 10 (December, 1965), 7–9.

† Dr. Banda, as Prime Minister of Nyasaland, has followed a policy of open dealings with South Africa and Portugal. He rejects the possibility of military action against either the Union or the colony of Angola, and he does not support political independence for Africans across-the-board.

British Commonwealth depends on what he does. He is in a grave situation, and the confusion of the British electorate, and the confusion or worse of the Conservative Party, only makes his responsibilities more frightening.

Here in white South Africa, and in white Rhodesia too no doubt, Mr. Wilson is portrayed as the seller-up-the-river who has been routed by Mr. Smith in the shining armour of Christianity and Western civilisation. That is not the opinion of Professor Arthur Keppel-Jones [a noted South African historian] writing in the *Natal Mercury* of November 29, 1965. He writes: "The many millions who watch these events [on television] have not recognised in Mr. Wilson a dogmatic, uncomprehending Leftist; they have watched the emergence of a Lincoln." Those are strong words indeed and no one can lightly dismiss them. Let no one believe that Mr. Wilson has been routed.

If Mr. Wilson were to be routed, many white South Africans would be jubilant, not realising that the world had moved into a new era, where the white nations were finally ranged against the rest. This is the greatest danger that confronts us, and if Mr. Wilson were to back down, it would be brought decisively nearer. Who knows that better than Mr. Wilson himself?

It is encouraging to hear that the Catholic bishops of Rhodesia have now joined the other churches (except the Dutch Reformed Church) in condemning UDI. They have accused Mr. Smith of making a mockery of Christian and Western civilisation by claiming that he declared UDI to preserve it.

This pattern is already familiar to us. In South Africa parents are separated from children, wives are separated from husbands, workers are debarred from employment in the name of Christianity.

A few days ago I made my first acquaintance with a remarkable poem by Solomon Bloomgarden.*

---

* Solomon Bloomgarden (1870–1927) was born in Lithuania and emigrated to the United States in 1890. He wrote in English and Hebrew but mostly in Yiddish under the pen name Yehoash. This poem, translated from the Hebrew by Marie Syrkin, appears in Mark Van Doren (ed.), *An Anthology of World Poetry* (New York: Harcourt, Brace & World, 1929). Reprinted from the *Menorah Journal.*

In the blossom-land Japan
Somewhere thus an old song ran.
Said a warrior to a smith
"Hammer me a sword forthwith.
Make the blade
Light as wind on water laid.
Make it long
As the wheat at harvest song.
Supple, swift
As a snake, without a rift,
Full of lightnings, thousand-eyed
As the web that spiders spin,
And merciless as pain, and cold."
"On the hilt what shall be told?"
"On the sword's hilt, my good man,"
Said the warrior of Japan,
"Trace for me
A running lake, a flock of sheep
And one who sings her child to sleep."

Such a sword is UDI.

V. Out of the Depths

BEWARE OF MELANCHOLY*

In his address to the annual congress of the Liberal Party on July 12, 1965, Paton expressed the conviction that the Government had set out to destroy the nonracial Liberal Party by raids, arrests, and intimidation. "Beware of Melancholy" is his advice to fellow Liberals of all races caught in the frustration and depression of this difficult situation.

ALL THE VISITORS ask me—the American, the British, the Scandinavian—"What is the future?" They ask me as though I had some special knowledge. South Africans ask me too. Experience has taught me the answer, and the answer is "I do not know." At the moment it is possible to believe that nothing will change, that Afrikaner nationalism will never consent to any change that threatens its own position of power, however remote that threat may be. In its treatment of its enemies, it is becoming quite merciless. Those who openly oppose *apartheid* (or separate development, to give it its sweeter name) are going to suffer more, not less. It is plain to me that the only opposition that will be allowed to continue will be an

---

* *Contact,* VIII, No. 7 (July, 1965), 2–3. "Beware of Melancholy" was first published in the United States in *Christianity and Crisis,* XXV, No. 11 (November 1, 1965), 223–24. It is reprinted here by permission of *Christianity and Crisis;* copyright 1965 by Christianity and Crisis, Inc.

opposition that differs only in respect of the way *apartheid* is implemented. It is plain to me that ex-members of the banned organisations are going to face punishment even if they meet together as friends to discuss the events of the times. It is plain to me that the Government, believing that it has crushed subversive action, is prepared to move more ruthlessly into the field of ideas. In the eyes of the Government, if you are a member of a political organisation, and that organisation is banned, it is your plain duty to stop thinking politically. It is your plain duty, in fact, to change your character and personality, and if you do not, you will be put in prison. I have no doubt whatever that if the Government were to bring in a bill making it an offence to speak of separate development in a way considered by the Minister of Justice to be contrary to the public interest, it would be passed by a large majority, only Helen Suzman and a few others opposing.

There is another thing that is plain to me, and it is not a pleasant thing either. Any person who, at the expiry of his or her ban, picks up public life where he or she left it off will be banned again immediately. This person too has to change his or her character and personality, or has to accept a life cut off from the life of society.

The full meaning of a ban and the full legal implications of a ban have not yet been clearly established, but there is the shocking possibility that judicial interpretations will become stricter and stricter, and that ultimately a ban will be interpreted as meaning a complete severance of all personal relations outside the immediate family, if the banned person has one.

These facts are shocking. Much more shocking than [the recent] sex scandal and municipal corruption in Stellenbosch. In a way, I hesitate to write them down, but write them down I must, and look at them we all must, for this is the immediate future that I see.

For how long will this future last? My answer is "I do not know." To me there is another question: "How long can I last?" And there is still another question: "Is it worth trying to last?"

People answer this question in different ways. Some leave the country. Some leave politics. Some stick to their course, even if they expect certain consequences. And even this last group is diverse, for some would face *any* consequences and some would not.

What is my own answer to this question? I must give my own answer, because I would not dare to answer it for anyone else. I think it is worth trying to last. It is worth something to me, even if it apparently achieves little.

If someone were to ask me, "What would you and your wife do if you had young children?" I would answer, "We would have two choices: to stay here and to give our children a father and mother who put some things even above their own children's safety and happiness, or to leave and to give them a father and mother who put their children's safety and happiness above all else." Which would I choose? They are both good courses, are they not? I hope I would choose the first.

To those who want to stay, whether out of love or duty or just plain cussedness, I direct these few words:

Stand firm by what you believe; do not tax yourself beyond endurance, yet calculate clearly and coldly how much endurance you have; don't waste your breath and corrupt your character by cursing your rulers and the South African Broadcasting Corporation; don't become obsessed by them; keep your friendships alive and warm, especially those with people of other races; beware of melancholy and resist it actively if it assails you; and give thanks for the courage of others in this fear-ridden country.

THE LONG ARM OF PERSECUTION*

> Government intimidation and harassment led several Liberals, in 1966, to go into self-imposed exile. In the following essay, Paton writes of these and of those who remain behind. Adelain Hain, mother of four children, Secretary of the Pretoria branch of the Liberal Party, was banned in

* *Contact*, IX, No. 2 (March, 1966), 7–9.

1963; her husband, Walter Hain, Pretoria Chairman of the party, was banned in 1964. In 1966, they left South Africa. Ann Harris, who lived with the Hains during her husband's trial (see "John Harris," pages 213–16), also left the country. In 1965, Maritz van den Berg, who succeeded Walter Hain as Pretoria Chairman, received a "magisterial warning" of a ban if he continued political activity, and Ann Tobias, editor of *Contact* and Cape Province Vice-Chairman, was banned in 1964—each left South Africa. Although no accusation was ever brought against any of these banned Liberals, they, and others like them, could no longer carry out their normal occupations or live normal lives.

WHEN THIS IS published, or soon after, Walter and Adelain Hain and their children, Ann Harris and her small son, Ann Tobias, and Maritz van den Berg will have left South Africa to make a new home for themselves in Europe.

The Hains are going because Walter Hain, an architect, can no longer make a living in this country. Ann Harris is going because her son's future is her paramount consideration. Ann Tobias is going because she is the kind of young woman who must have a purpose to live for and the freedom to work for it, and finds life without them intolerable. Maritz van den Berg, a future architect, is going because his difficulties are much the same as those of Walter Hain.

There will not be a Liberal in the country who will presume to judge any of these, their colleagues and ex-colleagues, for their decision to leave their country. The Liberal Party has cause to be grateful to them for their work, and to admire them for their courage. We all wish for them that they find a use for their talents and a purpose for their lives, for that achievement after all is the nearest we get to happiness.

Why are they going? I have already given the immediate reasons. The antecedent reasons are that these Liberals challenged the Nationalist policies of *apartheid* and separate development, that they did not observe the ruling customs of *apartheid* either in their own lives or in the work of the party, and that the Government, with its almost absolute powers, so confined and restricted them that their lives became intolerable. That the creation of this intolerableness was as much the purpose of the ban as was the restriction can hardly be doubted. Nor can it be doubted that the making of life intolerable is one of the duties of the security police.

The Government has been cleared by the courts of the charge that its prisons are cruel,* but history will have no doubt as to its cruelty towards its political opponents (and in these I do not include the United Party, nor as yet the Progressives). Many of these opponents broke laws, notably those relating to the continuance of their political activities after these had been declared unlawful. The punishment for these offences goes far beyond anything that can be called just. But what is worse, persons are charged, say, with the offence of carrying on the work of a banned political organisation, and when they emerge after long prison sentences are charged with some second offence, such as collecting funds for a banned political organisation. This is not the long arm of the law, it is the long arm of persecution. At no time in the history of the nationalist struggle were its fighters subjected to such insatiable vengeance.

While it is not an offence to charge the Government and its laws with cruelty, it is regarded by many white South Africans as an act of treachery. They hold a kind of belief that if cruelty is bad, to denounce it publicly is worse. It is to me a fact of great significance that more than once recently, when anyone protested or began to protest against some abuse of power, a statement was issued warning people against perjury. And the chances are that if you make a hundred charges, and can only substantiate ninety-eight of them, that is exactly what you will be found guilty of.

* During 1965, there were many allegations in the press relating to cruel treatment of political prisoners. Several persons who made these allegations were charged with making false statements. One of these, prison warder G. J. van Schalkwyk, pleaded guilty when charged in the Johannesburg Regional Court, on August 16, 1965. He was convicted and sentenced to prison. Another, Harold Strachan, whose allegations had appeared in the *Rand Daily Mail*, was brought to trial in Durban on August 28, 1965, and convicted of supplying false information.

The majority of white South Africans no longer have any protest to make against the inhuman powers that are used in the defence of law and order. Some of these people are of the kind that like to see their enemies persecuted. Some are of the kind that so fear authority that they would never dare to criticise it. And yet others don't like being left out in the cold; they see the bandwagon driving past, with its noise and blare, and want to get on it as fast as possible. It is a human failing to want to belong, not to a party with principles, but to a party with power.

Who is mad? This white South African majority, or myself? I like to think it is not myself, or the Hains and their fellow victims. Whatever attraction there may be in separate development (and the fall of Nkrumah has done nothing to lessen this attraction), it cannot be carried out without cruelty. This cruelty is called petty *apartheid,* but there is nothing petty about it. It is unspeakable. And it is applied, not only to the unenfranchised and the disenfranchised, but to the enfranchised who oppose it.

May the day come when the Hains and our other friends can return to us, to help in the building of the nonracial and democratic society in which we most profoundly believe.

NATIONALISM AND THE THEATRE*

A proclamation of February 12, 1965, imposed a ban on the presence of members of more than one racial group in "any place of public entertainment." The proclamation prohibited mixed attendance at, for example, sporting or musical events without permit; it also prohibited mixed audiences or interracial casts in theater performances in privately owned halls. This proclamation caused great public confusion in the spheres of entertainment, cultural activities, and sport. The Johannesburg *Star* commented, on February 17, "There are almost as many opinions on the legal effects of the Gov-

* *Contact,* VIII, No. 3 (March, 1965), 2–3.

ernment's proclamation on mixed audiences as there are lawyers."

THE APPETITE of extreme nationalism is never satisfied. Its fears are never stilled. Its hates are never lessened. One might suppose that it would direct its hates against a few specific enemies, such as Communism, but it does not. In this country extreme nationalism never stops making enemies. It thinks nothing of attacking an ex-chief justice [the Honorable van de Sandt Centlives]. It turns on its own ministers of religion, and then accuses them of dividing the Church. It despises its best writers, excepting poets, whose work it does not understand.

Its enemies besides Communism are legion. Some of them are liberalism, the Black Sash, the Institute of Race Relations, ex-judges who enter politics (on the wrong side), NUSAS, the United Nations, any African politician who does not support the Government, the Russians, the Chinese, and the British Labour Party. It will be fascinating to see if our brilliant legal team at The Hague will be able to conceal this universal phobia, for to reveal it would be to place a powerful weapon in the hands of our accusers.*

Nationalism has two striking characteristics. It is cool and calculating in its *apartheid* strategy, which it conducts with skill so long as it remains cool. But it is also emotionally vulnerable in the extreme, and is capable of destroying some strategic gain with irrational anger. When it has just convinced some part of the world of the beauty of separate development, it shocks it by banning mixed audiences. When it has won over that obtuse man, Sir Stanley Rous,

---

* On July 18, 1966, the International Court of Justice rejected the case brought by Ethiopia and Liberia (as former members of the League of Nations) in respect of South Africa's administration of the mandated territory of South West Africa. The decision was reached on the technical grounds that individual member states had no power to institute actions in the Court in regard to the administration of a mandate. On the following day, July 19, the Liberal Party issued a statement, signed by Alan Paton and Edgar Brookes, which described the judgment as giving South Africa an "unexpected last chance to put her house in order." It added, "The natural sense of relief which many people feel must not lead them to think that this is an acquittal, much less an approval of South Africa's policies."

of the Federation of International Football Associations, it slaps him in the face by banning mixed crowds.* Its officials publicly turn away Coloured people from concerts at places from which they have never before been excluded. And all this, mind you, when our lawyers at The Hague are trying to convince the Court that separate development is the finest compound of love, justice, and duty that any government has ever devised. It is hard to conceive of a greater stupidity. But extreme nationalism just cannot help being stupid.

It should not surprise us when some of the enemies of extreme nationalism show themselves to be inimical. It should not in the least surprise us when overseas playwrights decide that they do not want their plays produced under such conditions. Extreme nationalism and its enemies sometimes come to blows; and then people who would rather not be involved get hurt.

Overseas playwrights have certainly dealt South African theatre a heavy blow. I have been asked whether I would not use what influence I have to get them to reconsider their ban. It is argued that it is not the producers, actors, and theatre-goers who want segregated audiences, but the Government. It is argued that producers and actors are only obeying orders.

Under no circumstances would I ask overseas playwrights to reconsider their decision. I myself do not wish any play of mine to be presented before segregated audiences. I have had to forgo the pleasure of having an actor like David Horner read my short stories from the stage, but I would choose to forgo that pleasure rather than have people excluded from the audiences on grounds of race and colour. South African producers and actors must learn a hard lesson. So long as we have *apartheid,* just so long must we pay a price for it, and one of the prices is cultural isolation. Our cultural isolation is growing, just like our sports isolation and political isolation. The more white South Africans who learn that lesson, the

* In 1961, the (soccer) Football Association of South Africa (FASA) was suspended by the Federation of International Football Associations (FIFA) on the grounds of racial discrimination. In 1963, this suspension was lifted after a two-man FIFA commission, headed by Sir Stanley Rous, visited South Africa.

better. The only white South Africans who won't care are the extreme nationalists, for to them culture and isolation are one and the same thing.

Better no theatre at all than colour-bar theatre.

ST. GEORGE DESERTS TO THE DRAGON*

J. S. Thomas, a prominent Coloured Anglican churchwarden, informed the 1964 synod of his church that he intended to enter his son at St. George's Grammar School (choir school of St. George's Anglican Cathedral, Cape Town) and his daughter at Herschel Anglican School for Girls. On January 28, 1965, the St. George's Council of Governors issued a statement declaring the application unacceptable: "while having every sympathy with the application now before the council, the custom and practice of the community together with the trend of legislation make the immediate admission of the boy unacceptable, and it is premature to try an experiment of this nature." The Dean of Cape Town, the Reverend E. L. King, dissented. The case drew national attention and was debated in Parliament. Government spokesmen distinguished between the kind of education provided by the Bantu Education Act, which offers education "suitable" for the Bantu, and the ordinary liberal education offered to nonwhites in mission-run schools, describing the latter as an attempt to make "imitation whites." For instance, on the same day that the Council of St. George's issued its statement, the Minister for Bantu Administration and Development, M. D. C. de Wet Nel, said in Parliament, with regard to the St. George's case, "The English Church tried to make an imitation of the white man. It tried to select certain black people and give them equality with whites, and thereby separate them from the masses of their own people. This can never be done successfully and is the reason the English Church is today hated and has difficulty in continuing its mission work." But, unlikely as it was that the government authorities would countenance a racially mixed An-

* *Contact,* VIII, No. 2 (February, 1965), 2.

glican school, Alan Paton felt the Council of Governors
should have gone on record to show that the Anglican
church would.

THE DECISION of the Council of St. George's Grammar School
not to admit the son of Mr. J. S. Thomas is a Christian scandal.
The fact that the decision was taken—so I understand—by a narrow majority is little cause for comfort. The fact that it was taken
at all is a disgrace to the Anglican church.

It horrifies me to think that this Council has in its keeping not
only the honour of a Christian school, not only the honour of a
Christian church, but also—in some degree at least—the future of
Christianity in Africa. For what non-Christian would be attracted
to a Christian church one of whose schools behaves in this un-
Christian fashion? And what will the young Coloured boys and
girls of Cape Town think of the church to which so many of their
elders have been devoted? It is hard to survey this havoc without
the most intense anger.

It is nauseating to read that the Council had every sympathy for
the application, but thought that the "custom and practice of the
community" made admission unacceptable. Unacceptable to whom?
Would it have been unacceptable to Christ, the Lord of St. George's
Grammar School? Or would it have been deemed by the Council
to be in some way offensive to God, whose creatures the members
of the Council are, indeed whose instruments they are, did they
truly understand their place and duty? Since when have the "custom and practice of the community" become the criteria by which
a Christian body determines its action?

Of course I am writing as though Christ really has something to
do with St. George's School, and as though it is really God's school,
and as though the Council really has some special duty to its Lord,
as distinct from its duty to the community whose custom and practice it has so handsomely endorsed. That is unrealistic, is it not?
It is more realistic, is it not, to consider our earthly lords below,
and to see that their will be done on earth, even if not in heaven?

The Council further resolved that a decision to admit would be premature. And who knows? Perhaps St. George was premature in killing the dragon. Perhaps he should have waited a little, until the dragon ate him up, as it has eaten up the school that was named after him in hope and piety.

For some people any action which challenges the established order is premature. Does the Council think, when it reflects on the way that white South Africa is moving, that it will soon be less premature?

It sometimes happens that Christians outside politics reproach those who are within that they have lost their true religion, that they have substituted social programmes for commandments, slogans for worship, and propaganda for prayers. I myself am proud to be an Anglican, but I am also proud to be a member of a political party which would never deny admission to any South African on the basis of his colour. For that brand of religion which condones such action, I have no use whatsoever. Whatever it is, it is not Christianity.

The Council of St. George's has been caught in a trap of its own making. It is faced, as Christian white South Africa often is faced in moments of crucial importance, with a choice between its white South Africanism and its Christianity, and it chose the first. By so doing, it brought shame on the Anglican church, and distress to every Anglican who takes seriously the pronouncements of his Church on matters of race.

Let us hope it will repent of its sin.

WAITING FOR ROBERT: THE KENNEDY VISIT*

In 1965, NUSAS invited Senator Robert Kennedy to visit South Africa and address several of its meetings. The Senator accepted the invitation, and, on June 4, 1966, he arrived in

* *Contact*, IX, No. 4 (July, 1966), 7–8.

South Africa. In contrast to *Waiting for Godot,* almost fren-
zied activity marked the period of "Waiting for Robert."
Although the Senator was granted a visa, the Government
made it clear that he was not welcome. On May 11, a five-
year banning order, issued under the Suppression of Communism Act, was served on Ian Robertson, NUSAS' President, who had extended the invitation to Senator Kennedy.
The Government then announced that no foreign correspondents would be permitted to enter South Africa during
the Senator's visit, and, in spite of two requests by Kennedy,
no member of the Government was willing to meet him. On
June 7, Senator Kennedy attended a dinner in his honor, in
Durban; there, he met Alan Paton, Archbishop Dennis Hur-
ley, two Zulu chiefs, and the leaders of the Indian community. He addressed student groups in Cape Town, Durban,
and Johannesburg and visited Chief Albert Luthuli in
Groutville. On June 9, Senator Kennedy left South Africa.
In the following essay, Paton evaluates the effects of the
Senator's visit.

THE KENNEDY visit can only be described as a phenomenon. The
phenomenon resides not solely in him nor solely in the vast ex-
pectant crowds. It is the conjunction of the two that is phenomenal.
These long waits, this excitement, those outstretched hands, what
are they but the signs of a hunger and a thirst, greater than we
imagined? And who better able to satisfy them than our visitor?

It was exhilarating to hear again those truths that have been
driven into hiding by the enemy, by the blaring trumpets and the
shouting hooligans, by the promises of security and the imputations
of treachery, by the vested interests and the need for import
licences [for books], by the bans and the threats and the cruel
laws. It was exhilarating to hear again that totalitarianism cannot
be fought by totalitarianism, that independence of thought is a
strength not a crime, that security and self-preservation are not the
supreme goals of life, that to work for change is not a species of
treachery.

And what was the excitement? It was to feel part of the world again. Reginald Reynolds the Quaker observer of Africa once brilliantly and wittily likened white South Africa to a room full of men and women smoking and drinking with doors and windows closed; when a stranger came in and exclaimed, "My, what a fug in here!" they cried out at him, "How do you know? You've only just come in!" Kennedy was like a fresh wind from the wider world, reassuring those who had said there was a fug that they were right after all.

It is said of course that his only reason for coming to South Africa was to benefit himself politically. This may well have been one of his reasons. I am sure that if Dr. Verwoerd could benefit himself politically by touring abroad, he would do so, if he could find a country to go to. But even in my short acquaintance with the Senator, I was convinced that he really believed in the things he was telling us. I could not help thinking that he would be welcome in almost every country of the world, whereas Dr. Verwoerd would have to confine himself to Portugal and its so-called provinces, Rhodesia, and perhaps Spain. Algeria is off the list, and even Mississippi is slipping. Nor could I help thinking that if Dr. Verwoerd visited Soweto, where would be that multitude of outstretched hands, waving in greeting, trying to touch him maybe?* And the simple reason is that Kennedy has something in him that Dr. Verwoerd has not, some warmth for all people, not just his own.

It would be a mistake to imagine that the Kennedy visit has made our world anew. What he in effect said to us was this, "I know all about your situation, about the bans and the threats and the imputations of treachery, and I've come to tell you that you've been fighting for the right things, and to encourage you for tomorrow."

* On June 8, after visiting Chief Luthuli in Umvoti, Natal, Senator Kennedy flew to Johannesburg and toured the complex of African townships known as Soweto. (The name is not African; it is an acronym for "South Western Townships.") Approximately 500,000 people live in Soweto. The Senator received an enthusiastic welcome. He stood on top of his slowly moving car, waving to cheering crowds, stopping at times to shake outstretched hands. Outside the Catholic cathedral, his party was surrounded by thousands of excited African schoolchildren. Soweto, which has no political campaigns, had never seen anything like this reception.

He can't fight our battles for us, and it is we who have to live our particular South African tomorrow. One feature of that tomorrow will be a sustained campaign to shut all the doors and windows again. And we must face the possibility that during the campaign some people are going to get hurt.

Contact, and the Liberal Party also, expresses its thanks to the National Union of South African Students for their imaginative invitation, and to Senator Kennedy for accepting it, and for giving us so invigorating and encouraging an experience.

IN PRAISE OF FOLLY*

> S. E. D. Brown publishes the monthly South African Observer, which consistently attacks what it calls "liberalists" and "liberalistic tendencies." In July, 1966, a conference of the Afrikaanse Studentebond (ASB), the student organization of Afrikaans-medium universities, passed a motion in praise of Mr. Brown. Shortly afterward, the South African Observer questioned the true Afrikanerskap (loyalty to the Afrikaner people) of certain prominent men including the Principal of Stellenbosch (Afrikaans-medium) University. On August 9, 1966, some 1,300 Stellenbosch students signed a petition dissociating themselves from the ASB motion in praise of Mr. Brown.

IT LOOKS AS though Mr. S. E. D. Brown, the editor of that nauseating paper the South African Observer, has at last come unstuck. He can't grumble, for he has had a good run. As an example of pathological athleticism he can't be beaten. Not even Mississippi has ever produced his peer.

Mr. Brown held the view that there was a perennial struggle between the forces of good and evil. This view has been held by much clearer and better minds than his, and it is not the point at issue. The point at issue is Mr. Brown's idea of evil, which indicates

* Contact, IX, No. 5 (September, 1966), 7–8.

a mind morbidly obsessed, for Mr. Brown's idea bears little relation to the thought of the greatest and deepest thinkers of the human race.

Mr. Brown is not concerned with the evils of cruelty, injustice, mercilessness, arrogance. To him racial mixture and racial mixing are the greatest evils. Criticism of laws to prevent racial mixing is to him a far greater evil than the cruelty of the law which forbids it. Indeed any criticism of the status quo is vicious, and should at all costs be punished, no matter how vicious the punishment.

Mr. Brown's great weapon in the war which he declared on racial mixing and the disturbing of the status quo was character assassination, parading, as it often does, as loyalty to South Africa, devotion to law and order, and love of Christian civilisation. He tried to topple others into the slime—Liberals, Progressives, churchmen, race-relationers, and the rest of this sickly brood. His nemesis was that he toppled none of them; it was not they who fell into the slime. It is a just irony that this should be so, just as it is a mark of an Infinite Compassion that the polecat is revolted by the smells of other creatures.

Mr. Brown was doing fine, enjoying the support of some of the most virulent Nationalist reactionaries.* Yet his success went to

* During 1966, an extreme right-wing group known variously as the *Afrikaner Orde* and the Constantia Group (because of its office in the Constantia Building, Pretoria) emerged within the Nationalist Party in the Transvaal. Dr. Albert Hertzog, Minister for Posts and Telegraphs, and the Reverend J. D. Vorster (the Prime Minister's brother) are among its leaders. It supports the National Council Against Communism, which, in 1966, sponsored an international symposium on Communism. The symposium was under the chairmanship of the Reverend Mr. Vorster, and its chief foreign speaker was Major Edgar Bundy, of the Anti-Communist Church League of America, who alleged that the U.S. State Department had been infiltrated by Communists. He spoke of the World Council of Churches as a "Communist front" and called South African member churches "tools for advancing Communism." The *Afrikaner Orde* has a following in Afrikaans-speaking student groups such as the ASB, and it is said to be using S. E. D. Brown's *South African Observer* as a mouthpiece. The *South African Observer* has links with extreme right-wing groups in the United States. It reprints articles on Communism from the John Birch Society's organ, *American Opinion,* and from similar journals (especially articles alleging sexual promiscuity among civil-rights workers); S. E. D. Brown, in turn, has contributed to *American Opinion.*

his head, as it had done thirty years earlier to the head of Adolph Hitler. Hitler committed the unbelievable folly of turning on Russia, and Mr. Brown the unbelievable folly of turning on Dr. Dönges, Mr. Anton Rupert [a tobacco magnate], Dr. A. J. van Eck [Chairman of the Government-supported Industrial Development Corporation], and Dr. Thom, Principal of the University of Stellenbosch. If he had been given time, he might in his obsession have turned on Mr. Vorster himself. But before he fell he was awarded the shining accolade of the *Afrikaanse Studentebond*, than which one can go no higher or lower.

It was then that the students of Stellenbosch, clad in the snow-white armour of the very pure, came out in revolt, and denounced Mr. Brown as a danger to Afrikanerdom. It happens so seldom that Stellenbosch denounces anything or anybody on the right that many one-time believers in liberty, their senses dulled by years of captivity, felt new hopes stirring in their breasts, and tapped messages to one another in their dungeons, "Youth is all right, *die jeug* [the youth] is O.K." Alas, my view is otherwise, and the cowardly part of my self wishes it need not be, so that for once I could give praise to those whose views I have condemned so often.

But I am not able to do so. The students of Stellenbosch have turned on Mr. Brown, not because he has done anything mean or wrong, but because he has threatened the unity of Afrikanerdom. When he attacked others in his unbridled and bitter way, and in a manner which exceeded the bounds of decent and responsible criticism, the students of Stellenbosch had nothing to say. They have no views on character assassination as such, only on character assassination of their own people. Not in them the spirit of Voltaire, who said, "I disagree with what you say, but I will fight to the death for your right to say it."

There is only one comfort to be drawn from this unedifying chapter, and that is the character assassination of Mr. Brown. Or rather it was a suicide, for he did it himself. And of all such jobs he has done, this one is most to be praised.

IN MEMORIAM: ALBERT LUTHULI*

On July 21, 1967, Albert Luthuli was struck down by a freight train while crossing a narrow railroad bridge near his home in the village of Groutville. A crowd of some 7,000 Africans and a few hundred whites gathered to pay final tribute to him on July 30, when he was buried in the graveyard of the Groutville Congregational Church. Alan Paton paid tribute to Luthuli's memory in the following address delivered at the funeral service. Because Luthuli was a banned person, Paton was forbidden by law to quote anything Luthuli had ever said or written even prior to the time he was banned.

IT IS AN honour to be standing here today to pay tribute to the memory of a noble man. It is an honour to be invited by Mrs. Luthuli and her children to do so. I am not allowed by some foolish law to tell you what he said, but I can tell you what he did.

He did what other heroes have done. He stood up for the rights of his people, for the rights of all people, for the rights of the dispossessed, for the rights of the poor, for the rights of the voiceless. For this he had to choose between his chieftainship and his rights as a man to fight for what he thought was good. He knew, though I am not allowed by this foolish law to repeat the memorable words he used,† that he might have to suffer for his choice; he was prepared even to die.

They took away his chieftainship, but he never ceased to be the

* *Christianity and Crisis,* XXVII, No. 5 (September 18, 1967), 206–7. Reprinted by permission from *Christianity and Crisis;* copyright 1967 by Christianity and Crisis, Inc.

† When Luthuli was dismissed from his chieftaincy in 1952 for refusing to resign from the African National Congress, he issued a statement entitled "The Road to Freedom Is via the Cross." The text of this statement, which contains the "memorable words" to which Paton refers, but which he cannot quote, may be found in Appendix A of Luthuli's *Let My People Go* (New York: McGraw-Hill, 1962), pp. 235–38.

Chief. They took away his temporal power, but he never ceased to have his spiritual power. They took away his freedom, but he never ceased to be free. He was indeed more free than those who had bound him. He was given the honour of the Nobel Peace Prize, and many of us to-day remember the great crowds that gathered in Grey Street and at the airport to wish him godspeed. To them he was still their Chief.

At the airport the crowd was tremendous. It surged into the main concourse; and when the flight was announced, it threatened to surge onto the tarmac. The authorities were afraid of this and wanted to control the crowd. Whom did they get to control it? Why Luthuli, of course. He stood on a chair or pillar and told them that no one was to go onto the tarmac. And no one did.

I do not think that on an occasion such as this one should talk what is called politics. We should talk about a man. But one cannot talk of Albert Luthuli and not talk about the banned African National Congress. It was to be the head of the Congress that he gave up his chieftainship. He put all his power, his great power as a speaker, his great power to move men and women, his power as a leader, into the African National Congress. I have heard him speak on many occasions. He had a voice like a lion, and it was because he had a lion's voice that he had to be silenced. So was silenced a great and noble man.

It is tragic that he is dead, but the real tragedy, which is not only his tragedy but the tragedy of us all, is that those great gifts could not be used, that his great voice could not be heard in the service of our country, South Africa. And we shall never reach the solutions that we all so desire so long as we have to silence such men in order to do that. And history will say, and because history cannot be banned I can tell you what history will say, that a noble voice was silenced when it would have been better for us all if it had been heard.

I once went to visit him at his little shop above the railway lines. But he would not let me stay. Instead he directed me to the railway reserve [right-of-way], and I stayed on the side of the fence that was in the railway reserve and he stayed on the side of the fence that was in the African Reserve. Because if I had been caught in the railway reserve I might have been fined ten rand; but if I had been caught in the African Reserve, who knows what might have happened to me!

There are some people who will think that his life was a failure. Some will think he went too far and some that he did not go far enough. But that is not the real story of his life. The real story of his life is the story of his fortitude. If you win in life, you are a successful man. If you lose, you are an unsuccessful man. But if you go on whether you win or lose, then you have something more than success or failure. You keep your own soul. In one way Luthuli lost the world, but he kept his own soul.

Although he was silenced, history will make his voice speak again, that powerful brave voice that spoke for those who could not speak.

On behalf of the Liberal Party of South Africa, many of whose members have paid the price of their beliefs even as he did, I bring sympathy for Mrs. Luthuli and her family, for the African people, and for the people of all South Africa. The sun rises and the sun sets, and tomorrow it rises again.

Nkosi sikelel' iAfrika.
God save Africa.

Epilogue: "Dr. Hendrik Verwoerd—
A Liberal Assessment"

Prime Minister Hendrik F. Verwoerd died of stab wounds inflicted on him, on September 6, 1966, in the House of Assembly. His assailant was Demitrio Tsafendas, a parliamentary messenger, who was later found to be insane and unfit to stand trial. (In an earlier attempt on his life, on April 9, 1960, Dr. Verwoerd had suffered severe head wounds.) The Prime Minister was assassinated as he was preparing to address Parliament for the first time since the general election, in which his party had, once again, increased its majority over all opposition parties (Nationalist, 126; United, 39; Progressive, 1). This proportion is far greater than the proportion of Afrikaner Nationalist Party members to other white South Africans. Alan Paton's assessment recognizes Dr. Verwoerd's success in winning over the majority of whites to his policy of separate development, which Liberals consistently opposed as unjust.

DR. VERWOERD detested Liberals and liberalism, and said so publicly. Liberals detested the policy of *apartheid,* and said so publicly also. Nevertheless, the Prime Minister's death and the manner of it shocked us.

The killing of a public man and the suffering (for the second time) of his wife and family are not things that give pleasure to us, although there are people who suppose that they do.

268

In any event what change could such an act bring about? Powerful and influential as Dr. Verwoerd was, neither his life nor his death could change the nature of the forces that moulded even him. He could guide them, he could manipulate them, but in a fundamental sense he was their creature.

I can remember well the first attempt at assassination, and the public reaction to it. To many people the news was exciting, to some even pleasing. To this last event the reaction was grave and solemn; neither political friends nor political foes regarded it as anything but useless and terrible, except, perhaps, those of the latter who had come to hate him.

Why is there this difference? One can think of many reasons. When Dr. Verwoerd died he commanded the support of a larger number of white South Africans than he had five years earlier. Not only had he changed, but the world had changed. And in particular, Africa had changed, so that many who had thought him dangerous now looked upon him as a bulwark against danger. The swing to the right and the swing to Dr. Verwoerd were pretty much the same thing.

There is another reason why the reaction is different, and that is, I believe, a growing revulsion against the use of violence in our politics. I know that in some cases this revulsion is strongly motivated by a desire to preserve the status quo, which means to preserve white power and privilege.

But in other cases the revulsion is caused by the realisation that violence in our South African context only exacerbates the conflict.

It is generally conceded that the use of violence in Palestine led to the establishment of the state of Israel, but our situation cannot be compared with this. The position of the white people in South Africa and that of the British in Palestine are quite different. The white people of South Africa are, to all intents and purposes, indigenous; the British in Palestine were alien.

Of course there are some South Africans who feel so deeply and disturbedly about the injustice of the status quo that they declare that violence is the only solution left, and they declare that a person like myself secretly wishes to preserve his own state of privilege, or is simply a coward. I can well understand these views, but I have no intellectual trust in them. If a situation seems unchangeable, there is no reason to believe that violence will change it. One draws back from the prospect of an unending history of murders and assassinations.

There is, I think, a third reason why the violent death of Dr. Verwoerd produced such a grave reaction. I ascribe this to the changes that took place in Dr. Verwoerd himself, particularly after he became Prime Minister [in 1958]. I would have no hesitation in describing the Dr. Verwoerd of the 1930's and 1940's and early 1950's as a racialist.

As editor of *Die Transvaler* [1937–50], he poured contempt on those organisations that held mixed conferences, he often wrote contemptuously of nonwhite people and published photographs of black and white consulting together, with the intention of condemning black and white and conference and all.

In a peculiar way he changed remarkably; in his later years he showed an impersonal geniality toward black people which was entirely absent in his earlier life. But racial consultation remained for him a matter for group leaders, not for persons, and he expressly warned the students of Stellenbosch not to try to do in the field of race relations what was better done by officials. Indeed, the whole machinery of the Group Areas Act is designed to keep racial contact to a minimum. Nevertheless, in the last few years, the public impression deepened of a Prime Minister who, though certainly not to be trifled with, was essentially benign. Innumerable smiling photographs helped to confirm this impression.

In my opinion Dr. Verwoerd's greatest achievement was the way in which he took his predecessor's concept of *baasskap,* that is, white supremacy, and replaced it by the concept of separate development, which is sometimes called, even more grandly, separate freedoms. By so doing he stilled many an uneasy Afrikaner conscience, and won back to his side the troubled Afrikaner intellectuals and churchmen. On the positive side he also gave opportunity to many idealistic Afrikaners to feel that, in directing soil conservation in the Reserves, in planning the new towns and villages, in directing the higher education of Coloured and Indian and African students, in working in the various departments of Bantu affairs, they were also serving their own country and people.

Dr. Verwoerd liberated Afrikaner idealism from the sterile narcissism in which it was captive, and by so doing strengthened Afrikaner progressivism, and weakened Afrikaner reaction. What had happened in himself he was now able to let happen in others. The quality of leadership which he showed in this direction was considerable. I myself did not venerate Dr. Verwoerd, but I can understand why others did.

Is the concept of separate development really different from the concept of *baasskap?* To the Afrikaner nationalist, and especially to the Afrikaner idealist, they are certainly different. But to the liberal South African, and to the politically awakened nonwhite South African, the element of *baasskap* is an essential element in the concept of separate development.

We critics of separate development are often thought churlish in our refusal to concede its ethical purity. We are often accused of doctrinaire criticism, but our criticism is based on harsh and unpleasant facts.

That there is an element of cruelty in *baasskap apartheid* and in separate development seems to us incontrovertible. I often used to wonder whether Dr. Verwoerd knew that, under the Group Areas Act, one could expropriate a man's house, one could make him pay rent and rates for it while withholding the purchase money from him, and that one could, while making him pay rent and rates, deny him the interest on the purchase price.

I used to wonder whether Dr. Verwoerd had ever heard of a man like Mr. Abraham Ngwenya who, in 1911, at the persuasion of the Town Board of Charlestown, bought a piece of land and a house in that village. He set up business as a blacksmith; most of his customers were the white farmers of the district. But, forty-two years later, it was decided to move all African families to Buffalo Flats, forty miles away, with no compensation for loss of livelihood. "I am eighty years old," said Mr. Ngwenya. "This move to Buffalo Flats has knocked me down, and I feel almost too old to get up again. I would rather die soon and escape this bitter ending to a hard but happy life." His wish was granted.

I believe that injustices are intrinsic in any programme of separate development, for the simple reason that separate development is something done by someone with power to someone without power.

I believe that the concept of separate development is there primarily to serve the purposes of Afrikaner nationalism, but that it serves another equally essential purpose, and that is to make it possible for nationalists, and others, to reconcile their religion with their own self-interest.

Does that mean that separate development is an hypocrisy? It certainly has hypocritical elements. But it is, rather, a gigantic self-deception, so that if one believes in it one is also able to believe that the Transkei, the rags and tatters of Zululand, the rags and tatters of a dozen other places, are going in some way to duplicate the extraordinary industrial development that has taken place on the Witwatersrand, in Durban, Port Elizabeth, and Cape Town; that tremendous cities (not merely a conglomeration of cheap houses) are going to rise there; and that the African inhabitants of the "white areas" are going to return in increasing numbers to the homelands, until presumably white South Africa is completely white.

Did Dr. Verwoerd really believe in that kind of separate development that would lead to separate freedoms, that is, to independence? I am prepared to believe that he did, but I am also sure that he knew that such an independence could never be, for example, the kind of independence that white South Africa enjoys.

The independence of the Transkei was the price which Dr. Verwoerd persuaded white South Africa to pay for the right to deny to Transkeians and all other Africans any prospect of achieving permanent residence or of attaining quite ordinary freedoms of movement, employment, and so on, in the so-called white areas. The element of cruelty is readily apparent here, but it is less noticed than it used to be, because Dr. Verwoerd put the separate freedoms in the shop window, and kept the cruelties under the counters.

Indeed the whole purpose of our information services is to hold separate freedoms steadily before the eyes of the world and to keep quiet about the ordinary freedoms. Many overseas visitors who come to see me testify to the courteous and untiring attention rendered by information officials and to the warm and friendly relationship that grows up between them, and to the unhappiness and embarrassment that is caused when the visitors ask difficult questions about black spots, group areas, Job Reservation, and restrictions on sport and entertainment.

Yet Dr. Verwoerd gave to the whole philosophy of *apartheid* an extra dimension, which gave its exponents more room for manoeuvre. He found a strong moral motive for a programme which most of the world found immoral, and convinced many by affirming the morality and denying the immorality. He—and the changing world—made it virtually impossible for any politician to return to the *baasskap* of Mr. Strijdom.

This finding of a strong moral motive, which I contend Dr. Verwoerd did not have in his earlier career, had a profound effect on himself, and accounted for the growing benignity. He himself said he lived at peace because he knew he was right.

Does one judge him for this? I don't like answering this question, because all or most of us deceive ourselves in some way or other, but if one presumes to assess the life and work of a man, one cannot avoid answering it. I would say that he was both the child and the creator of this world of deception. He was the child of a race that wanted both to be just and to be boss.

And I think that if you want to be both those things simultaneously, you must indulge in self-deception. If you make your security the supreme aim of your life, then it becomes your supreme moral value. But, because you feel uneasy about doing that, you must argue that it is only if you are boss that justice will be done to all, and that, therefore, being boss is a kind of supreme moral value after all. That was the way General Hertzog [as Prime Minister, 1934–39] reasoned thirty years before Dr. Verwoerd.

There is another important factor to be considered in any assessment of the late Prime Minister. I think history will say he was ruthless (and by that I mean merciless) towards any South African who opposed vigorously the policy of separate development, and who believed in a common society and tried to propagate such an ideal. I think history will say he was ruthless to a degree not necessary even by his own standards. He permitted the banning of people whose only offence was they had showed a courage and tenacity equal to his own.

Why was this so? Why was liberalism, and why were liberals, the victims of an oppression that went beyond all reason? There can be only one answer to that question and that is that the fear of them went beyond all reason also. The danger of subversion and revolution was exaggerated to a tremendous degree, partly because of this fear, partly because of vindictiveness, partly because it helped to have another enemy at hand now that Communism, according to the Minister [Mr. Vorster], had been crippled.

In all this Dr. Verwoerd's role is remarkable. More and more he became the benign figure, more and more Mr. Vorster became the terrifying one, each role being congenial to the player. But it was not Mr. Vorster who shook the foundations of the rule of law, it was his master.

Was Dr. Verwoerd a great man? In the eyes of Afrikaner nationalism and white South Africa, he certainly was. Will the outside world ever so regard him? This seems to me to be highly improbable. He may be recognised as a man who, within the confines of his narrow philosophy and narrow loyalty, was of considerable stature, and possessed considerable intellectual and political and administrative gifts. Whatever he was, he was not small or small-minded, and there can be no doubt that his rise to power and a high place in the esteem of white South Africa enabled him to shed much of the narrowness of his earlier career.

I cannot help reflecting that had Dr. Verwoerd been born into a wider world, where his gifts could have been used for the wider benefit of mankind, he might have achieved more than this limited greatness. Cassius found in himself, not in his stars, the fault that limited him. But, of Hendrik Verwoerd, the opposite was true. He could have been great under different stars, but he was born into a society whose definition of greatness is not accepted anywhere else, except in those societies and those minds dedicated to the same ideals of white security, white survival, and, inescapably, white supremacy, by whatever grand name they may be called.

Appendix A:
List of Banned Liberal Party Members

The following list of banned office holders and leading members, while not complete, reveals the extent to which political bannings affected the party organization. This list does not include approximately thirty leading Liberals detained under the ninety-day clause of the General Laws Amendment Act (1963), or those otherwise restricted.

Patrick Duncan	March, 1961	Member National Executive; *Contact* editor
Joe Nkatlo	April, 1961	Cape Vice-Chairman
Peter Hjul	February, 1963	Cape Chairman; *Contact* editor
Randolph Vigne	February, 1963	National Deputy Chairman
Jordan Ngubane	May, 1963	National Vice-President
E. V. Mahomed	July, 1963	National Treasurer
D. F. Evans	August, 1963	Natal Provincial Committee
Adelain Hain	October, 1963	Pretoria Secretary
Hammington Majija	October, 1963	Member Cape Executive; *Contact* staff member
H. J. Bhengu	November, 1963	National Vice-President
John Harris	February, 1964	Transvaal Provincial Committee
Elliot Mngadi	March, 1964	National Treasurer
Eddie Daniels	May, 1964	Member Cape Executive
Peter Brown	July, 1964*	National Chairman
Terence Beard	August, 1964	Cape Vice-Chairman
Harold Head	August, 1964	Cape Provincial Committee
Walter Hain	September, 1964	Pretoria Chairman
Dempsey Noel	October, 1964	National Committee

* Further restricted, 1966.

Ann Tobias	October, 1964	Cape Vice-Chairman; *Contact* editor
Eric Harber	October, 1964	Cape Vice-Chairman
Joe Tsele	October, 1964	Pretoria Vice-Chairman
David Rathswaffo	December, 1964	Pretoria Secretary
Eddie Roux	December, 1964	Transvaal Provincial Committee*
S. Bostomsky	February, 1965	Member National Committee
Max Thomas	February, 1965	Transkei Secretary
E. Ndziba	February, 1965	Cape member
Selby Msimang	March, 1965	National Deputy Chairman
Barney Zackon	March, 1965	Cape Chairman
Alban Thumbran	March, 1965	Transvaal Vice-Chairman
Fred Prager	March, 1965	Transvaal member
David Craighead	June, 1965	Transvaal Chairman; National Chairman of Defence and Aid Fund
John Blundell	June, 1965	Cape Town Chairman of Defence and Aid Fund†
Michael Francis	July, 1965	Cape Executive Committee; *Contact* editor
John Aitcheson	July, 1965	Office bearer both the Liberal Party and NUSAS
St. Leger Kerr Pillay	July, 1965	Johannesburg member
Godfrey Beck	July, 1965	Johannesburg member
Richard Triegaart	July, 1965	Johannesburg member
Jean Hill	September, 1965	Pietermaritzburg Secretary of Defence and Aid
Laura Hitchins	September, 1965	Johannesburg Secretary of Defence and Aid
Heather Morkell	March, 1966	Pietermaritzburg Secretary
C. K. Hill	March, 1966	Natal member
Ruth Hayman	April, 1966	Transvaal Vice-Chairman

* Roux was not a member of the Liberal Party at the time he was banned. Because he had been a member of the Communist Party in the 1930's—when it was a legal party in South Africa—he was a listed Communist and, on that basis, had been forced to resign from the Liberal Party in 1963.

† Technically, Blundell was "deported," not banned; he was ordered to leave South Africa within ten days because he was not a South African citizen.

Appendix B:
Checklist of "The Long View" by Alan Paton

Starred items have not been included in this volume. Where titles in
THE LONG VIEW do not accord with the original, they follow in
brackets.

FIRST SERIES: 1958–59

1. "Towards a Nonracial Democracy," *Contact,* I, No. 1 (February 8, 1958), 11.
2. "Nigeria," *Contact,* I, No. 2 (February 22, 1958), 11.*
3. "The Archbishop of Cape Town Views Apartheid," *Contact,* I, No. 3 (March 8, 1958), 11.
4. "Liberals and the United Party: Sir de Villiers Graaf," *Contact,* I, No. 4 (March 22, 1958), 11.
5. "A Calm View of Change," *Contact,* I, No. 5 (April 5, 1958), 11.
6. "Liberals and the Nationalist Party," *Contact,* I, No. 6 (April 19, 1958), 11.
7. "Nonracialism in a Racial Society," *Contact,* I, No. 7 (May 3, 1958), 11.
8. "SABRA Talks with Nonwhites," *Contact,* I, No. 8 (May 17, 1958), 11.*
9. "Bantu Education: The State Must Not Run the Universities," *Contact,* I, No. 9 (May 31, 1958), 11.
10. "Tribute to the Bravest Liberal of Them All" ["Christopher Gell: Salute to the Brave"], *Contact,* I, No. 10 (June 14, 1958), 11.
11. "Racial Juggernaut Moves on Indians," *Contact,* I, No. 11 (June 28, 1958), 9.

12. "Group Areas Act Cruelty to the Indians is un-Christian," *Contact,* I, No. 14 (August 9, 1958), 9.
13. "Hooliganism Reveals the True Nature of *Apartheid,*" *Contact,* I, No. 16 (September 6, 1958), 9.*
14. "An Open Letter to Dr. Verwoerd," *Contact,* I, No. 17 (September 20, 1958), 9.
15. "Raise Production by Treating African Labour Humanely" ["The Wages of the Poor"], *Contact,* I, No. 18 (October 4, 1958), 9.
16. "Verwoerd's Claim to Divine Guidance," *Contact,* I, No. 19 (October 18, 1958), 9.
17. "A Foolish Man Imagines an 'Indian Menace,'" *Contact,* I, No. 20 (November 1, 1958), 9.*
18. "Alan Paton Invites Mr. Ekkis Blindendoof to Take the Short View," *Contact,* I, No. 21 (November 15, 1958), 9.*
19. "The *Cape Argus* and a Planned Utopia: Totalitarianism or Liberalism?" *Contact,* I, No. 22 (November 29, 1958), 9.*
20. "Michael Scott: What Kind of Man Was He?" *Contact,* I, No. 23 (December 13, 1958), 9.
21. "The Accra Conference," *Contact,* I, No. 24 (December 27, 1958), 9.
22. "Precepts of a Cabinet Minister," *Contact,* II, No. 1 (January 10, 1959), 9.
23. "The Days of White Supremacy are Over," *Contact,* II, No. 2 (January 24, 1959), 9.

SECOND SERIES: 1960

1. "A Man Called Brown," *Contact,* III, No. 8 (April 16, 1960), 5.
2. "Our Rulers' Latest Blunder," *Contact,* III, No. 9 (May 7, 1960), 5.
3. "Margaret Ballinger," *Contact,* III, No. 10 (May 21, 1960), 5.
4. "The United Nations in Africa," *Contact,* III, No. 11 (June 4, 1960), 5.*
5. "A Nonviolent Third Force," *Contact,* III, No. 12 (June 18, 1960), 5.
6. "Keep the Party Clean," *Contact,* III, No. 13 (July 2, 1960), 5.*
7. "The Congo," *Contact,* III, No. 15 (July 30, 1960), 5.
8. "End of an Age," *Contact,* III, No. 16 (August 13, 1960), 5.*

9. "Our New Bishop: Trevor Huddleston," *Contact*, III, No. 17 (August 27, 1960), 5.

THIRD SERIES: 1964–66

1. "A Toast to the End of the Colour Bar," *Contact*, VII, No. 2 (January 24, 1964), 2.
2. "A Dubious Virgin," *Contact*, VII, No. 4 (March 13, 1964), 2.
3. "An Example for Us All: Elliott Mngadi," *Contact*, VII, No. 5 (April 10, 1964), 2.
4. "Solving Our Problems," *Contact*, VII, No. 6 (May 8, 1964), 2.
5. "His Crime is Loyalty [Chief Albert Luthuli]," *Contact*, VII, No. 7 (June 5, 1964), 2.
6. "Liberalism and Communism," *Contact*, VII, No. 8 (July 3, 1964), 2.
7. "Intimidation," *Contact*, VII, No. 9 (July 31, 1964), 2.
8. "Peter Brown," *Contact*, VII, No. 10 (August 28, 1964), 2.
9. "No Genade at Genadendal," *Contact*, VII, No. 11 (September 25, 1964), 2.
10. "Something to Be Proud Of," *Contact*, VII, No. 12 (October 23, 1964), 2.
11. "A Plea For the Freedom of Monkeys," *Contact*, VII, No. 13 (November 27, 1964), 2.
12. "The Ninety Days," *Contact*, VII, No. 14 (December, 1964), 4.
13. "Ideas Never Die," *Contact*, VIII, No. 1 (January, 1965), 2.
14. "St. George Deserts to the Dragon," *Contact*, VIII, No. 2 (February, 1965), 2.
15. "Nationalism and the Theatre," *Contact*, VIII, No. 3 (March, 1965), 2.
16. "John Harris," *Contact*, VIII, No. 4 (April, 1965), 2.
17. "Ham-Handed Hildegard," *Contact*, VIII, No. 5 (May, 1965), 2.*
18. "Defence and Aid," *Contact*, VIII, No. 6 (June, 1965), 2.
19. "Beware of Melancholy," *Contact*, VIII, No. 7 (July, 1965), 2.
20. "Marquard on Liberalism," *Contact*, VIII, No. 8 (September, 1965), 5-7.
21. "Rhodesia," *Contact*, VIII, No. 9 (October, 1965), 7.
22. "In the Blossom Land," *Contact*, VIII, No. 10 (December, 1965), 7.

23. "The Ndamse Affair," *Contact*, IX, No. 1 (January, 1966), 7.
24. "The Long Arm of Persecution," *Contact*, IX, No. 2 (March, 1966), 7.
25. "The Trial," *Contact*, IX, No. 3 (April, 1966), 7.*
26. "Waiting for Robert," *Contact*, IX, No. 4 (July, 1966), 7.
27. "Mr. S. E. D. Brown" ["In Praise of Folly"], *Contact*, IX, No. 5 (September, 1966), 7.
28. "On Poverty," *Contact*, XI, No. 6 (October, 1966).*

Bibliography

The following is a selection of writings by Alan Paton on topics related to those covered in THE LONG VIEW; it omits fiction, drama, poetry, and contributions to newspapers and periodicals:*

BOOKS AND PAMPHLETS

* *The Non-European Offender* ("Penal Reform Series," No. 2). Johannesburg: South African Institute of Race Relations, 1945.
* *Freedom as a Reformatory Instrument* ("Penal Reform Pamphlets," No. 2). Pretoria: Penal Reform League of South Africa, 1948.
* *South Africa Today* ("Public Affairs Pamphlet," No. 175). New York: The Public Affairs Committee, 1951; London: Lutterworth Press, 1953.
* *Christian Unity: A South African View* (Peter Ainslie Memorial Lecture). Grahamstown: Rhodes University Press, 1951.
* *Salute to My Greatgrandchildren* ("St. Benedict's Booklets," No. 5). Johannesburg: St. Benedict's House, 1952. (Cover title incorrectly printed: *Salute to My Great-Great Grandchildren.*) Letters to the twenty-first century, with commentary on nonracial democracy.

The Land and People of South Africa ("Portraits of the Nations Series"). Philadelphia: J. B. Lippincott, 1955; London: Lutterworth, 1957 (with variant title: *South Africa and Her People*).

Hope for South Africa. New York: Frederick A. Praeger, 1958; London: Pall Mall Press, 1958. An account of the Liberal Party and its place in South Africa during the period 1953–58. *The Long View* is a sequel to *Hope for South Africa.*

* *The People Wept: Being a Brief Account of the Origin, Contents, and Application of That Unjust Law of the Union of South Africa Known*

* Titles preceded by an asterisk are pamphlets. A more complete bibliography may be found in Edward Callan, *Alan Paton* (["Twayne's World Authors Series," No. 40], New York: Twayne, 1967).

as The Group Areas Act of 1950 (since consolidated as Act No. 77 of 1957). Kloof, Natal: Alan Paton, 1958. Extract included in *The Long View*.

* *The Christian Approach to Racial Problems in the Modern World* (A Christian Action Pamphlet). London: Christian Action, 1959. Reprinted in London, 1961.

* *The Charlestown Story.* Pietermaritzburg: The Liberal Party, 1960. Extract included in *The Long View*.

Hofmeyr. Cape Town: The Oxford University Press, 1964. This fine biography is probably Paton's most important single work of nonfiction.

South African Tragedy: The Life and Times of Jan Hofmeyr, abridged by Dudley C. Lunt. New York: Charles Scribner's Sons, 1965.

Instrument of Thy Peace. New York: Seabury Press, 1968. Explores the deeper meanings of Christianity for the modern world.

INTRODUCTIONS AND FOREWORDS TO BOOKS

Durban: A Study in Racial Ecology by Leo Kuper, Hilstan Watts, and Ronald Davies. London: Jonathan Cape; New York: Columbia University Press, 1958. Introduction by Alan Paton.

Brief Authority by Charles Hooper. London: Collins, 1960. Introduction by Alan Paton.

Non-racial Democracy: The Policies of the Liberal Party of South Africa. Pietermaritzburg: The Liberal Party, 1962. Introduction by Alan Paton.

* *This Is Apartheid* by Leslie Rubin. London: Christian Action, 1959. Foreword by Alan Paton. New edition by Leslie Rubin and Neville Rubin, with an additional foreword by Chief Albert Luthuli. London: Christian Action, 1965.

CONTRIBUTIONS TO BOOKS AND SYMPOSIA

"Religious Faith and Human Brotherhood," in *Religious Faith and World Culture,* ed. A. W. Loos. Englewood Cliffs, N.J.: Prentice-Hall, 1951. Reprinted in T. C. Pollack *et al., Explorations.* Englewood Cliffs, N.J.: Prentice-Hall, 1956.

"Trevor Huddleston," in *Thirteen for Christ,* ed. Melville Harcourt. New York: Sheed & Ward, 1963.

"The Challenge of Fear" ("What I Have Learned Series," XVI), *Saturday Review,* L, No. 36 (September 9, 1967), 19–21, 46.

Index

285